RESISTANCE

The author and Václav Havel during the pre-revolutionary days of opposition to the communist regime

RESISTANCE AND REVOLUTION

VÁCLAV HAVEL'S CZECHOSLOVAKIA

Rob McRae

Carleton University Press

© Carleton University Press, 1997

Printed and bound in Canada

Canadian Cataloguing in Publication Data

McRae, Robert Grant
 Resistance and revolution: Vaclav Havel's Czechoslovakia

Includes index.
ISBN 0-88629-316-2

1. Czechoslovakia—Politics and government—1968-1989. 2. Czechoslovakia—Politics and government—1989-1992. 3. Havel, Vaclav I. Title.

DB2228.7.M37 1997   943.704'3   C97-900390-3

Cover Design: Your Aunt Nellie
Typeset: Mayhew & Associates Graphic Communications, Richmond, Ont., in association with MfL Graphic Productions

Carleton University Press gratefully acknowledges the support extended to its publishing program by the Canada Council and the financial assistance of the Ontario Arts Council. The Press would also like to thank the Department of Canadian Heritage, Government of Canada, and the Government of Ontario through the Ministry of Culture, Tourism and Recreation, for their assistance.

The views expressed in this book are those of the author, and not the views of the Department of Foreign Affairs and International Trade.

This
book
is
for

Lynn, Kevan, Laura, and Sean

CONTENTS

	List of Illustrations	viii
	Acknowledgements	ix
	Preface	xi
1	1968-1988: The Emergence of Public Protest	1
2	Glasnost—Not!	9
3	Living in Truth	15
4	Jan Palach	21
5	The Political Trials	27
6	The Symposium	35
7	The Resistance Spreads	41
8	A Few Sentences	49
9	Writers East and West	53
10	Means and Ends	59
11	The East German Exodus	63
12	The Symposium II	71
13	Too Little, Too Late	75
14	Czech Pens	79
15	The Twilight of Communism	91
16	The November 17 Massacre	99
17	The Student Strike	107
18	The Birth of Civic Forum	111
19	Don't Start the Revolution Without Me!	115
20	A Kingdom for a Balcony	123
21	The Return of History	129
22	Workers Unite!	135
23	A Communist Intermezzo	139
24	Alexander Dubcek	143
25	The General Strike	147
26	The Regime Strikes Back	153
27	The Government of National Understanding	161
28	Thomas Bata's Homecoming	169

29	The Campaign for President	181
30	The Deconstruction of Communism	187
31	President Havel	191
32	The Canadian Connection	197
33	Human Bridges	207
34	A New/Old Political System	215
35	The Economic Challenge	221
36	The Rebirth of Party Politics	225
37	Constitutional Crisis	231
38	Dubcek Remembers	239
39	Slovak Nationalism	243
40	An Independent Foreign Policy	247
41	The Campaign	259
42	The First Free Elections	267
43	The End of Czechoslovakism	273
44	The National Awakening	279
45	1968 and 1989	289
46	Hello Good-bye	295
47	The Disappearing Country	301
	Postscript: The Next Revolution	323

ILLUSTRATIONS

1	The author and Václav Havel	frontispiece
2	The author, Martin Palouš, and Ivan Havel	16
3	The author and Zdeněk Urbánek	77
4	"It's all over"	119
5	Alexander Dubček	145
6	"Havel to the Castle!"	182
7	Barry Mawhinney, the author, and Havel	199
8	The opening of the 68 Publishers exhibit	211
9	Pierre Guimond, Vladimir Dlouhy, Barry Mawhinney, and the author	236
10	Jirina Šiklová, Jiří Dienstbier, the author, and Gordon Skilling	281
11	Ivan Havel, Martin Palouš, Ivan Chvatik, Paul Wilson, Václav Malý, and the author	317

ACKNOWLEDGEMENTS

I would like to thank Stanislav Chýlek, Ambassador of the Czech Republic in Canada, for his friendly encouragement and help throughout this project. I am grateful to Mr. Thomas Bata Jr., Dr. Jennifer Simons and the Simons Foundation, Joseph Kuchar, and A.K. Velan, for their generous support of Carleton University Press in aid of publication. I would like to thank my wife, Lynn Massicotte, who provided superb drawings for the chapter headings. Finally, Ivan Havel, Martin Palouš, Josef Škvorecký, Paul Wilson, and Gordon Skilling read the book at different stages and offered invaluable insights.

PREFACE

THIS IS A PERSONAL MEMOIR of a special time and some extraordinary people. It is something I felt bound to write, given the unique circumstances in which I found myself. I was one of the few foreigners who came to know the Czechoslovak dissident opposition before, during, and after the revolution of 1989. As we now know, this was one of the great turning points in the history of this century. It also seems, sadly, to have been a brief idyll in the history of Czechoslovakia. A philosopher king overturned the dark forces of totalitarianism, and for a time it seemed as if the future of Czechoslovakia was there for the making. The golden age of the First Republic, under President T.G. Masaryk, seemed reborn in a new president who captured the hearts and minds not only of his countrymen but of the world. Perhaps the victory had been too complete. Perhaps the brilliant successes only better masked the forces of dissolution and deceit. There were some early signs of danger, but none of us understood fully the currents of history at work. Could it really have come out differently? Perhaps these days of division are in their turn a passing phase, and the noble ideal of Czechoslovakia may yet prove itself in another, more tolerant, age.

When my wife, children and I drove up to the Czechoslovak border in August 1988, we knew little of this country that was to become our second home. As a member of the Canadian foreign service, I was being posted with my family to Prague for three years. The timing could not have been better. Lynn and I were looking forward to living in the city of a thousand spires. Golden Prague it was called, and it soon lived up to its advance billing. I was looking for a quiet assignment, having just completed a demanding job at headquarters. We were to laugh about that later. At the time communist-ruled Czechoslovakia was a sleepy if Kafkaesque outpost of the Soviet empire. It was also brutal to anyone who refused to go through the motions of ritualized obeisance.

The border guard took our diplomatic passports and meticulously examined each one. He looked at our children, Kevan, then five, and Laura, then two, in the back seat of the car. We were to have our third child, Sean, during our rather eventful time in Prague (he was conceived during the revolution). The guard gave a smart salute, and we were off. I took this as a good omen for the future. I was surprised to have been greeted with such courtesy, given that I was no doubt viewed by some as an agent of Western imperialism. But problems on that score would come soon enough. We fell in love with this country and its people from the first day. The rolling hills, the Bohemian forest, the ancient castles, and the Czechs, whose civilization was truly "old-world." Our house was on a hill in Prague, with a large balcony that looked down towards the Castle and St. Vitus Cathedral. The city, neatly divided by the winding Vltava river, looked in the distance like something out of a child's fairy tale.

We met many wonderful people during our time in Prague. But there was a small cast of characters we came to know well, whose lives passed through the charged scenes of dissent and revolution. In a way, this is as much their story as ours, if not more so. But it is a story seen through the eyes of a foreigner from the West, one of the few to have witnessed these events at first hand. And so this narrative is much like one of those "I was there" adventure stories, accompanied by reflections of a totally personal character. These reflections mirror the intellectual and moral preoccupations of the principal actors, and provide a subplot to the main story. Of course the protagonist of this play is Václav Havel. He pervades each scene, even when he is not present. One might almost say he is really the dramatist, pulling the strings of the many actors. But no, the story is too real, the decisions too immediate, the outcomes too uncertain. It is life, after all, and the world a makeshift and temporary stage.

1

1968-1988
THE EMERGENCE OF PUBLIC PROTEST

WE CROSSED THE BORDER a week before the twentieth anniversary of the Warsaw Pact invasion of Czechoslovakia. This invasion, which took place on August 21, 1968, had crushed Dubček's Prague Spring democratic reforms. It remained the most significant political event in the living memory of most Czechs. But by 1988 certain steps, surprising for the time, had been taken in Hungary and Poland to further the cause of reform and openness. Czechoslovakia, however, was still one of the most repressive hardline communist states. Havel's years in prison, like those of a fair number of other opposition figures, provided ample testimony. Nonetheless, I wondered if something might happen during my assignment there as number two at the Canadian Embassy. The common wisdom was that Czechoslovakia would be the last to reform, and even then only very slowly, probably long after my departure. As it turned out, fate was to intervene and, at least this time, on the side of the angels.

It was a warm and pleasant summer day in August 1988, as we drove along the highway from Dolní Dvořiště and Tábor in the south toward the old imperial city of Prague. I noticed that the two-lane highway was well-maintained and that the lines on the road were freshly painted. It was a pleasant surprise, given my experience of roads during a posting a few years earlier in Yugoslavia. Driving along the tree-lined highway past carefully groomed Czech villages with their red tile roofs I was struck by the fact that, though there was not the kind of material wealth in Czechoslovakia that was evident in Austria or Germany, a Central European civilization clearly pervaded all three. It had something to do with a premium placed on technical skill, even in literature, together with a deep spirituality that in the case of the Czechs had occasionally inspired revolutionary social movements.

Miraculously, we managed to navigate by map through the old city and made our way right to our villa at Za Hanspaulkou 2 without getting lost. Prague had never been seriously damaged by war for over a thousand years. It had never been subjected to the kind of clearances that preceded the creation of grand boulevards found in most other European capitals. The result was that the streets of the city followed the winding medieval footpaths, making travel by car an adventure. Our quarter was called Dejvice, lying north and west of the old town. It was largely residential, with villas scattered among orchards atop rolling hills. There was a variety of fruit trees bearing apples, cherries, and especially pears. In the spring, these hills were a sea of pink and white blossoms, their perfumed scent wafting in at the windows. The villas were built mostly in the late nineteenth and early twentieth centuries. They exuded the architectural dreaminess of art nouveau, with sweeping curves and floral emblems.

Our house was built at the end of this period, in the 1920s, reflecting the art deco style then in vogue. There was a certain Bauhaus feel to it, reinforced by a utilitarian layout. The architect had built it for himself and his family. It seemed he could not keep himself from adding spectacular cut glass windows above the entrances and doorways, depicting scenes from Bohemian country life. It was all a little incongruous, but we loved it. A large balcony looked down the hill across more orchards and towards the Prague Castle and St. Vitus Cathedral in the distance. In our backyard, there were five or six pear trees, and a few apple and cherry trees. The yard, and the neighbourhood, was slightly overgrown with bushes and long grass. It was the Czech way, a little wild and unkempt, but pleasant, and it added to the timelessness of the place. Only very occasionally, a small Škoda would struggle up the hill, sounding like a runaway lawnmower. For the most part, life in Dejvice was quiet and undisturbed. You could be excused if you were not quite sure if it was 1888 or 1988. At first glance, there did not seem to be much difference.

We were pruning bushes in the back yard on Saturday, August 21, when our friends and fellow-Canadians, Louise Parent and Pierre Guimond, drove up to our front gates. Pierre was my colleague in the political section of the Canadian Embassy. He jumped out of the car and I could tell by his seriousness that something was up. He said that a small demonstration was going on downtown in Wenceslas Square. About fifty people had gathered in front of the equestrian statue of King Wenceslas. It seemed they were protesting against the 20th anniversary of the Soviet invasion of Czechoslovakia. Pierre said the police had not yet intervened. I was incredulous. I had not expected anything to happen on the anniversary, and the event came as a wake-up call in this, the most tightly controlled society of the East Bloc.

Pierre and I jumped into the car and sped off. As we wound our way down the hill beside the renaissance arches of the Belvedere, or summer palace, I could hardly believe our luck. We had only just arrived and already one of the most significant events in terms of public opposition to the regime was taking place. I had no idea what to expect, except that the communists were not likely to tolerate such protest very long. The lack of reaction on the part of the authorities probably meant they were as surprised about the demonstration as we were.

We parked the car in Malé Náměstí, an out-of-the-way spot near the Old Town Square. From there we ran across the medieval square, turned under a baroque archway, and jogged up through the narrow cobblestone streets to Wenceslas Square. Wenceslas Square was both broad and long, its buildings dating from the relatively more recent period of the nineteenth and early twentieth centuries. Trees lined the sidewalks on either side. The square extended uphill to the massive National Museum at the far end. The museum was topped with a brilliant gold dome, and in front of it was a huge bronze statue of King Wenceslas riding on horseback, carrying his standard.

Halfway up the square, to my amazement, a small crowd of people, now numbering perhaps a hundred, were standing in front of the statue. They looked like a fairly scruffy lot, but seemed intent on becoming the heroic successors of their patron saint. Most had long or longish hair, jeans, sweaters, and sandals. It was a counterculture look, as if released by a time capsule dating from the sixties. I soon learned that this was the style of the opposition in Prague. I felt at once both nostalgic and at home.

The difference from the sixties, or from more recent protest movements in the West, was that these protesters were not drawing attention to the environmental practices of a local company, or condemning the export of weapons to the Third World. They had decided to take on Big Brother himself, knowing full well what had happened to others who had done the same in the past. They had decided to gather in what was probably the most sacred place in Bohemia, to applaud youthful speakers calling for free speech and basic human rights.

The protest had started hours before, and the first thing that struck me as odd was that the police had made no attempt to break it up. There were now as many onlookers crowded onto the sidewalks on either side of the demonstrators. They watched and no doubt wondered how long this would go on. Some of the bystanders joined the demonstration as time passed, perhaps not fully aware of the existential decision they had just made. The StB, the Czechoslovak communist equivalent of the KGB, would ensure they paid for it later. And yet, this was already the most significant public revolt in twenty years, since the time of the Warsaw Pact invasion of Czechoslovakia.

Standing near the edge of the crowd, an American colleague, Bob Norman, introduced me to Karl Srp, the head of the so-called Jazz Section. It was in fact the jazz section of the musician's union, but under Srp the section had become a hotbed of underground music and video production, as well as *samizdat* (clandestine) publishing. Srp was no longer young, a man of about fifty now. He had spent over a year in jail for publishing banned books, producing audio tapes of banned groups, and launching a video news service. He too found the whole demonstration somewhat unbelievable, and laughed, wondering when the police would arrive.

I found it odd that, other than Srp, none of the other more well-known opposition figures were present, at least none that I recognized. I was to learn that some had been detained by the police the day before. Others were at their small weekend houses in the country, like the great majority of Czechs. The speakers in this crowd were young, indeed from a younger generation than the more well-known dissidents associated with Charter 77. They had recently begun forming their own opposition groups, such as the Independent Peace Initiative.

One of the best speakers on that day was Tomáš Dvořák, a man in his late twenties and one of the leaders of the IPI, who had a vigorous and direct approach. For me, what was most striking about the protest was that a core of young people had decided to confront the regime regardless of the consequences. They had made the leap of faith, like the medieval cleric Jan Hus before them. That core was still small, nascent really, but on this day in August 1988, they had opened the door, if only a crack, into another world.

After about an hour and a half of hanging around on the sidewalk and then walking through the crowd of protesters in order to speak to a few people, Pierre and I decided to go home. What I did not know, but should have guessed, was that the StB had taken a considerable interest in my presence. On that day, I was the most senior Western diplomat to have become so directly involved in opposition activities. What made it worse, in the eyes of the regime, was that it had happened only days after my arrival. The authorities would come to hold this against me, and much more besides, and eventually move to expel me from the country. Part of their ammunition would be photos they took of me at this first demonstration.

But the bottom line for Canada was that I was present to monitor the regime's compliance with international human rights accords, accords freely entered into by the regime itself. Incredibly, those who held power were under the impression that the signing of such accords would be a sufficient gesture of support for human rights. They assumed the West would turn a blind eye to what was happening on the ground. The Canadian government, for one, was not going to play ball.

As we drove home, Pierre and I were uncertain about the significance of what we had just witnessed. We knew that any kind of demonstration in such a tightly controlled society was an important event. We were surprised that the police had not yet intervened to break up the gathering, and assumed that eventually the demonstrators would wrap up their discussions and go their separate ways. Our assumptions showed how little we understood the political dynamic at work between the regime and the opposition. Only hours after we left, the crowd grew to about 10,000. No doubt word began to spread about what was going on downtown. More and more people decided to join in. It was Sunday night, and a lot of them were returning to Prague from weekend cottages in the country. I heard later that, as more people arrived, the demonstration took on a more vocal character, becoming less a sit-in and more properly a demonstration. Suddenly people in the crowd felt they had to do something. There were calls to march from Wenceslas Square to the Old Town Square. The crowd set off amidst shouts of "Dubček!" and "freedom!" On this 20th anniversary, the humiliation of 1968 was still seared into people's, memories.

At the Old Town Square they listened to the young speakers I had seen earlier. Dvořák was trying to draft a proclamation. But then the crowd, intoxicated by its apparent freedom and the lack of police intervention, decided to march on the president's office. To do this, it had to cross the Vltava River by one of the bridges in order to get to the Castle, where the communist President Husák had his office. It was at this point that the police blocked the march and broke up the crowd with dogs and truncheons. Later, Pierre and I would come to understand why it had to end that way. The regime knew, instinctively, that any crack in its authority would bring it to the precipice. But what made this demonstration a turning point was that it was almost completely spontaneous, and that the issues were entirely political, and of the most fundamental kind.

The communists must have been surprised by the anti-government protest, especially the willingness of onlookers to take part. It may also have been that the communist Prime Minister Štrougal had decided to take a hands-off approach, at least until the end when the riot police finally intervened. The hardliners in the regime must have viewed this decision as a miscalculation when they saw how quickly the number of demonstrators grew in the course of the evening. It must certainly have contributed to his removal as prime minister about a month or so later.

We had hardly had time to consider the meaning of all of these events when the Independent Peace Initiative, the opposition group behind the protest of August 21, called for a demonstration on the last Saturday of every month. Accordingly, on September 24, 1988, a few hundred people managed to gather in Wenceslas Square before 150 riot police with white helmets and truncheons emerged from the subway entrances. They lined up above and below the crowd in the square. Ten paddy wagons pulled up at the top of the square, while police loudspeakers warned the crowd to disperse. No one moved. Then the riot police marched into the crowd with truncheons swinging.

Plain-clothes StB agents grabbed people from within the crowd and shoved them down, and then dragged them by the hair to the waiting paddy wagons. You got to recognize the plain-clothes types after a while. The StB had a kind of expressionless look as they kicked people on the ground. They were the epitome of the worst in all of us. They almost certainly did not believe in communism as an ideology. They believed in it as a force, as the legitimate expression of the "winner" in 1948 of the communist coup d'état they called "Victorious February." Essentially, it came down to the fact that some people, who were in power, wanted certain things done, and were willing to provide both latitude and perquisites to those that did them. The worst thing was that most Czechs realized the StB reflected a part of human character present in us all: everyone is capable of treachery and brutality.

Warily taking note of the regime's antics on this Saturday in September, Pierre and I were standing at the edge of the crowd beside a Reuters correspondent. A policeman asked for my identity card and then told me to get out. They took the Reuters correspondent a few yards away, took his notebook, held him down, and intentionally broke his right thumb. Then the riot police began clearing the square of the several thousand people by pushing them out into side streets. The whole thing was over in forty-five minutes. It had been a public display of superfluous force to make the point that a repetition of the August 21 demonstration was not on.

But there was something about this demonstration that had impressed me. Just before they were beaten the demonstrators started singing the Czechoslovak national anthem, which dated from the founding of the country in 1918. Again, history was deployed in the struggle with the state. The protesters stood there, singing this anthem, while the riot police walked into them hitting them to the ground. It made you feel terrible inside, although the dignity of these protesters and the strength of their ideals was incredibly moving. In the end, I was overwhelmed with disgust at the brutality of the police. By the time I eventually got home, I had a difficult time telling Lynn what had happened. I told her the facts, but there was this heaviness in my soul I could not shake. Political work at the Embassy had taken on a new meaning. Issues and ideas had acquired a human face, and it was profoundly troubling.

At the same time I was struck by the fact that resistance against communism in Czechoslovakia had suddenly taken a radical turn. Since 1969, opposition had been largely the affair of "dissidents," as they were called in the West. Protest took the form of meetings, publications, music, and art. The resistance was headed up by exceptional individuals who led by example and were willing to pay an unbelievable personal price. All that changed in August, 1988. Protest had taken to the streets. A small, symbolic gesture by a younger generation of dissidents had acted like a spark in an underground mine. The tremors were felt everywhere on the surface, even if the pattern of life had not yet changed.

It was at about this time that Pierre and I, together with Ambassador Barry Mawhinney, sat down at the Embassy to map out our strategy for dealing with the regime. We looked at a lot of factors, and decided that we would pursue Canada's human rights concerns to the limit, in order to increase pressure on the regime. We would refuse to be intimidated by a totalitarian government and would continue to support fully the opposition, in accordance with the human rights provisions of the Helsinki Accords. Without exaggerating, I can say that the Embassy's actions which followed our decision were regarded by many in the opposition in the months to come as both forward-looking and a model of effective representation abroad.

Both before and after the revolution, Barry, Pierre, and I became well-acquainted with Havel and with the circle of people close to him. This was, at the time and even more so later, greatly to the benefit of the government of Canada, and the Canadian people. I think our decision to do the right thing, when it came to the pursuit of human rights, also brought the three of us at the Embassy closer together. By the time my assignment in Prague was over, our adventure had created the kind of friendship that is usually forged in the trenches.

2

GLASNOST—NOT!

IN EARLY OCTOBER, unexpectedly, the politburo proclaimed October 28 an officially sanctioned national day. Until that time, the national day of communist Czechoslovakia had been May 9, the day of the Soviet liberation of Prague at the end of the war. October 28 had previously been passed over in silence because it was the date of the founding of the capitalist Czechoslovak Republic in 1918. Hence October 28, 1988, was the seventieth anniversary.

I wondered if the government might be appealing to a latent Czechoslovak nationalism to reinforce the independence of the communist regime, at a time when Gorbachov was going his own way. Communists in Yugoslavia would soon adopt the same tactic, with devastating results. About a week before the anniversary, a central committee plenum of the Communist Party had replaced Štrougal with Adamec as prime minister. Štrougal had been "compromised" by the delay over police intervention on August 21. In the very same week in which Štrougal was ousted, there were warnings over the radio and TV that any unofficial demonstration on October 28 would be broken up. As justification for this action, it was claimed that such demonstrations were inspired by "anti-socialist forces backed from abroad."

The regime's celebration of this new national day was in fact held the day before, on October 27, in Wenceslas Square. I was invited as a representative of the Canadian Embassy and decided to see how the other half lived. Thousands of loyal party members were bused in from across the country. There was a podium for the regime's leaders and the resident diplomats, and I saw President Husák, General Secretary Jakeš and the others at close range (small grey men without exception). The Prague party boss, Miroslav Štěpán, who looked like a boxer, made a terrible speech and received at best polite applause. There was a rendition of the International and the national anthem. Suddenly, I realized the hearty choruses were from tape recordings being broadcast from speakers attached to lamp posts up and down the square. No one, not even the leaders, actually sang them. Then everyone filed back into the buses, collected their bonuses, and went home.

The demonstration on October 28 was rather different. I saw it as a litmus test for the depth of commitment by the opposition after the brutality of September 24. I was not disappointed. By 4 P.M. about 10,000 people congregated in the square and shouted "Masaryk!" and "freedom!" Someone read out a Charter 77 proclamation calling for a return to parliamentary democracy. As if on cue, hundreds of riot police emerged from the subway entrances and from trucks parked on the side streets. First a young man, and then a couple in their 70s, tried to place flowers at the foot of King Wenceslas. They were dragged away by the police, and the crowd hooted. As the riot police moved into the crowd with their truncheons, people broke into the national anthem even as they were clubbed to the ground.

Trucks with water cannons emerged from the side streets and forced the crowd off the square into the streets. The riot police charged these smaller groups with guard dogs. After the last demonstration, Pierre and I had decided to exchange our brogues for sneakers. Now we ran as fast as we could down the narrow streets, chased by riot police wielding truncheons. We were certainly going to the wall for the Helsinki Accords. The panic and sheer force of this crowd, charging down these narrow streets to escape the police and the dogs, was frightening, and dangerous. To fall in the midst of this stampede would have been fatal. The street we found ourselves in was typical of many, with scaffolding along some buildings. During the panic, I was shoved into one of the scaffolds and badly bruised a shoulder. Fortunately, I managed to keep my balance.

We finally eluded the police and followed the demonstrators as they made their way to the Old Town Square. Soon there were about 5,000 people in the cobblestoned square shouting slogans. Then I heard a rumbling sound echoing in the narrow medieval streets just across the way from where we were standing. It was not the sound of paddy wagons. Three black armoured personnel carriers rolled into this ancient square, like ghosts from 1968. They were sinister and threatening, totally incongruous against the pastel yellows and pinks of the baroque facades behind them. I looked at Pierre and said this was starting to get serious.

The armoured personnel carriers were like little tanks with six wheels, a small turret with a cannon, and heavy machine guns. They lined up on the cobblestones. The crowd was cornered against the medieval town hall on the spot where prominent Czech citizens had been executed by the Habsburgs in the fifteenth century for leading the Hussite revolt. These army vehicles were joined by four water cannons and twelve more paddy wagons. Suddenly, without warning, the armoured personnel carriers drove into the crowd at high speed.

We ran down side streets and the trucks with water cannons lobbed tear gas canisters after us. The tear gas did not really affect us much. We made our way down toward the river and then doubled back into town. The next two hours were spent running from street corner to street corner, the riot police playing cat and mouse with pockets of demonstrators, mostly boisterous young people roaming around downtown. People were beaten and kicked when they were caught and there were many injuries and about 200 arrests.

But the protest had been an unqualified success for the opposition. They had called for a demonstration and got a relatively large one, within the confines of a highly controlled society. It proved that the August 21 demonstration had not been an accident. It also proved that a significant minority had made a commitment to oppose the regime publicly. I was convinced that, through these demonstrations and other acts, this minority was undergoing a political apprenticeship. The regime, on the other hand, was shown to be perfectly capable of massive overreaction. This combination would eventually provide the spark that set off the revolution.

The pressure exerted by the StB on Western diplomats was mounting, and at the end of 1988 it was particularly bad for those of us who had close links with the dissidents. For a while there was a Lada containing two large men parked in front of our house, following my every move. When I went to the square to observe the police actions sponsored by the Czechoslovak Socialist Republic, a state signatory to the Helsinki Accords on human rights, I had a couple of StB agents literally ten feet behind me at every turn. It was an attempt to intimidate, but I was unconcerned by such gestures, perhaps foolishly. Pierre's predecessor in the political section of the Embassy, Peter Bakewell, had also been subjected to a lot of StB attention because of his contacts with the opposition at the time. After the revolution, Peter would be invited back to Prague by his Czech friends to attend a special Charter 77 celebration.

Of course surveillance occasionally had its comical moments. It so happened that, around the end of October, we were going to a Halloween party at the Embassy. Lynn and I, and Louise and Pierre, decided to dress up as cavemen. We used old synthetic shag rugs as a substitute for bearskin clothing (orange shag rugs, as I recall). We cut some branches to make wooden clubs, put charcoal on our faces, and some grease in our hair. Halloween is a North American ritual and it was not well known in Europe, especially in communist Czechoslovakia. I still wonder what the StB agents sitting in their Lada must have thought as the four of us drove off to the Embassy in our shag rugs. They followed us, as expected, and we laughed all the way.

The harassment we faced that fall was nothing compared with the treatment meted out to the dissidents. There had definitely been a change in the atmosphere, with much greater repression and heavier surveillance. A closed door seminar on Czechoslovak history chaired by Havel was broken up by the StB. Havel was detained for a few days as a warning. It seemed that even the discussion of history was subversive in the eyes of the regime. And so it was. The Communist Party daily, *Rudé Právo*, published boiler-plate about the Western imperialists, and their so-called diplomats, as daily fare. But I knew that Havel and the other dissidents were not about to go softly into the night.

It was at this time that Gorbachov's architect of reform, Alexander Yakovlev, came to Prague to talk with the Czechoslovak leadership. I called on my counterpart at the Soviet Embassy afterwards to obtain a briefing on the results of the discussion. Who would have thought, only a few years ago, that one had to go to the Soviet Union to get the inside story? Two chairs and a table were set up in the middle of a cavernous baroque ballroom. It was a little strange, even eerie. But the Russian told me Yakovlev had criticized the regime's crushing of the protests in Prague. He had also attacked the dogmatism of a regime tied to the heritage of Brezhnev. In his public remarks Yakovlev said, "Instead of a process whereby the state was to have been swallowed up by civil society, civil society has been swallowed up by the state and subjected to the dictates of a bureaucracy." God knows what the Stalinists in the Czech regime thought about that. But it was increasingly clear that the regime was out on a limb, all by itself.

As the December 10 UN Human Rights Day approached, the regime let it be known it would permit a demonstration in Škroupovo Square in Vinohrady, a district of Prague. This gesture seemed less surprising when it was announced shortly after that President Mitterrand would be visiting Prague on that day. The communists obviously wanted to make a good impression. The square in question was small and completely surrounded by apartment houses, so that everyone present could easily be identified. Perhaps for that reason no more than about 5,000 people came out. It was nonetheless well organized, with individuals designated by the opposition to control the crowd and keep people off the shrubs and flower beds. Václav Havel, Václav Malý (the underground priest and Charter signatory), and others spoke into a makeshift speaker system. There was even a banner or two. The crowd was enthusiastic and everyone sang the national anthem. Pierre and I were there, and Barry Mawhinney, our Ambassador, with his wife Islay. Though we were all jammed together in that small square, the Czechs exuded a sense of dignity, standing up and saying what they thought without the intimidation of a police presence.

I still felt a little disappointed afterwards. I had assumed that if a legal demonstration was permitted the whole city would come out. I obviously did not understand the political dynamic at work. I believed at the time that if the regime would have the foresight to permit peaceful demonstrations, the thrill of protest would fade after the initial demonstrations, and eventually the numbers would diminish. The regime would thereafter avoid being attacked by the West at regular meetings of the Conference on Security and Cooperation in Europe (CSCE), which had been created to monitor implementation of the Helsinki Accords. Moreover, why not loosen up if the kind of demonstration we saw on December 10 was all that would result? Within days, the demonstration was condemned by Jan Fojtík, the regime's ideology chief, for being not a human rights rally but an anti-socialist rally. He said another such demonstration would not be permitted. Obviously the demonstration that was permitted was window dressing for the Mitterrand visit the same day. The Czechs had understood this better than I. Most were not about to lose their jobs over participation in a human rights rally with no chance of affecting the regime. Or so it seemed.

Hence, just when we thought there might be light at the end of the tunnel, that Gorbachov might finally be having some influence, things looked bleaker than ever. At the end of December 1988, a plenum of the central committee of the Communist Party gave only tepid support for Gorbachov-style economic reforms. As for political change, the conservatives consolidated their position further. There would be no glasnost here, whatever Yakovlev said.

This was significant for the future. Czechoslovakia would not experience a transition from communism to liberal democracy: there would be no intermediate stage of glasnost or perestroika (restructuring). That stage had already been passed in 1968. In fact the non-communist Czechoslovaks knew exactly what they wanted. It was the kind of affluent democracy they had already possessed before the communist takeover in 1948. Perhaps this was why the regime instinctively rejected any kind of liberalization. Given an inch, people would have demanded a mile.

3

LIVING IN TRUTH

I FIRST MET VÁCLAV HAVEL at a Christmas Party in 1988 for Czech dissidents given by Bob Norman, an American diplomat. There were no diplomats present besides Bob, Pierre, and myself. Even a party like this was regarded by the regime as a provocation in those days. I had already got to know well the writer Zdeněk Urbánek, a white-haired gentleman in his 70s, whom many regarded as the grandfather of dissent. If Václav Havel had a best friend, Zdeněk was it. My wife and I found him witty and charming. He had a special way with the ladies.

Martin Palouš was a philosopher (like me) who had once been taught by Jan Patočka, the most important Czech philosopher since the war, and a founder of Charter 77. Martin would often punctuate his intense ruminations on the care of the soul, and its implications for political action, with a touch of irony and a broad smile that conveyed more than words ever could. Even when the going got tough, Martin retained an enlightened perspective on things, guided by a sure sense of principle like an internal compass.

Ivan Havel was a brilliant theorist of the information revolution, a Berkeley PhD, and Václav's younger brother. The bearded Ivan was the glue that held much of the opposition together, his quiet strength pervading any gathering of Charter signatories. Václav might have been the intellectual star of the opposition, but Ivan was its human reality. His weekly meetings of intellectuals, artists, and others in the opposition were something akin to the "salons" of pre-revolutionary France.

The author, Martin Palouš, and Ivan Havel

It is only with hindsight that we can now assess their key role in laying the groundwork for revolution, eerily reminiscent of their 200-year-old antecedents.

Václav Malý was a Catholic priest who was banned by the regime from practising publicly because of his political views. He epitomized the "underground" church, celebrating mass in the apartments of those who opposed the government, at least in part in the name of religious freedom. His hair, his earthy style, and his revolutionary fervour reminded one, paradoxically, of Martin Luther.

Ivan Chvatik was a bearded and bespectacled publisher of *samizdat* novels, essays, and poetry, and especially the writings of Jan Patočka. He exuded the careful attention to detail and that respect for the word you would expect to find in any major publishing house in the West. Ivan would help with the *samizdat* publication of my own philosophical treatise that would form the basis of an underground seminar.

These individuals became our special circle within the resistance, and our friends. They were all writers and thinkers and a pleasure to talk with about Czechoslovak affairs, or anything at all. Each was involved in a different dimension of dissent, motivated by principle as the touchstone of their existence. Yet they all acknowledged Václav Havel as both the intellectual and the moral leader of the opposition.

When I first saw Havel at Bob's party, he hardly projected this image. He was not a large man, and he walked with a barely perceptible limp, almost a shuffle. He had rather cool blue eyes, but it was difficult to see this because he mostly looked down, occasionally glancing at his interlocutor as if eye contact was more than he could bear. He appeared to be extremely shy. He arrived late, and made his way among the guests to say hello to each one. When he got to me, Pierre said I was an admirer of his writings, which was true. He just said "mmmm" without looking and shook hands and moved on to get a drink at the bar. He was totally withdrawn and somehow concentrated. None of the others approached him, only one or two old friends had a few words with him. He spent most of his time there standing by the door some distance off, talking with an elderly lady I did not recognize. He left early, and Olga did not come at all. I had wanted to meet Havel for a long time, and could not help feeling let down at the outcome.

I talked with Martin Palouš about the Czech philosopher Jan Patočka. Patočka, along with Havel and Jiří Hájek, had created Charter 77 towards the end of 1976. Hájek had been the foreign minister in the short-lived Dubček government in 1968. These three became Charter's first spokespersons. The idea was that new spokespersons would be appointed each calendar year. Becoming a Charter spokesperson for a particular year was a great honour, and a great burden, since it also meant police harassment and even jail. I talked with Martin about the philosophical considerations that lay behind the decision to become a Charter spokesperson. Martin was about my age, and as a young man had attended some of Patočka's underground philosophy seminars. Patočka was influenced by Husserl and Heidegger, but in a more profound way, I think, by Socrates. Patočka's notion of the "care of the soul" and his admonition to act in an authentic manner was a recipe for dissent under the communist regime. The regime enforced artificial obedience from the outward man, but was incapable of penetrating to the essential privacy of the inner life, as it found expression in family and among friends.

Patočka was offered the rare opportunity for a philosopher to act on the basis of his principles, as had happened to Socrates over 2,000 years before. After founding Charter 77 with Havel and Hájek, Patočka was harassed and during one of his interrogations by police died, tragically, of a heart attack. This was early in 1977. Havel and Patočka had been close intellectually, both taking up the admonitions of Jan Hus and T.G. Masaryk to always speak and live in truth. The importance of this was that Havel and Patočka, and the other members of Charter 77, were always more than dissenters from communism, which is what the unfortunate word "dissident" implies. They did not merely dissent, they had a positive view of society.

This ideal society was both pluralistic and moral, not in the sense of a moral code, but in terms of sensitivity to the rights and responsibilities of individuals. It valued the free movement of people and the free expression of their energies and aspirations. But the beliefs of the opposition amounted to more than political pluralism and a commitment to the market economy. There was a spirituality and a certain anti-materialism implicit in their views on modern life. Sometimes this was channelled into devout Catholicism, as with Václav Malý, or found expression in the mystical notions of Being evident, for example, in Havel's writings.

How this moral life was to be reflected in political structures was never clear. There seemed to be little of a political program in the various documents issued by the opposition groups, other than a call for genuine democracy and restitution of ecological and cultural patrimony. In their own lives, they refused to divorce their inner life from the outer shell of obedience to the regime. They insisted on living as normal individuals, as "whole persons." It brought them repression, and sometimes jail, but it was what "living in truth" meant. They were true to their inner life, to the value of human dignity, and to their political and cultural heritage. This often led to detention by the regime, and so living in truth regularly meant being interrogated by police, being watched and harassed, and living in prison.

Opting to oppose the regime, therefore, became an absolute, either/or, existential decision for the individual. Either you obeyed, at least outwardly, the ridiculous and dehumanizing constraints of the regime, or you threw everything away, job and material prosperity, sometimes friends, to live authentically. Most people naturally accepted living the lie at work and in public generally, while complaining about it in the relative safety of their living room. For Havel and others in the opposition this was no life at all, but rather a twilight existence in which time itself had come to a stop.

The stagnant quality of communist society, the slow technological progress and—for the Czechs—a decline in the standard of living from pre-communist days reinforced the feeling of a society frozen in history. Indeed, change was nothing else than slow decay, as buildings and the environment, and people's health, slowly deteriorated. This process was punctuated, as if to underline the fact, by the occasional grotesque steel and glass hotel, built with the expensive help of a Western company, destroying the ambience of the neighbourhood unlucky enough to include the site.

During the communist regime, it was history that had withered away. But the decay was one not only of buildings and atmosphere: it was above all a moral decay. For someone like me, it was immediately evident in public life, in the very faces of the leadership, in their meaningless statements that were the medium of violence, both real and implicit. They talked of heroism and sacrifice and the people, when one heard only of threats, lies and revenge. They privately squandered money on themselves while pretending publicly to poverty and solidarity. Newspapers, films, TV, books, theatre, the word in general, spoke only their words, played only their very dangerous language games. A furrowed brow was enough to sidetrack a career, a misplaced book or comment enough for an arrest. The glory of "victorious February," the 1948 communist coup d'état, was not to be besmirched, not by even one word, or a few, forty years later.

The moral decay was not only observable in the faces of the regime, it was evident among the people too. They had got used to being threatened, openly and implicitly; to being lectured without being able to reply; to being infiltrated and spied upon. They had become a sorry lot, but whom could they trust? And so when they met on the street, their inner debate was, "how far can I talk with this person, up to what point can I say what I think?" Inevitably, what was thought was hardly spoken at all. There was left only the charade, whose object was evasion at all costs. In this way, the inner world, one's thoughts and one's family, might be cut off and somehow preserved and protected, might somehow survive.

The surgical division of the inner life from the world around provided the feeding-ground for immorality. Not that most of us do not compromise when difficult options are presented to us. Few have the courage, or will, to resist the evil in society that we see, to try to overcome it in ourselves and in the world. This, alone, is corrupting over time. It is a kind of cynicism that obviates any responsibility. But there is always some element of responsibility, no matter how dire the situation.

I remember hearing, soon after arriving in Prague, the commonly accepted excuse for collaboration with the regime. Some Czechs would say that it was in the Czech character, a character formed by three hundred years of Austrian domination and then Nazi rule during the Second World War. The argument was that the Czechs were used to bending with the wind, to finding a way of living with repression. My standard reply was to question the easy self-justification of this generalization. I would point to the Hussite struggle against all of Catholic Europe, and to the victory of Masaryk in leading the country to independence. If it wasn't for President Beneš' mistaken capitulation in 1938, the Czechs would have fought the Nazis too. Hence, at a minimum, the jury was still out on the Czech character. But my instincts were to be confirmed by the events of November 1989.

It was true that for the twenty years after 1968 society seemed to be paralysed. The communists were easily able to intimidate most Czechs and Slovaks into quiescence. But even during these dark days, seemingly without end, Havel and the others of Charter 77 spoke out against overwhelming odds. The underground river of discontent flowed everywhere in society, and by the time I arrived, it was beginning to emerge through cracks in the glacis. Courage was catching.

4

JAN PALACH

AS THE REVOLUTIONARY YEAR 1989 began, we knew January was shaping up to be a test of will for both the regime and the opposition. Another anniversary was upon us, this time the 20th anniversary of the self-immolation of Jan Palach, a philosophy student at Charles University. Palach had committed suicide on January 16, 1969, in Wenceslas Square, by dousing himself with gasoline and setting himself on fire. He had wanted to protest the crushing of Dubček's Prague Spring reforms by Russian tanks. Charter 77 and other independent groups called for a peaceful commemoration of Palach's death.

It was difficult to exaggerate the way in which that death had reverberated in Czech minds down through the years. After the revolution I talked with the doctor who had attended Palach as he lay dying in hospital from his burns. Palach had said that he wanted the Czech people to realize what the Soviet invasion and the brutal end of the Prague Spring meant for Czechoslovakia. Dying, he kept asking the same thing, "Do they know why I did it? Do they know why?" The answer would come, twenty years later.

The day before the anniversary, on Sunday, January 15, protesters tried to gather in front of the statue of King Wenceslas and lay flowers. Army trucks and buses rolled in and about 1,000 riot police were deployed, together with regiments of the People's Militia. The People's Militia was the paramilitary arm of the Communist Party. They tried to seal off Wenceslas Square and the Old Town Square ahead of time, but about 5,000 people slipped in first. I was among them. Thousands more people stood at the barricades. Some protesters tried to throw flowers towards the foot of the statue of King Wenceslas over the heads of the police. As riot police formed in long lines in front of them, the crowd began to sing the national anthem. This was the signal for the riot police to do their work. They beat anyone within reach and chased the rest out of the square. They charged after smaller groups of people down side streets while trucks with water cannons tried to corner them. The water cannons were everywhere and fired indiscriminately at tourists, theatre goers, old people, children, anyone who happened to be downtown. I could count six armoured personnel carriers and ten fire trucks mounted with water canons.

It seemed the regime was determined to escalate the use of force. Pierre and I leaped into doorways as police cars careened down side walks at high speed in order to injure the protesters. They would then screech to a halt and two policemen would jump out, grab someone, and roar off again. It was surreal. Pierre and I finally went home remarking that these demonstrations were becoming increasingly hazardous to our health. On the next day, the actual anniversary, there was a smaller demonstration, at which Havel watched others try to lay flowers on the spot where Palach had set himself on fire. It was in the upper corner of the square, close to the Museum of Natural History. This was exactly what the regime had been waiting for. Havel was arrested and charged with inciting the demonstration.

Then, unexpectedly, on the following day, there was another demonstration, as news of the arrests spread. About 5,000 people came out and the riot police attacked again. In fact as soon as the white helmets appeared, most people fled. The rest of us were again chased down streets by police with guard dogs and water cannons. The amazing thing was that this happened every day that week—except Wednesday. There was no police intervention on that day. There was an amazing feeling of elation, of victory, in the crowd. Speeches were made and there was a new-found sense of dignity from participating in an open political forum. It so happened that Wednesday was the day the regime signed the latest CSCE document on human rights in Vienna.

As could be predicted, the next day even more people came out, and the police were even more brutal. But the real impact of this week of demonstrations was that more people from different walks of life were now involved, especially the artists, actors, and intellectuals upset at Havel's arrest. There were a few high-school kids, but still no university students. Towards the end of the week, I noticed that the police adopted a new tactic. Before the appointed hour, they threw up barricades across the streets leading to the square and blocked the metro entrances. Inside the square hundreds of city police were stationed even before the riot police emerged. By Friday night of that week, this had the effect of suffocating the demonstrations, though people in the side streets on the other side of the barricades still gathered to protest.

There was one particularly humorous moment during Thursday's otherwise brutal demonstration. The protesters had been forced from Wenceslas Square, but a large crowd regrouped in front of the philosophy faculty of Charles University. As I mentioned, Palach had been a philosophy student, and the square in front of the faculty would be renamed by the students of 1989 Palach Square in his honour, during the first days of the revolution. But on this Thursday in January 1989, a vocal crowd gathered to commemorate his sacrifice. At one point, a black Tatra limousine, reserved exclusively for the communist elite, was let through the square. It turned out to be the car of the regime's hardline ideologue, Jan Fojtík, who was with his wife. As they drove through the crowd of protesters he smiled and she waved. Two months previously she had published an article in *Rudé Právo* praising Stalin. As she drove by, she seemed to be saying something. I might have been wrong, but I think her lips said something about cake. Moments later the riot police attacked the crowd and I saw a policeman hold a nine-year-old boy with his arm behind his back, while two other policemen kicked his father as he lay on the ground.

The opposition groups wanted this week of protest to culminate with a pilgrimage to the grave-site of Jan Palach. It was to take place Saturday morning in Všetaty, a small town about half an hour's drive from of Prague. It was in this rather desolate place that Palach had grown up, and where he was now buried. I went with Pierre, Ole Mikkelsen (a Danish diplomat) and Cliff Bond (an American diplomat). We took one of the Canadian Embassy cars. It soon became clear that the police were stopping cars on the way to the town. We later heard that even the train was prevented from stopping in Všetaty. Many of those who had tried to come by train were detained all day and then taken far out into the countryside and let off in the middle of the night to make their way back to Prague on foot.

Our car, with diplomatic licence plates, was finally stopped on the outskirts of the town. There was one uniformed policeman together with five or six plain-clothes StB officers. The uniform took our identity cards and gave them to the StB. Other StB types filmed us with a video camera. It could not have been very interesting viewing back at StB headquarters. I suppose the idea was, once again, to intimidate, though I was only struck by the absurdity of it all. It seemed that graves could be revolutionary too.

After some fuss over our diplomatic cards, and some glares from the StB, we were finally allowed to go. They said that the road into town was closed for "technical reasons." We drove away from town. But we were not about to be deterred by such games, and worked our way back through the fields on side roads so that we approached the town from another direction. Všetaty was quiet, as if politically radioactive. There was literally no one on the street. We drove to the local cemetery, where Palach was buried. It was devoid of any living soul, except for two policemen patrolling the short stretch of road between the town and the cemetery. Temporary no parking signs had been installed along this stretch. The police waved us back into town. We parked on a side street and walked out to the cemetery. We arrived at exactly the time that there was supposed to be a commemoration of Palach's death, but no one else had made it. All of the Czechs had been stopped, detained, or turned back. When we got to the cemetery, it too was closed and barred, and there was a sign hanging from the gate that said "closed for technical reasons."

Walking back towards town we were surprised to see another car come slowly toward us. As the car approached, it was evident that there were a couple of StB agents inside. The one in the passenger seat was filming us with a video camera, and I took my hat off to provide a better shot. The whole encounter was a bit of theatre worthy of one of Havel's plays. We were alone with the StB, caught up in a confrontation over human rights on a deserted road in the middle of nowhere. At least that was how we saw the encounter. God knows what was going on in their heads. They just drove by slowly, disappearing down the road into the distance.

This event turned out to be my spot in the communist limelight. The next day there was a front page editorial in *Rudé Právo*, the Communist Party daily, that referred in the opening line to diplomats from the Canadian Embassy who had been in Všetaty, apparently to foment trouble. As we drove back through town on our way home, we came across an Austrian TV crew looking for the action. They seemed somewhat forlorn, standing with their equipment in the deserted square of the small town. Closed for technical reasons. Along the highway that led back to Prague, there were a number of Czech cars en route to Všetaty that had been pulled over by the police. People were lined up against the cars and were being questioned.

The odd thing was that there were no more anniversaries in the spring of 1989 that could be used by the opposition to launch new demonstrations. Moreover, the riot police had perfected their technique by the end of that week of demonstrations in January. They began using barricades to close off Wenceslas Square and the Old Town Square, and the streets in between, before the appointed hour. They fielded thousands of policemen to do so. If you managed to get into Wenceslas Square before the barricades went up (and this meant you had to be there hours before time) you found policemen stationed every few feet. If anyone started to loiter in front of the statue of the King, they were soon hustled off. The Independent Peace Initiative, still calling for demonstrations on the last Saturday of every month, failed to get any kind of turnout, because the sites were just too well controlled by the police.

The first phase of street protests had come to an end. What had been gained? The protests had broadened the base of opposition, and focused both Western and Soviet attention on the regime's anachronistic policies. The battle over anniversaries, over history, had been won. But the overwhelming majority of Czechoslovaks had yet to make the move from private to public resistance.

5

THE POLITICAL TRIALS

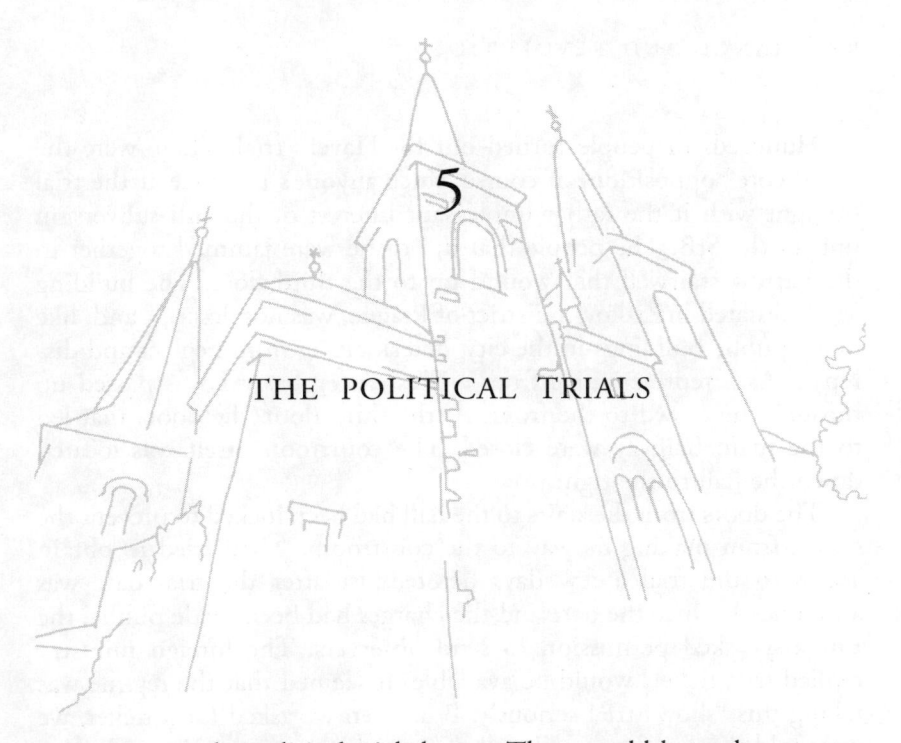

IN FEBRUARY, the political trials began. They would keep the pressure up, on both the regime and the opposition, in a way rather different from the street protests. During the week of demonstrations in January not only Havel but hundreds of opposition people, and people protesting for the first time, had been detained. Most were charged with relatively small crimes, and after a week in jail and a fine they were let out. Havel and some others from Charter 77 were charged with more serious crimes. Tomás Dvořák and Hana Marvanova, from the Independent Peace Initiative, had been kept in jail since the October demonstrations. There had as yet been no trial.

To reinforce the expression of continuing Canadian concern about these travesties of justice we decided that I would go to Havel's trial. Pierre would attend the trial of eight others being prosecuted together. We wanted to make it clear to the communist regime that the Canadian government was monitoring the regime's human rights performance in terms of its commitments to the Helsinki Accords. The regime, for its part, seemed perfectly willing to sacrifice its obligations under the Accords, and its international image, in the pursuit of domestic control. Havel was charged with incitement because he had invited people to commemorate peacefully Palach's death. A whole new range of stiffer penalties for opposition activities had been introduced by the regime only a few weeks earlier.

Hundreds of people turned out for Havel's trial. These were the "hard core" opposition, of course, since anyone's presence at the trial brought with it the rather unpleasant interest of the anti-subversion unit of the StB. The people that did come were jammed together in the narrow stairwell that wound up to the third floor. The building itself, situated in Žižkov, a district of Prague, was nondescript and, like many public buildings in the city, deteriorating from neglect and disrepair. As a representative from a Western embassy I was passed up through the crowd to the front. At the third floor, the doors that led to the main hallway were closed. The courtroom itself was located down the hall to the right.

The doors from the stairs to the hall had been locked to prevent the crowd from making its way to the courtroom. I had tried to obtain access to the trial a few days before, just after the trial date was announced. Once the date and the charges had been made public, the Embassy asked permission to send observers. The foreign ministry replied that tickets would be available. It seemed that the regime was taking this "show" trial seriously. But when we asked for a ticket, we were told that, unfortunately, all of the tickets were gone! On the day of the trial, the courtroom was mostly empty except for Ivan and Dáša Havel, Václav's wife Olga, and one token Western journalist.

At the glass doors at the top of the stairs I presented my diplomatic identity card and made a pitch to the guard there that I should be admitted to the trial. He consulted his superior in the hallway and I was refused. So we waited, sandwiched together like sardines against the glass doors. I recognized a good number of the opposition people present, but there were one or two individuals mixed in the crowd who were clearly StB plants. A few words and a few looks were exchanged, but the general reaction was to ignore them. The opposition people had already lost everything the regime could take away from them. They had lost their real jobs and been offered jobs as stokers, street sweepers, or window washers. Either they or their children had been barred from university. Many friends and neighbours no longer spoke to them. The isolation and impoverishment sometimes led to divorce and alcoholism, and the effect on children could be devastating. The only thing they still had to lose was a further restriction of their physical freedom, since they could not travel out of the country, and travel within the country was complicated by the StB. Even one's own home was invaded by phone tapping and unexpected visits from the StB at any time of day.

The regime did its level best to restrict any kind of personal privacy for the opposition. This was countered by the personal friendships within the opposition itself, the support network that formed the basic organizational structure of the revolution. But the regime could take the friendships away too, at the end of the day, by simply jailing people. Standing in the crowd at Havel's trial were young people and people in their forties and fifties, all dressed in the sixties counter-culture clothes, and all with a kind of quiet determination that seemed essentially Czech.

Various communist officials passed in the hall on the other side of the glass. There was a woman judge, in her early forties. She seemed to be well-known among the opposition. They told me that she was the equivalent of a hanging judge, with a reputation for sending dissidents away for long stiff sentences regardless of what happened in the courtroom. I had heard that other communist judges had come up with a variety of reasons to excuse themselves from trying Havel. Perhaps they had calculated, rightly, that there would be a lot of international interest, and that the trial would be by definition a show trial. Perhaps some even wondered if one day the trial would not come back to haunt them, no doubt in the very distant future. All of the judges in the communist system, including this woman judge, were notorious for their almost total lack of formal education. They were appointed and given some kind of bogus party-school diploma as a reward for unfailing loyalty. Besides the woman judge, I noticed a young fellow on the bench in the hall, about eighteen or nineteen years old. He had apparently taken part in the demonstrations, and the StB had exerted pressure on him to identify Havel as having been at the January demonstration.

Then Ivan and Dáša Havel, and Václav Havel's wife, Olga, appeared in the hall and I said hello to them as they came over to the glass doors. At last came Havel himself, marched down the hall by two thugs holding his arms on either side. His hands were cuffed in front of him, despite the fact escape was anything but the remotest possibility. The crowd, jammed together in the winding staircase, started shouting "long live Havel!" and "freedom!" Despite the confusion and discomfort, it was a moving moment: this rag-tag group of people standing up to state power on the basis of fundamental principles, seemingly without the expectation of real change. This was the tradition of Thoreau and Gandhi. Havel managed a smile as he saw us through the glass, and raised his bound hands in the form of a salute.

He was wearing a black armband which stood out against his white shirt. It had been tied on by the police, a traditional means of identifying the accused. And then he was gone.

The long wait began, hour after hour. Suddenly there was a break in the proceedings. It seemed that the young man had, in court, refused to identify Havel as having been present at the demonstration. The student was not willingly going to play the role of Judas. The prosecution was thrown into confusion and the hanging judge called a recess. I spoke to Ivan Havel and Olga Havel in the street outside during the recess, and they were, understandably, downcast. Their only hope was that the prosecution might find itself in such difficulty that the final outcome would not be as bad as they expected. We went back into the court house. Those of the opposition who had gone outside for a smoke now found that they were blocked by the police from reentering. No reason was given.

I was let in, and joined those who had stayed on at the glass doors at the top of the staircase. The prosecution decided it would no longer aspire to a sophisticated process. It simply called on a couple of StB thugs to identify Havel as having been present at the demonstration. This decision removed the trial's last shred of pretence to objectivity, but in the end who really expected it? I was to learn later that the whole business of dealing with Havel, including the arrest, the charges, the trial, and the sentence, had been decided by the communist leadership in advance. The judge was simply presiding over a bit of theatre, all that her no doubt limited qualifications permitted.

We had at least managed to get a copy of Havel's own statement for his defence from his brother Ivan. It was a humane and profound discourse, without doubt completely incomprehensible to the communist officials listening. Havel ended his remarks by saying, "If sentenced to prison, I accept the verdict as a necessary sacrifice for doing what is right."

Then, finally, came the sentence. It turned out to be relatively harsh, given the nature of the case. Havel was sentenced to nine months in a second-category prison. This meant there was no option for parole. Equally worrisome were the physical conditions of the second-category prison system. Havel would be jailed with criminals who had committed violent crimes. There would be forced labour in conditions considered to be too dangerous for normal workers, whose workplaces were already dangerous enough by Western standards. Visits and letters were restricted to one per month. This was tantamount to isolation. For Havel, now over fifty and with recurring and serious health problems, the sentence would be a physical, if not a psychological, blow. Havel said he would appeal.

We filed out of the derelict building into the darkness. The cold was damp and smelt of sulphur from the burning of soft coal that was heating old Prague. Olga Havel and Ivan Havel were quiet and obviously worried, as were we all. There was nothing left to say. They, and Václav, and the others who had come to the trial, had committed themselves to the long fight many years ago. This was simply one more chapter. Some might have said another "hopeless" chapter, though hope and the tenuous thread that attached these people to the West was precisely what kept them going. It seemed my role was to be the somewhat frayed end of that long thin thread. It was, after all, not I that mattered, but that fabric of civilization, linking men and women of humane aspect across thousands of miles in the most different circumstances.

As we poured into that night, there were trials going on in other parts of the city, with others being jailed, many of whom I knew. There was a feeling that something was in the wind, for better or worse. There was a new sense of expectation that had not been there even a few months before. The atmosphere had changed. In reflecting on my time in Prague, I saw that a new civic society had begun to emerge outside the control of the state, with a whole network of underground publications, performances, exhibitions, videos, newspapers, artistic and literary "salons." These had started to reach beyond the opposition to the grey zone of individuals who were at least inwardly, if not openly, opposed to the regime.

This newly emerging civic society was bridging the gap between the inner and outer man, a gap that was the essential psychological prop to all communist regimes. The network of opposition was reinforced by Radio Free Europe, which provided an information service linking the various underground circles that were springing up all over the country. Of course it was still risky business to show the slightest resistance to the regime, and the average Czech who was found participating in unapproved activities or in possession of unauthorized material was regularly jailed.

The regime had agreed to stop jamming Czech language RFE broadcasts only after pressure from the Russians, and then only reluctantly. The USSR had agreed in January to stop its own jamming as a commitment under the Vienna Document of the Helsinki Accords. But even as the Czech communists signed on, they persisted in busting up demonstrations with a liberal use of violence, and jailed those who dared to speak out.

One can think of few more trenchant examples of hypocrisy than the spectacle of the foreign minister of the Czechoslovak Socialist Republic signing the Vienna human rights document and speaking in lofty tones about it while the regime's riot police were beating people up in Wenceslas Square. Their crime was the peaceful commemoration of the death twenty years before of Jan Palach, who was, admittedly, hardly a communist hero. Palach had, with his suicide, symbolized resistance against Soviet repression. How ironic that the Soviet communists were now pressuring the Czech communists to loosen up a bit.

Coincidentally with Soviet pressure on the Czech regime, the "correlation of forces" inside the country moved into a state of flux. At the end of January's week of protests I declared in a telegram to HQ that the continuing, perhaps precipitous erosion of the regime's authority in the eyes of a reawakened public would be the story of 1989. To diplomatic colleagues from other Western embassies it was a foolhardy prediction. Most thought I was wildly optimistic. But I pointed out that Czech society had become dynamic: social and political attitudes were changing rapidly, and the momentum of social change was putting pressure on an ossified regime seeking to keep change in check. It may have been a superficial impression, but the communist leadership seemed to me to be nothing more than a small group of old men who were out of touch with reality. The week of protests in January was reality knocking at the door.

In the weeks following the demonstrations and Havel's trial, those dissidents who had not been jailed began circulating a petition. The significance of this was not the petition itself, since no one expected the regime to act on its demands. The significance lay in who agreed to sign it. Over 700 Czech artists, writers, and intellectuals, including well-known TV actors, signed their names to a petition destined to Prime Minister Adamec protesting both the violence used to suppress the demonstrations and Havel's arrest.

Cardinal Tomášek wrote his own letter to Adamec voicing the same concerns. This was the first time that Tomášek had spoken out publicly on a non-church issue. The arrest and continuing detention of Havel soon became a focus for both domestic and international pressure. The Ambassador, Barry Mawhinney, and I made several diplomatic démarches to the foreign ministry conveying Canadian demands for the fulfilment of international human rights commitments. This international attention encouraged, and perhaps helped to legitimize, a broadening of the opposition to the regime to include the cultural community, scientists, the church, and a discontented middle class. With an economy now clearly in terminal decline, the middle class was coming to terms with reduced expectations. The protests of January had become a psychological milestone for a reawakened civic life. This reawakening was only strengthened by the paranoid and hysterical media campaign unleashed in the communist press, which saw subversives and NATO spies under every bed.

Tomás Hradílek was one of the three Charter 77 spokespersons for 1989. He wrote two open letters complaining about police brutality at the demonstrations and about the trials. One letter was sent to the regime's leadership, and the other to all CSCE states, including Canada. For this act, he was charged with "incitement" and with "damaging state interests abroad." If found guilty, he would be liable to five years in prison. In addition to the issues raised by Hradílek, his own prosecution was another flagrant human rights abuse, and we at the Embassy were committed to pursuing it too.

The first international conference to review the CSCE Vienna document on human rights would take place from May 30 to June 23 in Paris. Hradílek's trial was set for April 4. In light of this timing, we decided to make vigorous démarches to the foreign ministry both demanding an explanation for Hradílek's arrest and seeking information as permitted under the Vienna document. Relations between Canada and the Czechoslovak communist regime were brittle to say the least, and the regime repeatedly castigated both the Embassy and Canada for our aggressive defence of human rights. They called it interference in the internal affairs of another state. The experience of totalitarian regimes in the 1930s and 1940s in Europe and Russia had already rendered such a defence moot. And despite their rejection of our démarches we had an impact. Hradílek was found guilty, but he was given a lengthy suspended sentence, and was not jailed. The fact that Canada had championed his case had weighed in the balance. It was essential for those in the opposition to know that the world had not forgotten them, even when they were in the grip of the regime's repressive machinery.

6

THE SYMPOSIUM

MY OWN COMMITMENT to the defence of human rights in Czechoslovakia was, at least in part, the result of my becoming acquainted with the dissidents on a more personal basis. Foreign policy had taken on a human face, and policy options became existential choices. Perhaps this was the way foreign policy should always be made: as if it made a difference, as if your life, or someone else's, depended on it. My growing friendship with Ivan Havel, Václav's brother, led to his inviting me to lead a symposium at one of his Monday night intellectual gatherings. These were what I described earlier as Ivan's "salons." They were held in the apartment the two brothers shared. The topics for these evenings ranged from politics to art, literature and philosophy, and Ivan asked me to present a paper on Hegel. He had heard that I had previously published a book on the German philosopher.

The meetings were, of course, underground, to the extent that they were attended by people active in the opposition, mostly from Charter 77. They took it for granted that their attendance would be duly registered by the StB surveillance team. This underground quality gave the evenings a rather special atmosphere, since, though they were attended by the best and the brightest, there was an almost unquenchable thirst for intellectual contact with the West, something the regime had denied them for twenty years. It was the kind of audience most speakers could only dream about.

I suggested to Ivan that my topic would be Hegel's concept of the end of history. This was before the theme was more popularly expounded by others later that year. I wanted to focus on Hegel's ideas about the relation of civic society to the state, which seemed to me to be entirely relevant to the civic society being nurtured by the opposition within the communist regime. Then, with my paper in hand, I had to postpone my lecture two days before I was due to deliver it.

Life had become increasingly difficult for the few diplomats in Prague who had fostered links with the opposition. Barry, my Ambassador, was called into the Foreign Ministry and told that the StB was pushing to have one of Canada's diplomats expelled. The Czechoslovak foreign minister was inclined to agree. This would mean that the diplomat would be declared *persona non grata*. We referred to this in the trade as being "PNG'd."

The director of the third department in the Foreign Ministry, which covered Canada, said that he had opposed the proposed action. He had made the case to the foreign minister that expelling a Canadian diplomat now would only lead to retaliation on the Canadian side, and so on. As a result, the Czechoslovak foreign minister agreed that the Embassy would be spared this expulsion for a probationary period, on condition that it cease all activities which the foreign ministry deemed "inappropriate."

At the time, there was no question in my own mind that, in the eyes of the Foreign Ministry, inappropriate activities included my contacts with the Havels and the rest of the opposition. In fact we learned shortly after the revolution that the Canadian diplomat who had been on the verge of being expelled was me. Apparently the StB had quite a thick file. The Foreign Ministry had been supplied with all the gory details, including photos.

At the Embassy, we discussed the various acpects of the situation and concluded that the threat of expulsion was serious. Without more information from the foreign ministry, this was what we had to assume. We had known there might be a price to pay when we made our decision to pursue principle-based contacts with the opposition and to exert maximum pressure on the regime for its human rights abuses. It was clear that this would put us in the doghouse diplomatically, and it was already pretty well impossible for us to obtain a call on a communist minister. The Embassy's strategy, in response to the threat of expulsion, required me to ease up on my contacts for a month, and then return to the charge. This still left me the difficult task of telling Ivan, with only two days notice, that I had to postpone my philosophy symposium. Worse, I could not give him a decent explanation, since all matters relating to expulsions were closely held.

I went with Pierre to the apartment shared by Ivan and Václav. Ivan no doubt guessed something was up from the tone of my phone call. Pierre and I parked the Embassy car on a side street near the river embankment named after Engels, where the Havels' apartment was located. It was pouring rain as we scurried into the entrance of Ivan's building. The apartment block, originally built in art deco style by Ivan and Václav's father, was in bad repair. Like virtually everything in Czechoslovakia, it had been nationalized by the state and then left untouched for decades.

We decided to walk up the six floors rather than take the ancient elevator. Ivan and his wife Dáša were there, and they graciously served tea as we sat in an alcove by the window looking over the Vltava river. We talked a little while about the weekend cottage they were building together, a Czech pastime on both sides of dissent. Then I told him I would have to postpone my talk, and how disappointed I was about this. I vaguely hinted that it had to do with my role as a diplomat in the country. I said that without that role I would not be there at all, and that my continued presence in the country was at the whim of the communist authorities.

I am not sure Ivan got the drift of what I was trying to say, but I could not be more specific. I felt generally depressed about the whole thing. Ivan, in his usual polite way, tried to make light of the problem and understood that it was tied up with the arcane world of diplomacy. He did allude to the fact that, unfortunately, there was considerable interest in my talk, and that another underground philosophy symposium on the same evening had been cancelled so that all of Prague's philosophical opposition could be present at mine. This, of course, only depressed me more. He then wondered what he would tell the guests, so that it would not reflect badly on me or the Canadian Embassy. He could hardly say I was sick. I thought that if, at a minimum, there was somebody else to give a paper, that would lessen the inconvenience for those who would otherwise have come for nothing. Ivan thought that Radim Palouš, Martin's father, might have something in a drawer that he could use. Radim Palouš was a former philosophy professor at Charles University who had been fired because he had signed Charter 77.

Pierre and I made our way to Radim's cramped flat on Kampa Island in the Vltava River. Access to the island was via a steep staircase directly off Charles Bridge, or by a smaller bridge straddling a branch of the Vltava near the French Embassy. The small island looked desolate that day, the trees dark and barren under cloudy February skies. Faded yellow and pink buildings dating from the eighteenth century curved around a small square. There was a small café near the steps leading from Charles Bridge.

We found Radim's ground-floor flat with difficulty, since there was no obvious numbering system on the island. He came to the door and welcomed us in. I could make out rows and rows of books in the half-light. The whole flat had the feel of a comfortable study, and Radim with his beard and his girth seemed the perfect match for his surroundings. A very serious man, Radim was capable of thinking through virtually any problem with the greatest objectivity and allegiance to the strictures of logic. He understood perfectly my problem, and I was relieved that there was not the slightest criticism in his remarks. He would be more than happy to stand in for me at Ivan's philosophical discussion group. He thought he might have something in his top drawer that he could revise in time. I was not surprised, after the revolution, that Radim Palouš was acclaimed Rector of Charles University.

Though I was very disappointed about the postponement of my talk, I was at the same time determined to avoid expulsion. Ivan's evening went ahead as planned. I heard later that they did not in the end discuss Radim's paper. The debate focused on the conflicting obligations of politics and philosophy, and about whether the philosopher should make concessions to political expediency. I gather the debate was sharp indeed. It was curious to discover that Ivan and I both suffered restrictions on our intellectual life, and that, if anything, I had less freedom than he in the circumstances. The restrictions were, of course, part of the artificial situation created by the regime, where we were all exposed to the force of sanction, whether this be prison or expulsion. My reaction to the state's unjust interference in civic life made me all the more keen to present my paper a month later.

About this time, in the spring of 1989, the opposition and what had become known as the "grey zone" of the inwardly committed were increasingly active in a variety of initiatives. This was not evident on the streets: there were no demonstrations during these months. The use of arrests, detentions, barricades and a massive police presence had more or less pre-empted any public protests. But there were more and more independent groups popping up. One was called "The Society for a Merrier Present." They staged several events, one of which I witnessed on Charles Bridge.

On this occasion, the Society ceremoniously unfurled some banners on sticks and began marching up and down the bridge, wearing watermelon helmets. The banners were completely blank, but the Švejk-like parody of communist marches put a smile on everyone's face. The "happening" achieved apotheosis when the police arrived, confiscated the blank banners, and arrested the perpetrators. It was a media event, except that there was no media presence and hence no real hope. And the arrests were real. The Society's humour was black indeed. Not long after, the Society advertised a foot race along a street in downtown Prague named, incongruously, "Prisoners of Conscience." The slogan at the bottom of the hand-printed note said: "Today we race for you. Tomorrow you race for us."

7

THE RESISTANCE SPREADS

THE MOST SIGNIFICANT political event of the spring was the letter launched by the opposition calling for Havel's release from prison. From the start, people connected with the theatre were the strongest supporters, as well as Charter 77. This support soon spread to scientists, academics, artists, and musicians, a wholly new phenomenon. It seemed the inwardly committed of the grey zone, between the regime on the one hand and the dissidents on the other, were converting their convictions into public action. This civic action inside the borders of Czechoslovakia was matched by increased pressure on the regime from outside.

Some Western countries, particularly Canada, Britain, the United States and the Netherlands, persisted in the exercise of their new rights under the Vienna human rights document, which now formed part of the Helsinki Accords. This document, signed in January by foreign ministers from both East and West, gave all signatories the right to investigate human rights complaints in other countries, to institute impartial investigations, and to report on the results to the other signatories. We and a few others continued to pummel the communists with complaints and requests for information about Havel's arrest and the arrests of other dissidents.

I think that the regime, and especially the Foreign Ministry, were somewhat taken aback by the intensity of our activity on this score. Canada's Foreign Minister cancelled a scheduled meeting with his

Czech communist counterpart as a protest against the regime's treatment of its own citizens. The diplomatic protests and demands for information delivered by the Ambassador, Barry Mawhinney, and myself, were matched increasingly by European countries. The director of the Third Territorial Department in the Foreign Ministry, who was responsible for North America and Europe, stopped coming to work. We heard that he had had a nervous breakdown.

There was evidence of some Soviet prodding of the Czech communist leadership to loosen up, though this was going on in the background. All in all, the message was getting through, because the regime suddenly shortened Havel's sentence by one month. More importantly, the regime also decided that the sentence would be served in a first-category, as opposed to a second-category, prison. The first-category prison system was a minimum security regime, so that Havel would not be faced with forced labour under dangerous conditions. The switch also had the effect of making him eligible for parole after serving five months, in May.

Barry and I went to see Havel at his apartment a few days after his release. We drove in the official car, with the Canadian flag flapping from its standard above the front right headlight. We were not about to conceal our visit, as if Havel was some kind of disreputable character. The car pulled right up in front of the apartment block in clear view of the construction wagon that we knew housed StB surveillance. In addition to making a rather visible point about Canadian government support for Havel, I must admit that I also obtained a modicum of pleasure from thumbing our nose at the security apparatus. But when Václav opened the door, my exuberance vanished. He was thin and pale, and his health was obviously not good. He joked about the fact that his moustache had been shaved off and his hair clipped short in prison. He would proceed to grow them back.

What was most surprising, however, was his energy, determination, and optimism, despite his uncertain health. Havel was full of ideas and more intense than ever. The apartment had become a centre of activity since his release. The telephone and door bells rang incessantly and journalists from around the world were obliged with interviews over the phone. Between calls, he joked that he was expected to be an expert on everything, from developments in the USSR to China. At another moment, he huddled in the hallway with a representative of Solidarity, who was travelling from Budapest to Warsaw via Prague. Finally he sat down with us and said categorically that the atmosphere in Czechoslovakia had changed, that something had happened to people's attitudes.

In fact Havel said he would be glad to go to prison anytime if it generated the same kind of support. He was tremendously buoyed up by the spread of opposition to the regime, reflected in the many signatures appended to the petition for his release. Havel recalled that, already last December, when he was trying to launch a petition of his own for Ivan Jirous, a dissident publisher now in prison, he could see a shift in attitudes. Though few agreed to sign the petition for Jirous, many had said they would be prepared to come forward to support a well-known figure, such as Havel himself. And of course this is exactly what happened. The cultural community responded with surprising strength and unity of purpose in condemning his arrest and the brutal repression of the demonstrations. The government was increasingly in a corner, fighting off the rising tide of public opinion both domestically and internationally. Its actions had become hard to predict. As he recounted this and his thoughts about the future, we came to call the chain-smoking concentrated figure before us "the new Havel." He had always been thoughtful and intense, but now he was intensity in a hurry.

I took the opportunity to ask Havel about Dubček. Dubček had begun to emerge from twenty years of silence earlier that spring. Since the Warsaw Pact invasion in 1968, and his eventual overthrow and ouster from the Communist Party a few months later, he had been working as a mechanic in a forest products factory outside Bratislava, in Slovakia. All of this time he had been closely watched and virtually isolated from the society around him. He was not permitted to appear anywhere in public. In the communist newspapers, before the twentieth anniversary of the invasion on August 20, 1988, there were virulent editorials about him, calling him "that political wreck from 1968." They argued that he knew full well the Russians would invade, and had callously failed to inform the rest of the leadership or his people. Though Dubček had made mistakes, in my view due to a degree of political naivete, he was incapable of either the wilful deceit or the egotism of which he was accused by the party hacks.

In the spring of 1989, Dubček had managed surreptitiously to tape an interview with Hungarian TV. The Hungarian government was at this time determined to open every communist closet it could find to expose the skeletons hanging there. Both Hungary and Poland were well-launched on a path that was taking them from reform communism to anti-communism. This was not to be the route taken by the Czechs, who went straight from resistance to revolution without passing through reform. The Hungarian TV show, called Panorama, was a kind of muckraking Central European version of Sixty Minutes.

Panorama had decided to talk to Dubček about 1968, and somehow they pulled it off without having their tape confiscated.

Dubček, for his part, held nothing back. The show was broadcast in two parts, in April and May, and was received over the air not only in Hungary but in southern Slovakia too. Dubček spoke about his aspirations for Czechoslovakia in 1968. He talked about the political and economic reforms of the day and the popular support for his government. Then he described the pressure tactics used by Brezhnev, the invasion, and his kidnapping by the Russians. Dubček had been particularly disappointed by the fact that the other reformers of the day, such as Kadár in Hungary, had failed to support him and thus prevent the invasion.

The program caused quite an uproar, and the Czechoslovak communists protested against Hungarian "interference in internal Czechoslovak affairs." At the beginning of the next instalment of the interview, the Hungarian moderator said that the current Czechoslovak regime apparently did not like his interference with microphones in the domestic affairs of Czechoslovakia. On the other hand, the regime seemed to find interference with tanks entirely acceptable. The announcer then apologized that, unfortunately, he had no tanks at his disposal.

RFE rebroadcast the program over short wave across Czechoslovakia, and suddenly Dubček became a topic of conversation again. It has to be remembered now that, though Havel was a hero to Westerners and to the relatively small circle of the opposition, he was not well known, or even known at all, to the average Czech or Slovak. Sometimes the communist press hinted that he was a counter-revolutionary fascist working for the CIA. But Dubček, well, everyone knew who Dubček was. He still symbolized in the public mind that longing for the freedom that had been snatched away by the Russians.

Dubček's covert broadcast took place against the backdrop of uncoordinated agitation for more freedom that had spread beyond Prague. In the town of Plzeň, to the west, a surprisingly large crowd came out to commemorate the American liberation of that region of Czechoslovakia in 1945. It was broken up by the police. The same fate was experienced by a crowd of Slovaks just outside Bratislava who had gathered in memory of Milan Štefanik, a Slovak who had helped found Czechoslovakia in 1918 alongside Masaryk.

In Prague itself the May Day celebrations were normally a ritualized obeisance to communism and to the party as the vanguard of the proletariat. The parade in Wenceslas Square was a highly regimented deployment of communists from factories, mines, and railroads interspersed with the People's Militia. Scintillating stuff. So much so that it was carried live on TV. But this year, a few foolhardy members of the opposition had slipped into the parade and managed to arrive in front of the leaders and the TV cameras with a banner reading "keep smiling." They were hustled away by the police at the last moment, but everyone except the apparatchiks laughed. All of these events took place while rumours circulated that Gorbachov was going to force change in Czechoslovakia: he would condemn the Warsaw Pact invasion of 1968. This would have thrown the very legitimacy of the regime into question, with unpredictable consequences.

The very day that Havel was released from prison Dubček had gone to visit him at his apartment in Prague. Word of this had spread like wildfire through the city. Now, as Barry and I were talking with him, I asked Havel if he had discussed politics with Dubček. This was the first time the two men had met in over twenty years. Havel said he had been surprised by Dubček's visit. Dubček had been in town for "other negotiations" and, hearing about Havel, had decided to drop by. Though he had intended to stay only for a short while, Dubček talked with Havel for over three hours. Havel said that he liked Dubček, and that Dubček made everyone feel relaxed and friendly. He made people laugh. Havel said that though they spent the evening together, they did not discuss any concrete political action. They discussed only personal matters.

Asked what all this meant, Havel said that its importance lay in its symbolism. It evinced a common approach in opposition to the regime. He did not think that the meeting would have been possible a year ago. Dubček was the politician, and he had made a political assessment of sorts. Havel added that he, of course, was no politician. The fact that Dubček had made a decision about the current state of affairs obviously appeared hopeful to Havel. He said that Dubček must also have judged that the atmosphere was changing.

Havel thought that Dubček's goal was to rehabilitate the program of the Prague Spring and the millions of people who had lost their jobs and careers after the invasion. He seemed to feel close to Dubček, and the meeting forged an alliance that was to reemerge at a crucial stage of the revolution. I then asked Havel if he was an optimist or a pessimist when it came to the future, with regard to both the government and the people. He said, without hesitation, that as far as the people were concerned, he was an optimist.

The meeting of Dubček and Havel had created a bridge between the liberals of the 1968 Prague Spring and the dissident opposition that had developed in the 1970s and 1980s. But some, at the time, argued that the most important opposition group was neither the one nor the other. It was the church. And in some ways, they were right. Though Jan Hus was a Czech from Prague, and though the Czech Hussites had fought long—ultimately unsuccessful—wars against the Roman Catholic Church, the victory of the Austrians over the Czechs in the seventeenth century had ensured that the country was converted to Catholicism. Before the communist coup d'état in 1948 the Czech attitude toward the church had been somewhat laconic. True, the church was an integral part of society, but religious fervour was hardly widespread. Tolerance was the order of the day, and in the nineteenth and twentieth centuries Catholics, Protestants, and Jews interacted amiably. The communist takeover after the war changed the role of the church dramatically.

The regime banned religious orders, confiscated church property, and asserted administrative control over the ordination of priests, the assignment of parishes, and the nomination of bishops and so on. The strategy of the regime was gradually to suffocate the church, and the number of persons permitted religious schooling and ordination was systematically reduced. Perhaps more insidious was the fact that important jobs in a factory, on a collective farm, in just about any enterprise, or in government, required Communist Party membership, and such membership was considered incompatible with church attendance.

But, most crucially, the forced split between the inner and the outer man under communism led to the atrophy of ethical debate, even of conscience. By seeking to speak to the whole man, the church was seen as implicitly undermining the very basis of the regime. Not that the church did not try to fight back. By 1989, the struggle was taking a new turn.

Over the years the church and the regime had reached some accommodation on the nomination of certain ecclesiastical positions, though the church never gave up the principle of having sole responsibility for these appointments. By 1989, there was no agreement on the appointment of over ten bishops, and these seats were simply left empty. For his part, the Archbishop of Prague, Cardinal Tomášek, had slowly begun to harden his attitude against the regime. Though he had never supported the communists, his innate conservatism had held him back from rocking the boat. There was also the fact that a head-on confrontation with the regime might have led to the banning of the church altogether.

Tomášek refused to disown those priests who had been banned by the regime from celebrating mass because of their dissident views. These priests, such as Václav Malý, went on practising "underground," celebrating mass for people in the opposition in apartments away from the eyes of the authorities. Nor did Tomášek disown the pilgrimages that became literally mass movements, in defiance of the regime. But in 1989, a petition demanding religious freedom had been launched by a somewhat eccentric believer. It succeeded in obtaining over 600,000 signatures from both Czechs and Slovaks. The regime condemned the petition and committed the author to a psychiatric hospital. Just as he had refused to disown the underground priests and the pilgrimages, so Tomášek now refused to disown the petition. Tensions between the regime and the church, in the guise of an increasingly intractable Tomášek, were heating up.

They reached a high point in June, during Cardinal Tomášek's 90th birthday celebrations. He decided that he would receive Havel and Dubček, and each went separately to offer their best wishes. It is difficult now to appreciate how provocative this was at the time, at least in the eyes of the communists. Havel and Dubček were public enemies number one and two, though it was difficult to guess who had top honours. The fact that Tomášek received them, quite openly and publicly, confirmed the symbolic emergence of a new alliance. There was Havel, with support from Charter 77 and the other opposition groups, intellectuals, and artists; Dubček, and the not inconsiderable number of casualties from 1968; and Tomášek, at the head of a large mass of increasingly restless believers. And then something happened that gave yet another twist to the events of that fateful year. The massacre in Tiananmen Square.

8

A FEW SENTENCES

THE TIANANMEN MASSACRE of June, 1989 had a chilling effect on Czechoslovak society under the communist regime. The communist leadership, almost gleefully, announced its support for the Chinese communist party and the actions the Chinese regime were taking to crush dissent. Even the Russians did not go so far. Though the opposition was deepening and spreading, the massacre introduced a new note of uncertainty. There were rumours, probably started by the StB, that Jan Fojtík, the hardliner in the politburo responsible for ideology, had in a closed door party session argued for the use of live ammunition at future demonstrations. Undeterred, the opposition renewed its attack in mid-June with the launching of a new petition called "A Few Sentences."

The petition had been drafted sufficiently broadly to capture the support of many in the grey zone who were losing patience with the regime. Its title echoed a petition that had been circulated in 1968, called "A Thousand Words." The latter had been written by a Czech poet, Ludvík Vaculík. It had demanded much faster and broader reforms than even those that the Dubček government was undertaking. That first petition, which had received considerable support at the time, was later referred to by the Russians as one of the principal reasons for the Warsaw Pact invasion of August, 1968.

This time around, "A Few Sentences" recognized that more and more people were prepared to express their desire for change. Their wishes were running headlong into the inertia of the regime and threatened a crisis which no one wanted. The petition then asked that political prisoners be released, freedom of assembly be granted, censorship be abolished, religious rights be respected, industrial projects be assessed environmentally, and that the Prague Spring and "normalization" be discussed openly.

In an article published in the British newspaper *The Independent* days after the petition was launched, Havel noted that though Czechoslovak society had long ben decimated, silenced, and fragmented, it was slowly beginning to lose patience. He added,

As a result, even the 'dissidents' are ceasing to be just some kind of isolated handful of suicidal maniacs who might enjoy the tacit admiration of the public, but could not expect any visible help from it, as was for years the case.... The spontaneous independent demonstrations in August, October, and December of 1988, and the subsequent January demonstrations of 1989 and everything that has ensued since, provides clear evidence of this movement.

On hearing the crowds shout "long live Charter!" or "release Havel!" Havel saw that the onerous efforts of these "suicidal maniacs" had not been in vain, and were beginning to pay off.

Many individuals from the grey zone, such as academics, artists, and performers, were beginning to speak out. Havel described this aptly as a social awakening, which was given expression in the petition "A Few Sentences." Of course no one knew what would happen next, whether or not the regime would unleash a new wave of repression. He concluded, as had I, that "never in the past twenty years has the situation been as wide open as now." Havel then returned to one of his favourite themes, that Czechoslovakia was the crossroads of Europe for every imaginable spiritual and political current. Here, the fate of other countries was often decided, or their destinies foreshadowed. Hence the fate of "A Few Sentences" would provide a clue as to where Czechoslovakia, and Europe, were going. Impressively, the petition obtained over 4,000 signatures in its first week, mostly from those not previously involved in dissent.

Brezhnev's Czech heirs took the new petition very seriously. There was a lot of boiler-plate in the press about its so-called anti-socialist character. The petition was described as "an appeal for confrontation with the state, supported by forces active in the service of our enemy."

But there was also an indirect threat, too, which took on new meaning after the Tiananmen massacre. One of the front page editorials in *Rudé Právo*, the Communist Party daily, condemned the petition and finished off by saying that "those who sow the wind should be careful, since they may reap the whirlwind."

Havel was detained and interrogated. He was warned that he was still serving a suspended sentence and that if he did not stop giving interviews he would find himself back in jail serving the rest of his sentence. František Starek, the editor of the underground magazine *Vokno*, was put on trial and given a 2 1/2 year sentence in a medium security prison involving forced labour under dangerous conditions. He had been held in custody since February. Later that summer, those whom the regime thought were associated with the writing and organization of the petition, mostly in Charter 77, were arrested and detained indefinitely. They would only be released in the weeks of the revolution itself, as part of the bargaining between the opposition and a collapsing government.

9

WRITERS EAST AND WEST

IN JULY I CALLED ON HAVEL to discuss his invitation to the International Pen Congress. Pen is a kind of worldwide union of writers, of poets, essayists, and novelists. The 1989 Congress was to take place in Canada, and the Canadian organizers had invited him to give a keynote address. The theme of the Congress was to be the writer and freedom, and what better writer to speak to this than Václav Havel? The question, of course, was how he might free himself up to attend. I thought that my call on Havel might be an occasion to talk about literature, as opposed to Czech politics. Coincidentally, Allan Jones and his family, friends in the foreign service, came to stay with us at this time for a couple of weeks while they were still on assignment in New Delhi. I regarded Allan as not only a diplomat but, above all, as a superb writer. Two of his novellas had been published in annual anthologies of best Canadian fiction. Allan had a restless, critical mind, and it was he who had first directed my attention to Havel's writings. That was long before a posting to Prague was in prospect.

How appropriate, then, that Allan and I were going to see Havel at his apartment to discuss the International Pen Congress. It was a warm July day as we made our way through the traffic in downtown Prague to the Engels Embankment along the Vltava river. There in front of the apartment building was the familiar construction trailer. It must have been a little warm inside for the surveillance team. What we did not know was that there was another surveillance post in a baroque water tower located some way down the street. Allan was sensitive to the fact that what he wanted to discuss with Havel would be taped by the regime and could be used out of context to embarrass both Havel and the Embassy. Indeed, all of our conversations, whether with Havel or at home, were constrained by the regime's eavesdropping. Lynn and I took this for granted, but visitors like Allan reminded us how artificial was our situation.

We made our way into the dilapidated doorway of Havel's apartment block and up the darkened stairs. Allan is a big man, about 6'6" or so, with a dark beard, and we made our way slowly up the stairs. As always, there was deadly silence in the building. Finally at the sixth floor, I pushed the door bell. There was a button for Václav and a button for Ivan. Václav opened the door, smiling, shuffling backward with his barely perceptible limp as he invited us in. Always shy, he looked down as he spoke. I think he might have been a little surprised by Allan's towering height, but he took it all in his stride. We were invited to sit down in the small living room area made up of a couch and two chairs.

Above the couch was a large neo-expressionist painting. It had wide swatches of red and yellow and a couple of heads sitting on pedestals. On the other side of the room were some white bookshelves and lots of books and a TV and some video tapes. In a separate space, by the front window that looked out on the river and the Castle across the river, was a working desk. Havel was on his hands and knees looking under the desk for a pack of cigarettes. Then he went to the kitchen and returned with a bottle of bourbon and three shot glasses and proceeded to pour us each a glassful, which we drank before getting down to business.

I introduced Allan and then got into the question of the Pen Congress and the invitation for Havel to attend which had been extended by the Canadian organizers. He thanked the organizers for the invitation to present a paper in Montreal. Unfortunately, it was unlikely he would be able to deliver it in person. His passport had been confiscated long ago by the police. When he had applied again recently to obtain it he had been refused. He was still on probation after his recent release from jail, which made it even less likely he could obtain a passport. Unless, of course, the political atmosphere changed dramatically between July and September, when the Congress was to take place. Although he thought that things were changing, he did not believe that the changes would be rapid enough for the authorities to take a different view of him. And if, unexpectedly, he was given a passport in the present context, it would almost certainly be a ploy to get him permanently out of the country.

Havel did promise to write a short paper for the Congress that might be read by someone else. He said he was not sure what it would be about. Allan said he hoped it might raise questions for readers East and West. Western writers were aware of the shortcomings of communist societies, but Western societies had their own kinds of problems. He was particularly concerned with the ubiquitous nature of modern bureaucracies. Allan thought it might be salutary if the paper did not leave its Western audience too comfortable with the status quo. Indeed, Havel's writings had the singular appeal that they very often had as much to say to non-communist societies as to communist societies. They were really about life in the late twentieth century, life that was adapting to global bureaucracies made possible by technology.

Havel said that he appreciated Allan's sympathetic response to his writings, and that this visit might be just the thing around which to build his paper. This proved to be the case. The paper eventually delivered at the conference referred to Allan's remark, and went on to say that

In today's world, more and more people are aware of the indivisibility of human fate on this planet; that the problems of any one of us, or of whatever country we come from—be it the smallest and most forgotten—are the problems of us all; that our freedom is indivisible as well, and that we all believe in the same basic values, while sharing common fears about the threats that are hanging over humanity today.

We then talked about literature in general and I asked about the philosophical background to his work. Havel said that he did not know philosophy well, but that he had been influenced by existentialism in the 1960s, which had been very popular in Czechoslovakia. For the rest, in such books as *Letters to Olga*, he was just grasping for his own language to deal with philosophical issues that preoccupied him. I asked whether or not the hurdles that he faced, including his stints in prison, had influenced his writing? Was writing all the more necessary, as a way of dealing with his difficult circumstances? Havel replied that there was no doubt something to this, that difficulties could be a spur to creativity. And so the conversation went, Havel chain-smoking and looking intently down and occasionally at his interlocutors, and the three glasses of bourbon emptied and refilled again. Soon after this conversation, Havel left Prague for the countryside in order to build up his health and do some writing. I would not see him again until his birthday in early October.

During July, various opposition groups were as active as ever and there seemed to be no letup in the general desire to push the limits of the regime's authority. I was trying to keep Josef Škvorecký in contact with Karel Srp of the by then defunct Jazz Section. Škvorecký, with whom I had talked in Toronto before leaving for Czechoslovakia, was still well known to most Czechs from the novels he had written in his homeland in the 1950s and 1960s. But he was also known for the works critical of the regime that he had published in exile since 1968, and for the publishing enterprise he had launched with his wife, Zdena Salivorová. 68 Publishers had published all of the banned works of Czech authors in their original Czech, and had played a singular role in keeping Czech literary culture alive. Škvorecký, like Milan Kundera in Paris, had seen his own novels, translated into English, do well internationally.

Karel Srp had spent years in jail in the early eighties because of the activity of the Jazz Section in publishing banned books and producing underground music and video cassettes. His time in jail had clearly shaken him. Srp was nervous and secretive. He did not trust many of those in Charter around Havel, and the feeling seemed to be mutual. When I went to see him at his flat not far from our house in order to pass on some published material, Srp said that he was fed up with the dissident life and had no intention of going back to jail. He had made his contribution, and he was becoming too old to play the opposition's games. Despite these protestations, Srp was obviously fighting some kind of internal struggle. He was tense and spoke habitually in low tones as if his every word was being monitored. He may have been right.

To my mind, Srp was an example of how prison, and the security apparatus outside of prison, could bring people to the breaking point. His plan was to create a cultural network called Art Forum, that would have official approval but operate outside the official communist cultural organizations. Srp's idea was that more could be done by working with people in the grey zone than by isolating oneself in the dissident opposition. Those in Charter 77 who criticized Srp's lack of faith wondered out loud if he had made a deal with the authorities. Still, Srp sent to Škvorecký *samizdat* novels, journals, and underground music tapes, as well as some photos showing police brutality at the demonstrations. The latter subsequently appeared in Canadian publications.

The tension between Srp and Charter was palpable at the French national day reception on July 14, 1989. The event, hosted by the French Embassy, marked the two hundredth anniversary of the French revolution, and there was a lot of *liberté* in the air. The sun was shining on the magnificent pink and white baroque palace that housed the Residence of the French Ambassador and his Chancery. Copies of historical documents were handed out in the courtyard, revolutionary coins were minted by eighteenth century journeymen, and patriotic songs were sung by troubadours. Havel arrived, making the French Ambassador's day. What better representative of the revolutionary spirit?

But the opposition was not without its own problems, which was also something of a revolutionary tradition: splits in the ranks; pressure to get along with a regime which seemed as if it would last for years and years to come; the demoralizing fact that friends were jailed for trifles and families separated; and the overwhelming psychological and physical fatigue of trying to make a point which at times seemed to matter neither to one's fellow countrymen nor to the outside world.

At one point during the reception I was standing with Srp, after he and Havel had nodded to one another. It was the absolute minimum in terms of a gesture of recognition. Some around Havel simply refused to even acknowledge Srp now that he was talking about Art Forum as an officially sanctioned organization. Srp was miffed by what he saw as the snub, and complained that once Havel had used you as a rung on the way up the ladder, you no longer existed. From my knowledge of Havel, this was a little harsh, and underestimated Havel's genuine feeling for others.

To me, there was no doubt that Havel was single-minded in his pursuit of his goals, which were both worthy and important. In this single-minded pursuit, he could deal only with the pressing decisions of the day and the individuals involved in them. When others pursued different goals, he did not begrudge them, but he could not be all things to all people. His single-minded pursuit served him well during the revolution, but his biggest challenge when he became president was the need to become more things to more people, sometimes against his own inclinations. He would have to find the path that led from intellectual and moral leadership to the more prosaic role of politician.

But the difference between Havel and Srp raised a more pressing problem. There was still no sign the regime was about to fade away, as Havel himself had admitted. Srp's rather jaded, even cynical, views about the utility of dissident life represented a dilemma faced by everyone under the regime. It was the dilemma of all resistance movements. Yet the twentieth century has tended to bear out the importance of resistance, even if over the longer term. Living in truth has meant living with ideals, ideals that alone provide a glimmer of light and warmth in a sea of darkness.

10

MEANS AND ENDS

THE REGIME seemed to be lashing out in all directions that summer. Ideology chief Fojtík condemned counter-revolutionary forces in Hungary. Budapest responded by airing an interview with Havel that could be picked up in Slovakia. At a central committee plenum of the Communist Party, General Secretary Jakeš said that attacks on the regime delivered through the use of human rights mechanisms would be countered by an ideological offensive and mass political work. But he then said, curiously, "there is no need for the pessimism and nihilism which is beginning to penetrate also among party members."

I thought that the "also" was instructive. Even Jakeš seemed to realize that the foundation on which the regime had been built—ideological conformity backed up by brute force—was crumbling. There were persistent rumours that at successive meetings of Warsaw Pact leaders Gorbachov had lectured Jakeš about getting on with reform. Yet even modest economic reform proposals brought forward by Prime Minister Adamec were vetoed by the hardliners as the first step leading to what was anathema for this regime: political change.

One warm summer evening in July, 1989, Martin Palouš and Ivan Havel came over to our house to discuss philosophy. We sat on the large balcony overlooking the city, with a magnificent view of Prague Castle and St. Vitus Cathedral. As the darkness descended and the stars came out, Ivan remarked how strange it was to see the Cathedral at night from this side. The apartment he shared with Václav looked across the Vltava towards the Castle and the Cathedral perched on the hill. The side of the Cathedral they saw was always lit up with spotlights. Looking from our balcony, it was a silhouette etched by the light that shone like a halo around the edges. Ivan said that it was like seeing the dark side of the moon. For me, it was altogether normal.

We agreed on the details of a regular underground philosophy symposium that I would lead, with participants drawn from Charter and the other opposition groups. It would begin in September and be held in the apartment of Martin's mother-in-law, Dana Němcová. The apartment was situated at Ječná 7, not far from the Havels' apartment. Dana was one of the year's spokespersons for Charter 77. She had been arrested in the spring along with Havel, but fell ill while in detention and was later released pending her trial. She was liable to be rearrested any day for just about anything. She was no longer young. Her health, like that of many in the opposition ranks, was frail to say the least. But Dana was supported by a strong religious faith, and a friendly sense of humour. The fact that I would hold my philosophy symposium in her apartment would hardly endear her, or me, to the regime, and I appreciated her support.

Ivan, Martin, and I discussed some of the ideas in my latest manuscript, which was to provide the basis for the symposium. The manuscript, entitled "The Matter with Truth," tended to the poetic in its rendering of philosophical ideas. It was terse and often enigmatic, with a degree of word play that even Ivan and Martin, despite their excellent English, found hard to translate into Czech. But they were both keen to work on something out of the ordinary, and to overcome the obstacles as they arose. Ivan said he would arrange for the *samizdat* reproduction of the manuscript in time for the first session of the seminar in September.

As with all such projects in those dark days, when the regime was becoming more and more repressive and when arrest or expulsion was increasingly the rule, there was an element of unreality about our plans. There was the tacit, unspoken assumption that none of us were in a position to know for sure that we would be around when the seminar was to take place. For me, there was the consideration that two of my British colleagues had been expelled from the country in May, and an American colleague, Bob Norman, in July. I had worked rather closely with all three and, like Pierre and I, they had had regular contacts with the opposition.

We then talked about when the next demonstration would likely take place. There was bound to be something on August 21, the anniversary of the Warsaw Pact invasion of Czechoslovakia in 1968. All three of us had heard the rumour that the security units would be issued live ammunition this time around. Ivan felt that, even if this was StB disinformation intended to discourage a demonstration, Charter should inform people of the rumour and advise them to stay home just in case it turned out to be true. You just could not play politics with people's lives. Caught up in the élan of dissent, I was more inclined at the time to go toe-to-toe with the regime, and damn the consequences.

I was, in consequence, rather struck by Ivan's response. He had lived in opposition for twenty years now, and yet there was no bravado, no hubris. My own instincts only revealed the extent to which I had not absorbed what Charter was all about, and the extent to which I was a novice when it came to "living in truth." Ivan adopted a moral stand when it came to political issues, which was reflected in Charter's approach on most things. The means and the ends had to be consistent. Ivan would never be tempted by political expediency.

Some might have calculated that a demonstration in these circumstances could only succeed since, if the rumour was true, martyrs would be useful to the cause. But this calculation was never a part of Charter's philosophy. The unassailable occupation of the moral high ground was to be crucial during the revolution, when people's desire for the uncompromised, the clean, was to well up and wash away the dirt of the last twenty years.

In fact Charter did warn everyone about the rumour and the August 21 demonstration was smaller than the demonstrations in January. It was once again efficiently broken up by the riot police wielding truncheons. I watched the miserable affair on TV, while visiting my parents in Toronto. This did not deter me from stopping by to see Josef Škvorecký in order to tell him that things were definitely changing in Czechoslovakia. It was all just below the surface. Josef listened intently to my account of significant events, but he was still rather pessimistic. He seemed to have concluded that he would not likely see his country of origin again. I proposed we try experimenting with the regime, and that he mail me in Prague some of the recent books produced by 68 Publishers to see if they would get through.

Virtually everything the Škvoreckýs' small publishing house printed was banned in Czechoslovakia, including books in Czech by Havel, Klíma, Kundera, and Škvorecký himself. After the visit, I went by the brick townhouse in downtown Toronto where 68 Publishers were located and talked with Škvorecký's wife Zdena about the details of our scheme. She came to the door covered in printing ink and thought the plan would, at a minimum, be good fun. To our collective surprise, the books turned up in Prague a few weeks later and I took them along to a Pen International lunch that Barry hosted at his residence. The real political event of that August had nothing to do with the August 21 anniversary demonstration. Yet it was to have a greater impact on the future than almost anything that had happened so far. Paradoxically, that event took place hundreds of miles to the east.

11

THE EAST GERMAN EXODUS

AT THE END OF AUGUST, 1989 the Hungarian government decided to permit the free travel of its citizens across the iron curtain to Austria in the West. This was a revolutionary step for an East Bloc state. Incredibly, the new freedom of travel was also extended to other East Bloc nationals, such as East German citizens visiting Hungary. The East Germans were significant, because West Germany had made a commitment to all East Germans that it would extend them citizenship if they managed to get out of the German Democratic Republic (GDR). By taking their decision the Hungarians broke a bilateral agreement with the government of East Germany which was intended to keep East Bloc citizens bottled up in the Soviet sphere of influence. This bilateral agreement, one of a network of similar agreements between the communist regimes, left all decisions about the emigration of East German citizens in the hands of East German officials. For the whole communist bloc Hungary had suddenly become a hole in the fence through which their citizens could escape to the West.

When we heard of the decision at the Embassy we sat in Barry's office literally stunned by the logic of the situation. Given the offer of automatic citizenship, there would be huge numbers of East Germans trying to make their way to West Germany through Hungary. The Hungarian decision simply trumped the travel controls imposed by the other communist regimes. And it was these travel controls that were necessary to the very existence of East Germany. Why have a Berlin Wall when you could exit to the good life through the back door? And why have an East Bloc, if its principal raison d'être was the division of Germany? We were both convinced that the Hungarian initiative was the start of an unravelling of the socialist system, though it was difficult to predict exactly how this would happen and with what speed. But we knew in our bones that a door had been opened on the future, and that history had started moving again after being frozen in its tracks for decades.

The regime in Prague thought they had the answer to the Hungarian challenge: they closed their border with the renegade Hungarian state. All Czech and East German citizens were turned back at the frontier by Czech officials if they did not have some kind of official reason to travel to Hungary. This action backfired, as would many other similarly repressive steps in the months to come. Instead of returning to East Germany after being turned back at the Czech-Hungarian border many of the East German émigrés simply came to Prague and sought asylum at the West German Embassy. Within a matter of days, the numbers grew into the thousands. By the end of September and the beginning of October, the West German Embassy in Prague was filled to the rafters with East German refugees.

The West German officials began setting up tents on the grounds inside the Embassy walls and installing portable toilets. The German Red Cross provided the tents and the blankets, and helped provide the food and medical assistance as best as they could. The Czech police at first tried to seal off the Embassy, setting up road blocks around it to intercept East Germans. The police even pulled some refugees off the fence around the West German Embassy who were trying to get into the compound at the back. Western journalists and TV crews began coming to Prague once word of the situation got out, and there was good footage of the Czech police beating people back from the West German Embassy. This was hardly the image the communist regimes wanted to convey to the West. The Czech police suddenly ceased their operation and a new flood of East Germans arrived and camped in front of the West German Embassy. The Embassy itself, inside and out, was full to bursting.

During the period when the Czech police were trying to seal off the West German Embassy an East German émigré came to the Canadian Embassy. I went down to the visa reception area to talk with him. Fortunately, the room was almost empty. He was a man in his late forties, with a beard and somewhat threadbare clothing. He was obviously not a communist apparatchik. Between my elementary German and his less than fluent English, I understood that he was trying to get to the West German Embassy but that the way was blocked. He asked for my assistance, saying that he had left everything behind, his job, his family, everything. He would try to get his family out after. His only possession seemed to be a Bible, which he held in his hands. He said he could not go back home now, that he would be charged and perhaps jailed. I knew this to be the case from similar incidents in Czechoslovakia. He said that if he could not go to West Germany, then he would like to go to Canada.

The whole time we spoke he was shaking, holding his Bible tightly. He was frightened and desperate, though it was a quiet desperation that came with the realization he had made the leap, that he had burnt all his bridges, that his situation was totally precarious. Standing there, I was convinced I had to try to do something for this man. I recalled that at the beginning of the exodus of East Germans a colleague at the West German Embassy in Prague had told me that if an East German refugee turned up at our Embassy, a West German diplomat would be available to come and talk with him. I asked the poor chap in our visa reception area to wait a minute and went to telephone my contact at the West German Embassy.

Within minutes two of his colleagues arrived, and soon after it was agreed by all that the East German refugee would be escorted by the West German diplomats into their Embassy. The East German shook my hand vigorously and kept thanking me as if I had just saved his life. It was a small thing really, based on the use of diplomatic power and privilege within a totalitarian context. But it had made all the difference to him. I began to understand, if only a little, what some foreign diplomats, such as Wallenberg, must have gone through in Germany and in Nazi occupied states during the Second World War. How the tables had turned since then! The whole operation went off without a hitch.

A few days later, when the Czech police suddenly adopted a hands-off approach with regard to access to the West German Embassy, it became clear the regime had decided that the whole affair had to be worked out between the East German and West German governments. Nonetheless, the Czech regime closed its border with Hungary and established new border controls with East Germany in order to prevent more East Germans from travelling to Prague. This was not easy, because the "fraternal socialist states" had not expected they would need border surveillance and frontier controls between them.

After a lot of negotiation between Bonn and Berlin it was decided that this lot of refugees would go back to East Germany with the written guarantee that they would be given swift exit permission to emigrate to West Germany. This agreement ensured that the asylum extended to the refugees by the West German Embassy was genuine, despite their temporary return to East Germany. The return simply permitted the East German government to expel the refugees for having contravened socialist law. It seemed that the technicalities of socialist legality were to be upheld while "Rome burned."

The arrangement only made sense, of course, on the assumption that the influx could be stopped permanently. The Czechoslovak communists and East Germans tried their best to seal off the border between the two countries. This was virtually impossible because it was a rather long border with a lot of rough wooded terrain. The whole effort looked like someone trying to seal off compartments in a sinking ship. After the first lot had departed, more and more refugees arrived in Prague.

There were thousands of the tiny, rickety-looking Trabant cars lining the streets all over town, double parked even in front of our Embassy. All of them were abandoned, the occupants having made the last stretch on foot carrying their worldly possessions. The West German Embassy was located just down the hill from us in the Lesser Town. There were soon 5,000 new refugees jammed inside the West German Embassy and another 5,000 camped out front on the cobble stones in a small baroque square. The square was, of course, not legally part of the West German chancery, but the Czech police decided to treat all of the refugees as one problem.

This apparent benevolence was due to the fact that the regime had decided it had nothing to gain by wielding the sword on behalf of the East German government. Bad publicity in the West was thereby minimized. And, of course, it went without saying that good relations with West Germany were an important factor. West Germany was Czechoslovakia's largest Western trading partner, and the most important source of its hard currency. It was this hard currency, in the form of deutsche Marks, that helped pay for the regime's importation of Western foods and goods, most of which went to the regime's leaders. With the Czech economy in rapid decay, promises may well have been made by the West German government to encourage the regime to let the refugees go. After the revolution in Czechoslovakia, these promises no doubt turned out to be much easier to keep.

During this time, in September and October 1989, the spectre of desperate East German refugees haunting the streets of Prague was something we would never forget. Thousands and thousands of the ridiculous-looking Trabants were a reminder of how pathetic the communist economies had become compared with their Western counterparts. You could understand why there were few second thoughts about leaving the cars behind. Whole families, many young couples with children in tow, were carrying everything they could take from their former country. This was squeezed into a battered suitcase or two.

The grey, impoverished look of their clothing reminded me of refugee movements during the Second World War. This was not Africa, this was Europe. The children were carrying their knapsacks with a few favourite toys, their teddies flopping out on one side. There were a lot of photographs taken with old cameras, and a lot of spontaneous hugs between parents, between parents and children, and between friends. You almost expected a steamer to arrive to take them on an ocean journey to the New World. But no, the promised land was only about 200 kilometres to the West: so near and yet so far.

It was unseasonably cold in Prague that October. Those refugees unlucky enough to be camped outside were the worse for wear. Mothers piled up blankets on prams, trying to keep their babies as warm as they could. The temperature fell to about 5 degrees below zero centigrade. A collection of warm clothing was taken up in our Embassy to help ensure that the children and young mothers were properly clothed for the cold weather. Canadians seemed to have a generous supply of extra hats and gloves and boots and these were packed in boxes and sent off to the West German Embassy. The West German Red Cross was passing out hot soup and coffee as sustenance against the piercing damp cold. There were sleeping bags everywhere, with bleary-eyed refugees sitting on the pavement.

The children seemed to be all right for the most part. Many of them had been taken into the Chancery of the West German Embassy, and we could see them crowded at the second floor windows in the evening, silhouetted by the lights from inside. Throughout this episode, my wife Lynn and I were constantly worried about these children, wondering what must be going through their minds. They were the innocent victims of all this, embarking on some kind of adventure they could not comprehend. They too were leaving friends and family behind, taking with them a few precious toys, and aware, in their own way, of the great drama that had swept up them and their parents alike.

At last came the breakthrough. The East German regime agreed that the refugees could leave by special train directly for West Germany, though the train would pass through a corner of the GDR on the way. This brief transit through East Germany would permit the regime there to formally expel the refugees from its territory, since they were regarded as no longer fit to build socialism. There was jubilation among refugees inside and outside the West German chancery in Prague. There were many wives and children who were going on to join husbands and fathers who had left in the first wave.

The gamble, which had included the possibility that the husbands and fathers might not have seen their families again, had paid off. There were tears too, as grandparents decided they would let their children and grandchildren go on alone, while they themselves returned to East Germany. They were simply too old to start a life somewhere else, though they understood this to mean they would never see their offspring again. Suddenly, amidst all of this furore, an ambulance arrived in front of the West German Chancery. An East German woman inside the Chancery was brought out on a stretcher. She was about to have her baby. We could not help but wonder if she would be permitted to leave too, when everyone else had departed.

After the initial celebration, the mood turned more earnest as, hour after hour, the East German trains failed to arrive. Citing technical delays, the East German government said the trains would be delayed a day. The refugees spent yet another night in the cold, camped out on the damp cobblestones. This struck me as another, simply gratuitous cruel act of a regime on its last legs. We were to find out later that the trains had indeed been on their way. They had been stopped en route by people on the tracks who were trying to climb aboard the trains in order to flee East Germany. East German police had been called out to evacuate the trains of these interlopers and to keep the tracks clear all the way to Czechoslovakia.

Finally, the trains arrived at the train station in Prague. It was about 10 P.M. and the Czech regime provided buses to take the 10,000 East Germans from the Chancery, and the square in front, to the station. The refugees organized themselves into long lines down the side of the street connecting the square in front of the West German Chancery to the main street leading off the Lesser Town Square. In the dark, dimly lit night, everyone seemed to have a place, and there was no pushing or panic. A lot of this crowd control was done by young East Germans, very effectively. Over a period of some hours these thousands of people filed quietly on to the buses and then the buses disappeared into the mists that thickened in the narrow streets.

In the sudden emptiness after their departure, in the return of the repressive atmosphere of communist-ruled Czechoslovakia, you might have wondered if you had not simply dreamt the whole affair. That is, were it not for a telltale blanket left on the cobble stones, or the litter of paper coffee cups and other debris, that looked incongruously like the aftermath of a 1960s sit-in. I heard later that the route through East Germany on the way to West Germany was lined with people cheering on the refugees. This, like the flight of the refugees themselves, was an unexpected and spontaneous show of alienation from the East German regime. Both had less to do with the desire for material gain elsewhere than with the fact that people felt there was no future in East Germany or in communism. Like immigrants in the past, opportunity was the main attraction of the new life, and the exodus was symptomatic of a complete loss of faith in their current way of living. The artificial allegiance of the last forty years was collapsing. The common feature of the events involving the German refugees and the growing opposition in Czechoslovakia was the new sense of vertigo as expectations of change took hold. It was when these expectations were frustrated that unpredictable forces were unleashed, often as a chain reaction with unforeseeable results.

I noticed that as the East Germans had climbed on to the buses, some Czechs waved or flashed the victory sign. But when we talked with them afterwards it was obvious there were mixed emotions. The East German regime had been one of the main proponents of the Warsaw Pact invasion of Czechoslovakia that had crushed the Prague Spring in 1968. This fact was also mixed up in the minds of most Czechs with the fact of the Nazi occupation of Czechoslovakia during World War II. If there was muted joy on the part of the Czechs, it was joy nonetheless over the certainty that the East German regime, and Honecker himself, were in trouble.

More important was the subtle impact this whole affair was to have on the Czech psyche. It would germinate for six weeks and then suddenly bear fruit. The Czechs had experienced, if vicariously, the East German taste of freedom, and the exhilaration of going for broke. And they saw how, after all, the East German regime had feet of clay, and was collapsing under the pressure of people power. Over the past twenty years the East German regime had been the closest East Bloc ally of Czechoslovakia, especially in terms of its repressive policies. Yet how vulnerable it proved to be. The biggest surprise, however, was that Gorbachov, and especially Shevardnadze, had let it happen. It seemed that the Red Army would no longer be used to prop up unpopular, unchanging and bankrupt regimes. That, I think, was the main lesson of the East German exodus through Prague. This lesson was now percolating in the minds of the Czechs.

12

THE SYMPOSIUM II

BY SEPTEMBER, 1989 the Czechoslovak communist regime was beginning to reveal its own weaknesses. They had been accumulating a long time, but one particular event, more than any other, revealed them clearly. This was the circulation of an underground audio tape containing remarks by General Secretary Jakeš. The remarks were made to a closed door meeting of communist functionaries and had been intended for "communist ears only." Someone, obviously inside the party, had taped the event and before long it was broadcast over Radio Free Europe. The tape revealed that the politburo set out to deal with Havel and then constructed its case to produce a foregone conclusion: a guilty verdict. Of course we had suspected as much. But more damaging to the regime was the fact that Jakeš could barely express himself to his followers. He stumbled over words, made numerous mispronunciations, and came off sounding like a half-wit.

The tape became the talk of Prague and the General Secretary a laughing stock, to the point that it was played at parties as a guaranteed means of inducing general hilarity. There is no criticism more potent than ridicule, and I think this tape played its own role in eroding the authority of the regime at a time when the East German government seemed to be similarly losing control. I sent a message to headquarters about the regime which I called "The Long Goodbye," and could not help ending it with a quote from the Jakeš tape. The General Secretary at one point seemed to despair of the grass roots, and said, "we are quite alone, solitary, without a single word of support from below, from the population. No wonder they [the opposition] can manipulate the people against us." I could not have said it better myself.

Meanwhile, that same September, I had started leading my underground philosophy symposium. As I mentioned earlier, Ivan Havel and Martin Palouš had arranged for this to take place in Dana Němcová's apartment. Ivan Chvatik had generously arranged for "The Matter with Truth" manuscript, which I was using as the basis of the symposium, to be published as a little *samizdat*, with fairly modern photocopying techniques. I was startled when Czech friends like Zdeněk Urbánek would meet me on the street and say they had read my *samizdat* and liked it. I had the feeling I was becoming one of the gang, so to speak. There was something special about writing for a small circle of interested friends, something civilized and ancient that was unlike mass production in the West. The relatively few copies of the book made its way by hand from reader to reader. It was an experience that harked back to the first days of the printing press, or before.

Dana's flat was ideal for our seminar. There was a large living room with a long rough-hewn wooden table in the middle. The table had no doubt witnessed a lot of debate over many years, and our discussion ritually began with the arrival of a large pot of tea. This was the signal for many to light their pipes or cigarettes. Banned manuscripts were exchanged and impromptu reviews were given of the latest work of their colleagues. Then we got down to work. Almost all of the Czech participants of the seminar spoke English, but a few did not, so Martin and Ivan interpreted as we made our way through the terse, poetic paragraphs of my book. This led frequently to some comic moments, when there just did not seem to be a Czech equivalent to an English word or phrase.

It was difficult even in English to get at the meaning of a work that emphasized originality of expression over convention. Indeed, I think that the manuscript lent itself more to performance than to discussion, and when you added to this the intricacies of finding the equivalent rendering in Czech, the interpretation itself became a consummately creative task resulting in an entirely new and not uninteresting work. Of course some of the translation into Czech was simply hilarious. There were double meanings, sometimes off-colour, that were not present in the original English. Though Dana was hardly fascinated by the world of philosophy, she sat in for the considerable entertainment value.

The whole experience was rather mind-stretching for all of us. The intensity of the effort naturally found its outlet in exasperation and finally laughter. The word play in one language seemed to inspire more word play in the other. This process was interspersed, of course, by discussion of the substantive argument that was being made in the manuscript. That argument was fairly simple, some might say simplistic: assuming that sociobiology was correct in viewing language as a dynamic intimately linked to the survival of our species, what were the implications for philosophy? It might just be that language was a biological trick, like claws or coloured feathers, that simply helped us survive as a species. It was a fairly good trick, admittedly, and in association with other biological attributes, proved decisive.

When language "worked," it worked because it was integral to a survival strategy. On the other hand, language could not say what was true, at least true in terms of any meaning outside that strategy. This conclusion seemed something of an intellectual dead end, unless one argued that language could nonetheless point beyond itself to a truth; and this was where poetry, or art, came into the picture. This is not the place to summarize a difficult argument, but it is enough to convey the feeling that we were on new terrain, though none of us was sure where that terrain might be, or what paths might lead from it. What was impressive, however, was not whether the manuscript was prescient or wrong-headed, but that my Czech friends, after having been cut off from normal academic life for twenty years, could still bring a creative and fresh perspective to bear on just about any intellectual question. They were not afraid to give something a bit unusual, even marginal, a chance, and draw their own conclusions. Intellectual tolerance was definitely a mainstay of the Czech tradition.

I assumed that I was probably followed to those meetings. There was always a moment of anxiety when, under the dim light of the street lamps along Ječná street, I turned into a dark courtyard partly blocked by garbage cans where there was a winding stone staircase that led up to the floors above. There was a dilapidated lift encased in a metal cage that I never used. I made my way up the steps in the dark, briefcase in hand, until I reached Dana's door. As she opened the door on to the light and warmth of her apartment, I would immediately relax. If the StB had wanted to set me up for a little intimidation, that dark alley would have been a good place to do it.

What I was doing was the kind of thing the communists disliked most: a Western diplomat becoming a regular acquaintance of some of the key figures in Charter 77. But once I was with them in Dana's living room I was always buoyed up by their optimism and their determination. It made my own concerns look somewhat insignificant in comparison. When we gathered around the table and the tea pot, exchanged a few thoughts on the latest events, or ogled the most recent *samizdat* publications, I quickly felt at home.

Life is full of strange coincidences, and that fall seemed to have an extraordinary number of them. I learned from one of the Charter people that another philosopher would be visiting Prague for a few days. He would give a lecture at the French Institute, but he would also hold a seminar with opposition people. To my surprise, he was also to discuss Hegel. It turned out to be Pierre-Jean Labarrière, who had been the director of my own PhD thesis on Hegel. I had not been in touch with Labarrière for about eight years, so that I could hardly contain my excitement about running into him in Prague.

Labarrière taught at the Institut Catholique in Paris, and was perhaps one of the top three experts on Hegel in the world. He was for me something of a mentor, an ideal, with one of the finest minds I had ever had the privilege to know. This superb intellect was matched by a refinement of spirit and consideration for others that was remarkable. It turned out that Labarrière came regularly to Prague and was active in the underground intellectual and church circles. I arranged to attend his lecture on Hegel and the French Revolution, and afterwards we went out to dinner with our Czech friends. We laughed about the coincidence of our meeting, and it was a special treat to find an old friend in the strange circumstances of Prague in those days. They were dark days, but the darkness was penetrated by an undeniable light.

13

TOO LITTLE, TOO LATE

THROUGHOUT 1989, I was stubbornly optimistic about the prospects for change, despite the repression. My diplomatic colleagues from other embassies were rather annoyed at what they thought were my eccentric views. They argued that there would be no revolution, no change at all, unless the economy worsened first. I said that this was a Marxist interpretation of Czechoslovak society. I argued that one could have a *political* revolution, that there could be change that resulted from purely political factors. I felt that the fundamentals were right to produce that change. The Department flew me to NATO headquarters to make my case at a meeting of NATO experts. I described how the base of the opposition was broadening.

The loose alliance of the opposition groups, such as Charter, the church, and the reemerging leaders of the Prague Spring had helped turn passive dislike into active commitment for change. The youth seemed to be more politicized. They were channelling their energy into special interests such as ecology or alternative military service, and they were behind the myriad of new independent groups that were springing up everywhere. There was a vibrant new civil society made up of people engaged in underground publicity, art exhibits, newspapers and video news, and independent church groups. In sum, the underground had become an undergrowth and it was beginning to break through the undifferentiated glacis of communist conformity.

The regime's reaction to these developments was two-track. It made tentative contact with the 1968 reform communists, perhaps at Moscow's bidding, in order to split the opposition. And it came down hard on all those who did not recognize the "leading role of the communist party." But it was already too late for this gambit. Society was on the move. Not that change would follow the pattern of other East bloc countries. The opposition had no strong base among the workers, as had Solidarity. Nor was a significant segment of the leadership involved in reform, as in Hungary and the USSR. The economy was in difficulty but still supplied the basics. In fact the Czechoslovak opposition was informed by a complex of long-term historical and social traditions. These included a parliamentary past, political clubs, and a large, politically active middle class.

These traditions were now beginning to reassert themselves after being dormant for twenty years. There was a coordinated push for change outside the system, at a time when the regime was locked into a closed dialectic of dissent and repression. This was in part due to the fact that the Party had been so thoroughly purged of reformers. Now it was facing opposition not only at home but also from abroad. Newspapers and parliaments in Hungary, Poland, and the USSR were condemning the events of 1968, and questioning the legitimacy of the communists in Prague.

The regime, of course, never let up, despite what had happened with the East German refugees and in spite of the international criticism. People disappeared off the street for interrogation, others languished in jail without ever being charged. Those mixed up with the petition "A Few Sentences" or with underground publishing were especially targeted. But things could have been worse, as Zdeněk Urbánek pointed out one evening at the apartment of Pierre and Louise. Martin Palouš, Václav Malý, and Jan Urban (an opposition journalist) were also there. The occasion was a screening on videocassette of Jacques Rupnik's series "The Other Europe." Zdeněk was now over seventy, a white-haired gentleman with exquisite manners, impeccable English, and a wonderful sense of humour. You could not get it out of your head that he was the "grandfather" of the opposition.

Rupnik's series included a lot of material on Czechoslovakia, and we watched historical footage of the 1968 invasion, with Dubček heaving a heartbroken sigh over the radio as he asked people not to resist. But there was also a lot of material about the atrocities committed by the communists in the 1950s. Zdeněk remembered it all too well. There was Slanský, the former General Secretary of the

The author and Zdeněk Urbánek

Czechoslovak Communist Party, arrested on Stalin's orders and framed. He stood in the dock at his political trial, a pitiful figure, admitting in a meek voice all kinds of subversive deeds supposedly committed in collaboration with imperialist capitalism and the class enemy. He was executed shortly after.

As we sat there watching this we were reminded of the power of the regime to break people, to brainwash them, and then to turn them into the willing servants of so-called people's justice. Slansky might as well have been saying "I love Big Brother" for all the sense that he made. All of us had a kind of morbid interest in the footage. Our Czech friends had not had the opportunity to see it before. The regime, though occasionally flirting with Stalin's name, never associated itself with what were then regarded as Stalin's excesses. But neither did it show concern for Stalin's victims either. Zdeněk was not so much interested in the footage as repulsed by it. He had had the misfortune of living through this period as a young man. When we asked him what it was like, he exclaimed in his wavering voice, "It was horrible. Horrible." Then he said he did not know if he could watch any more, and we turned it off.

14

CZECH PENS

IT WAS NOW CLEAR that Václav Havel was not going to be able to attend the International Pen Congress in Canada. He had made some discreet inquiries about obtaining a passport and, as expected, had not got anywhere. He had promised to prepare a text for the Congress that might be read out by someone else, and Ivan duly called me up to say that he had returned from the country with it. In this text, Václav Havel referred to Allan Jones, whom I had taken to see Havel in June. It was a nice touch.

Havel always seemed to take his literary cue from day-to-day life. He was not one for artistic creation in a vacuum, and linked his various works, whether plays or essays, to some event in his life. He was intensely involved in what was going on around him, but then logically worked through, at a higher level, the questions posed by daily existence. It was a good way to work, and no doubt drew his many friends, who faced the same kind of questions, into a tightly knit group. The whole process was neither solely art nor solely philosophy. It was rather a kind of existential reflection, which took as its jumping-off point the presupposition that the unexamined life was not worth living. Under the communist regime this presupposition had explosive potential.

At the Embassy we decided that, in view of the fact that Havel would not be able to attend the Congress hosted this year by Canada, we would have our own International Pen lunch for the prominent Czech writers, almost all of whom were in the opposition. Pierre and I went to call on Havel on October 5 to obtain his thoughts as to who should be included. It happened to be Havel's birthday and he was in a good mood. The phone never stopped ringing and there seemed to be someone constantly knocking at the door. Olga said hello with her gentle, slightly worried look, and then sought refuge elsewhere in the apartment from the commotion. It also happened that the Nobel Committee was to announce that day its decision on a recipient for the Nobel Peace Prize. Everyone, including journalists from all over the world, thought that Havel was a sure thing, and were trying to get a few words with him on the phone. Despite all of this, Havel made time for us. He was his usual polite and deferential self. He would simply smile and raise his arms as the telephone rang again with another call from around the world. With a cigarette in one hand and the telephone in another, he spoke in his deep, even voice, answering directly, succinctly, and thoughtfully.

The Czech Section of Pen International had in fact been "asleep" since 1969. Havel and some other writers were looking to see how they might revive it, so as to permit the participation of writers now banned by the regime. Jiří Mucha, the son of Alfons Mucha the art nouveau painter, would be the president of the Czech Section. Mucha was a journalist and historian and, though no friend of the regime, was not particularly active in the opposition either. He was eighty years old, and a fascinating character.

I had come to meet him through Miroslav Galuška, a friend and the former liberal-minded Minister of Culture under Dubček in 1968. Miroslav, or Mirek as he was often called, told me that Mucha lived in an incredible house on the square that faced the Prague Castle. He said that he knew Mucha well and that we would go to call on him one day. We did so that autumn. The house was white stucco with a large wooden door and a fresco over the entrance. We knocked, but there was no answer. A window opened above us on the second floor. Leaning out was a young girl, about seventeen, dressed in a white nightgown and with long flowing red hair. She asked us what we wanted. I had the sudden premonition that I was about to walk into the nineteenth century. I did, for our entire visit.

Mirek replied, saying that Mucha had invited us over, and just then Mucha himself turned the corner and was walking toward us. Mirek told me in hushed tones that Mucha always seemed to have a seventeen-year-old girlfriend. A new version appeared on the scene at regular intervals, despite the fact that Mucha himself was hardly a young lion. I said hello to the elderly gentleman, who spoke perfect English with a British accent. The three of us went inside together as Mucha unlocked the heavy wooden door. The ground floor was dark and cluttered with furniture, the most recent pieces from the early years of this century. There were cobwebs and paintings and drawings everywhere. They all seemed to be by Alfons Mucha, and must have been worth a small fortune. Some were stacked together, others leaned haphazardly against walls behind pieces of furniture. Then we went up an ornate winding staircase to the second floor. At the top of the staircase was a huge painting, from floor to ceiling, of Sarah Bernhardt in the inimitable Mucha style.

I was simply stunned. As we made our way from room to room, Mucha paintings crowded the walls beneath chandeliers and velvet curtains. The house had not been touched, I think, since 1910. There was a large painting of Jiří Mucha and his sister when they were young children, with white clothes, straw hats, and green leaves. I was in art nouveau heaven. And it was not only because of the paintings. The rooms were full, and I mean literally every square inch, of decorated mirrors, glass of all kinds, stuffed lizards, bird feathers, hats, plants, exotic objects from all over the world, incredible inlaid furniture, and just about anything that one might imagine from an art nouveau aesthetic.

Light filtered in through the heavy curtains and lace to reveal a china teapot and some cups on a silver platter. There was a large four-poster bed with a canopy, and a fireplace beside it. Orange peels littered the hearth. Just then the young mistress in her long white nightgown, bare feet, and long red hair swept from one room into another down the hall. The picture was complete.

Strangely, I noticed a small silver cup of oriental design on a windowsill, and it was full of match boxes with Mucha paintings on them. This minute, subtle invasion of twentieth century marketing was oddly out of place and yet the boxes, with their reproduced Muchas, oddly belonged, too. It crossed my mind how much revenue must result from these reproductions, whether matches or posters. Since the sixties, Mucha seemed to be everywhere. Mirek told me that Mucha travelled freely to the West and that he had apartments in Paris and in Geneva. It was rumoured that his foreign accounts were rather sizeable. He nonetheless always came back to Prague. Some kind of modus vivendi had no doubt been worked out with the regime. I wondered what happened to the young girls after they moved on. Mirek smiled and shrugged.

Mucha was to become the head of the Czech section of Pen International. There were to be two deputy positions, and the regime would fill one slot with a communist writer and the other slot would be filled by Ivan Klíma. Klíma's novels had been banned by the regime since 1969. They were selling rather well outside the country in English translation and Klíma, Kundera, Škvorecký, and Havel were perhaps the best known Czech writers internationally. Even Havel would be part of the reawakened Czech section of the Pen International. These developments seemed to be incredible breakthroughs in the autumn of 1989.

When Pierre and I were talking with Havel about our planned Pen International lunch, Havel suggested that we invite not only Klíma but the regime representative as well. He was quite open-handed about the whole thing. He may well have suspected that the regime representative would not come anyway, and this in fact turned out to be the case. Mucha, too, could not come, as he was in Paris. Havel also suggested Ludvík Vaculík, a poet and novelist and the author of the infamous 1968 petition "2,000 Words." Some Czechs thought that, after Bohumil Hrabal, Vaculik was the best writer in Czechoslovakia, though not known outside his country. The "2,000 Words" petition had sought to force the Dubček government to go faster and further in making political and economic reforms. It was specifically cited by the Russians as one of the events justifying the Warsaw Pact invasion a few months later. Havel also recommended Zdeněk Urbánek, our friend and a prominent literary scholar.

After we had spoken about the Pen International, I could not help referring to the Nobel Peace prize. I expected, like the press, that Havel would receive it. I said that if it did turn out that way, it would be something of a personal tribute. He immediately played down the personal dimension. It would be a recognition of the work accomplished by Charter 77. He added that it would be helpful for all of those in Charter who had worked and suffered over many years to see some tangible recognition of their efforts. It would be a morale booster. Havel's own morale that day was excellent, and we wished him a happy birthday and found our own way to the door, since the phone was ringing again.

Our Pen International lunch took place a few weeks later, in late October. It promised to be stimulating company. Havel came of course, and there were Ivan Klíma, Zdeněk Urbánek, Ludvík Vaculík, Barry, and I. The lunch was at Hadovka, the Canadian Ambassador's official residence in Prague. It was a brisk but sunny fall day and the

Canadian Residence, in high gothic style, was as impressive as ever. Located on what was then Lenin Boulevard, our guests made their way in Škodas and on foot through an archway into a small interior courtyard. There was a small fountain, with steps leading up to flower beds and then a bower that opened onto the backyard. We had drinks outside on a patio overlooking the grounds and gardens. Barry and I couldn't resist taking a few photos. I knew Havel, Klíma, and Urbánek fairly well, but did not really know Vaculik at all. During our conversation, it became apparent that there were subtle differences within this group as to the approach each adopted in dealing with the regime. Such nuances corresponded to an increasingly uncertain political environment. Yet despite these differences, Havel was the unspoken leader. Not that he dominated the conversation in any sense. It had something to do with his moral presence, a presence that he projected in a remarkable way during the revolution and during his presidency.

At lunch I sat between Vaculik and Klíma and directly across from Havel. We were in the conservatory at the back of the residence, just off the patio. This room was full of natural light and the walls were pastel yellow. I said to Havel that I had heard his paper had been well received at the Pen Congress. He confirmed that the idea for the essay came from the conversation we had with Allan Jones in his apartment. Havel had wanted to speak about the role of the writer in a way that reflected life in both East and West. We inevitably talked about the difficulty for him in obtaining a passport to attend the Congress. This led to a discussion of the political situation in Czechoslovakia.

Havel was at bottom an optimist and believed that change would come eventually, though it was difficult to see any change in the regime. It seemed to be oddly paralyzed: the left hand did not know what the right hand was doing. Havel told us how someone from Kratký Film, a government-run studio that made documentary films, had told him that they wanted to make a film about him. At the same time he was being warned by the StB about his opposition activities and threatened with the cancellation of his parole. If his parole was revoked, he would end up back in jail. Havel asked what we were to make of these contradictions? No doubt the regime was confused by what was going on in East Germany, by the exodus of the East Germans, by the reluctance of the Russians to stop it, and by the persistent demonstrations in Prague.

On a more humorous note, we all laughed about the practical joke that had recently been played on *Rudé Právo*, the Communist Party daily newspaper. In the weekend editions there was habitually a page of birthday greetings to comrades. The greetings were supposedly contributed by fellow workers, and were often accompanied by little photographs of the birthday comrade in question. It had been Havel's birthday only a few days before, on October 5. Someone had sent to *Rudé Právo* birthday greetings for "Vaněk of Hradeček."

Vaněk was the name of the principal character in several of Havel's one act plays. He was a dissident, and the plays were largely autobiographical. Hradeček was the village in which Havel's weekend cottage was located, and it was here that he did most of his writing. Not only did the editor not catch the literary allusion to Havel, he even published the photograph of Havel that had accompanied the greeting. The irony of the Communist Party paper publishing best wishes to Havel was really too much, and all of Prague enjoyed this splendid practical joke. At our Pen International lunch, Havel wondered how long the people in charge of the birthday page would keep their jobs.

We talked about Dubček's reemergence. Havel's respect for Dubček was understated, but clear. He did not imply that the two were at all alike, or even shared the same political ideals. He was deferential too, saying that Dubček was a politician. Dubček's actions were the result of his own political calculations. Havel spoke about political calculations as if they were something mysterious that he did not pretend to understand. Since we were talking about Dubček, I mentioned to Vaculik that I had just read *Night Frost*, Zdeněk Mlynář's book about 1968. Mlynář had said that the petition Vaculik had produced in the spring of that year, called "2,000 Words," had been a serious miscalculation. Mlynář argued that the petition had been too radical, too far out in front of Dubček's Action Plan of political reform. In consequence, public attention, and public debate, focused on the "2,000 Words" instead of the government's reform effort.

It was the prominence given to the more radical demands of the "2,000 Words" that got the Russians' attention, said Mlynář in his book. And the Russians specifically mentioned the petition as a concern in the months leading up to the 1968 Warsaw Pact invasion. Vaculik, in replying, did not seem overly burdened by this accusation. He simply noted that "2,000 Words" had captured what people were thinking at the time. It was in the air. And so it could hardly have been a question of any miscalculation. Vaculik, unlike Mlynář, and rather like Havel, was not motivated by political expediency. He was concerned with what was right. This difference was related to another. Mlynář had, in the end, chosen exile in Vienna. Havel and Vaculik had not, though the regime no doubt wished they had. After the revolution, Mlynář reappeared briefly, fresh from exile, and tried to turn the Communist Party into something like it was in 1968. He seemed out of touch with the attitude of people in 1989, who basically wanted to hear nothing more from the Communist Party, whether reformed or not.

After lunch, we went into the living room for coffee. We were sitting as a group in front of the large gothic fireplace, with both Havel and Klíma on the sofa. There were wood-panelled walls, red damask curtains, and a grand piano at the far end. Klíma spoke about his interest in Kafka. Klíma was himself Jewish, though of Czech rather than German origin. He had spent time as a child in a Nazi concentration camp. We talked about the disappearance of the Jewish community in Prague. I told him about the first time I had gone to visit Kafka's grave.

I had looked up Olšany Cemetery on the map of Prague and found that it was a large cemetery located a little way out of downtown. It was on a main road and hard to miss, and I parked the car nearby. Inside, there were neat rows of graves and carefully groomed paths and tombs and a plethora of freshly cut flowers. There was a small army of widows renting watering cans or chatting together in the aisles. In the sunlight, it was about as cheerful a place as a cemetery could be. I walked up and down the rows thinking I knew where I was going but I could not for the life of me find Franz Kafka. The little old ladies smiled as I wandered by for the umpteenth time. Finally, I asked one of the ladies if they knew where I might find Kafka's grave. There was a long thoughtful pause, then a discussion with a neighbour, and a helpful gesture toward a remote corner of the cemetery. I thanked the lady and then proceeded to examine every grave stone in the general direction suggested.

After an hour of fruitless search, I was on the verge of giving up. I had the Kafkaesque sensation I was in a maze of the dead, a transmutation of the Castle into a thousand grave stones. I retraced my steps and asked the lady renting the watering cans. "Not here," she said. She pointed outside the cemetery altogether. I walked out through an archway wondering if I had in fact been told to leave. But no, the cemetery seemed to continue across the street. I finally made the connection. I had been in the Catholic cemetery. The Jewish section of Olšany was over there.

I made my way through a small door in a long wall. The cemetery was about the same size, but I found I was completely alone. There were no widows here. In fact there was no sign of life at all, as if the cemetery had been abandoned. The graves, the whole cemetery, was completely overgrown with long grass and bushes run wild. Tall leafy trees blocked out the light. It was as if the end of the world had come and civilization had been reclaimed by nature. The overgrowth and the silence created an eerie atmosphere. And of course the world had come to an end for the Prague Jewish community. The graves were overgrown because there was no one left to maintain them; there were few if any survivors. History had come to a sudden stop for these families. I looked at the grave stones, those going back to the nineteenth century, and those from this century. I tried to imagine what their lives must have been like. I am sure they never imagined within the normal cycle of life and death such a total calamity for their descendants, for their entire community. And then down along the wall I came to Kafka's grave. There was the tall gravestone for Franz, dated 1887-1924.

So he had existed after all. He had been a real person, who had lived and thought and felt and died. This realization, which one obtained not so much from his books but from the incontrovertible fact of his grave, made his writing all the more powerful. Those writings were like a balloon on a string floating over the horrible history of the twentieth century. Kafka's grave was the string. One was tempted to call it a heartstring. What made this confrontation with the grave even more difficult for me was the marble plaque that rested against Kafka's tombstone. It listed the names of his three sisters, their birth dates, and the approximate dates on which they had died in Nazi concentration camps.

These facts were like a blow to the chest. Kafka's own early death, and the deaths of his sisters, left me inflicted with both sadness and anger. It was difficult to conceive that such a tragedy could befall any family. And yet I was in a cemetery full of such families. Forty-five years after World War II, as I walked out of this dark place down the gravel path, I confess I was burdened by the shame of the realization that the Nazis had existed in our century, in living memory. It was a shame all humanity had to bear. I was angry about the fact that some, who still lived only a few hundred kilometres away, who shared responsibility for the fate of families like the Kafkas, had carried on since the war as if nothing had happened. This was a conundrum which I did not think anyone would ever be able to solve.

Klíma carried on our discussion of Kafka and talked about the Jewish community a little. He said that the Jews had mostly spoken German, although they also knew Czech. They tended to be sympathetic to Czech causes, unlike the large ethnic German community.

But the plight of the Jews was never an easy one. They often found themselves under pressure from both sides, sandwiched between pan-Germanism and Czech nationalism. Indeed, their cosmopolitanism occasionally made them suspect in both communities. There were still a few hundred Jews left in Prague, like him, who had survived the camps or who had escaped the country and come back after the war.

I had been to the Jewish community centre on Maislova Street near the Old Town Square and had a kosher lunch there. Inside this building, built in 1586, there was a gallery around the second floor of the main dining hall which, like the dining hall itself, was bursting with people. It was an unusual sight so many years after the golden age of the Jewish community in Prague. I felt as if I had walked into another century. My first thoughts were that communism could never penetrate here. In fact some of the leaders of the community, and of the Catholic and Protestant communities, had worked out an accommodation with the regime. This would, unfortunately, come back to haunt them after the revolution.

For all three communities, the main preoccupation was a determination to preserve their community and its traditions at all cost. Many Jewish artifacts, for instance, were held by the regime in dilapidated warehouses. There were fears that these would be lost unless action was taken by the regime to return them to the community or to provide them museum space. Alas, only after the revolution was this finally possible. And only then could many of the young people take advantage of the new ties with Israel to visit that country and, in some cases, meet relatives for the first time.

Amazingly, Klíma seemed to show no outward sign of the suffering endured by the Jewish community, nor of his own ordeal in the camps as a young boy. He was calm and always ready to laugh. He seemed determined to look for positive developments, even in those dark days in the fall of 1989. As we sat in the living room of the residence, he mentioned that a publishing house in Prague might actually publish one of his books. Of course it was a book that he had written before 1968. Klíma then pulled a contract out of his pocket and asked what was one to make of this? Havel, seated on the sofa beside him, showed no sign of either censure or envy. Havel had talked earlier about the novelist Bohumil Hrabal, perhaps the greatest living Czech writer, who was now well into his seventies. Hrabal had finally agreed in the 1970s, when he was already over sixty, to alter his novels in order to have them published in Prague. As a justification, he had said that, at his age, he would otherwise never see his books in print. He did not have time to wait for the new world that would come one day, the world for which Havel was fighting.

Havel was understanding of Hrabal, and said simply, "we know he is one of us." Each writer in his own circumstances had to make his own decision. Havel seemed disinclined to judge others, despite the rigorous standards he applied to himself. I met Hrabal several times after the revolution. Though almost seventy-five, he mostly wore jeans and a sweatshirt and often carried a knapsack over his shoulder with a few books in it. He had closely cropped hair, a broad smiling face, and sparkling, mischievous blue eyes. He seemed to have done every job imaginable, even the most menial.

Hrabal started writing late in life and his almost incredible personal experiences were a rich mine to plumb. In one of his novels, *Too Loud A Solitude*, the protagonist operates a machine to recycle paper waste. Under the regime, the waste is often banned books. The story follows a bizarre plot to say the least, and I remarked to Hrabal that it was one of my favourites. He laughed and said, referring to the main character, "you know, it's me, this book is me!" Hrabal was more like a natural phenomenon, or a child, than an adult, and you could not help liking him. I shared Havel's conviction that Hrabal's heart was in the right place.

Zdeněk Urbánek was his exuberant self at the party, with ready wit and smile. He too was over seventy, and fond of making fun at the frequently breathtaking idiocy of the regime. In addition to being an excellent essayist, he was a translator and specialist in English literature from Shakespeare to Joyce, Hemingway and Faulkner. There was a small cloud on his horizon these days, however. He had been invited to lecture in the United States and had been refused a passport by the communist regime.

Zdeněk wondered if he would be able to see the United States again in his lifetime. It was the same kind of dilemma that faced Hrabal. But Urbánek was not about to change his ways, or his friendship with the Havels. To its credit, the U.S. Embassy kept up pressure on the Czech regime to let Urbánek go, and made several high-level démarches that autumn. The regime finally relented and Urbánek was permitted to take up the American offer to lecture in the States for the 1989-90 academic year.

Urbánek left Prague only a few weeks before the revolution. During the events of November and December, he would keep in regular contact with Havel by telephone. The two would finally see each other again in February during Havel's official visit to Canada as President of Czechoslovakia. Urbánek did not return immediately to his country at the time of the revolution because he felt that he had to keep his commitment to his American friends. It had been these very people that had done so much to defend him from the regime, and had finally succeeded in pressuring the regime to let him go. He could not let them down now. This was the same kind of moral precision that Havel brought to bear on his own actions, and I came to see it as a specifically Czech characteristic. In retrospect, it was also true that the revolution turned out to be exhausting. It ruined the health of men and women half his age. Zdeněk was so close to the central figures in the opposition that I think the revolution would have been very hard on him physically. Perhaps fate would intervene in the lives of these Czech authors in more ways than one.

15

THE TWILIGHT OF COMMUNISM

IT WAS NOT EVERY DAY that I had the occasion to mix with the "dialectical antithesis" of Charter 77. The opportunity came on the East German national day, October 10. The East German Embassy was having a reception to mark the occasion and I was invited in my capacity as chargé d'affaires of the Canadian Embassy. I had never until then had the chance to visit the East German chancery, situated in a prime location on the banks of the Vltava river. Nor had they previously invited me to any kind of reception. But I found the whole affair rather illustrative of what must have passed for hardline communist protocol in days past.

I parked nearby and made my way through what seemed like hundreds of official cars and traffic police. The street adjacent was jammed with the black Tatra limousines and chauffeurs of high-level Communist Party officials and generals. I had my invitation checked at the door by a beefy StB agent, who looked at me as if there must have surely been a mistake. He finally let me go through with a shrug of the shoulders, deciding no doubt that, in any event, I was too insignificant to worry about. I made my way up the stairs and at the top shook hands with the East German ambassador and his senior staff. They all looked rather grim, without exception. Perhaps they already had an inkling, in mid-October 1989, of where the exodus of their compatriots was going to lead.

The receiving line led through an archway into a hall. Two doors led off the hall into a large reception room. Without paying much attention to what I was doing, I simply went through the doorway that was closest. I found myself in a small alcove, not particularly crowded, and slightly set back from the large reception room. The latter was now packed with hundreds of people elbow to elbow. The noise was deafening. The waiters squeezed between the guests, trays raised high, and I could just make out a few mangy-looking hors d'oeuvres. I could not understand why more people were not jammed into the alcove where I was.

Here in this tranquil oasis there were lovely hors d'oeuvres laid out on silver trays and small sandwiches and glasses of wine. There were only about ten of us, with lots of room to move and chat and there seemed to be a waiter devoted just to us. I sampled the smoked salmon from the richly laid table and then took a glass of orange juice from what appeared to be our own bar. Thus fully equipped I stood in the alcove at the point at which it gave on to the hall, looking out with perhaps a touch of disdain upon the masses who seemingly were not happy unless they were crowded together like cattle, shouting in each other's ear. How much better to contemplate the spectacle from a safe distance.

The waiters of the alcove were touchingly diffident, unlike their compatriots constantly harried by the plebs. But there was a certain hesitancy about them as I scooped up a couple more hors d'oeuvres. They seemed too shy to say anything. My first thought was—well, I checked and my zipper was up. I wiped my nose and mouth with the napkin served with the hors d'oeuvres. Feeling a little self-conscious, although still uncertain about what, I looked around to see if anyone else was looking at me. It was like one of those nightmares where you go about your daily business and suddenly realize at the bus stop that you forgot to get dressed. The others in the alcove were standing around, some of them alone, some in groups of two or three. They were just standing there as if unaware of me and eating their sandwiches. I remarked that they had terrible manners and were eating and talking with their mouths full and parts of the sandwiches were falling on the rug as they tried to shove the whole thing in their mouths. My apologies to the factory floor, but these were the manners that one might expect to see "on the factory floor."

About this time I noticed that that dull-looking chap over in the corner bore a remarkable likeness to the General Secretary of the Czechoslovak Communist Party. Hardly the sort to wield absolute power, though. But wait a minute, it *was* the General Secretary! And the others, too, standing around with me in the alcove, they all looked vaguely familiar. But of course! It was the politburo. And yet for all the world they looked exactly like the kind of stereotypical small-town mayor and his aldermen that one might see in a Hollywood movie. They had a provincial, even redneck, look: not particularly intelligent, and wearing ill-fitting clothes. They did not seem to mind having me there. They did not look put upon, or anything. But they made no move to speak with me or anyone from the hall either, and no one from the hall dared to speak to them. It was a little more complicated than a country club, I suppose. They could not be visibly snooty, since that would have given the lie to the comradeship thing. What I was doing was simply not done and the fact that it was not done was understood by the comrades both inside the alcove and in the hall. The leaders had the StB to be snooty for them, after all. On occasions like this they simply came, they ate, and they went. Alas, I realized I had to go too, and wandered as nonchalantly as I could into the hall sipping my orange juice and clutching an hors d'oeuvre. But the hall was awash with greasy-haired apparatchiks, and so I exited—through the front door.

While the repression exercised by the regime was worse than ever, there were a few inexplicable exceptions. It seemed as if the totalitarian machine was not working as intended. Perhaps what had not been fully understood up to this point was the extent to which any such machine was necessarily afflicted by entropy. The regime was both more laughable and more violent and isolated. Any Czech could be imprisoned from one day to the next. Without cause and without reason. There had also been the threat of expulsion directed at me. Barry, Pierre, and I were exerting maximum pressure on the regime through the use of the Helsinki human rights mechanisms. We seemed to be pummelling the government with demands and démarches every other day. But it could have had immediate, and unexpected, consequences for our own continued residence in the country at any time.

Another anniversary was only days away. This was October 28, the date of the founding of the Czechoslovak Republic in 1918. As we approached that date, the context changed dramatically. First there was the fiasco of the East German refugees in Prague. Then there was the spectacle of huge demonstrations in East Germany against the communist regime there. The demonstrations in Leipzig, with 200,000 people and more, left people in Prague speechless. There was the full expectation that Warsaw Pact troops would be deployed to crush the demonstrations, which would have been easy enough, given the number of troops stationed in that "front line" country. And all of this was going on a few hundred miles north of Prague! The clincher was the rumour, which was later seen to be confirmed, that Gorbachov had ordered Soviet troops to stay in their barracks.

The Czechoslovak regime responded to these developments by tightening the screws. At a central committee plenum of the Communist Party, Jakeš expressed grave concern about developments in Poland, Hungary and the USSR. He was incensed by the support given to the Czech opposition from those very countries. Then he warned all and sundry that the Communist Party would safeguard its leading role "at any cost." He promised an ideological struggle and a crackdown on underground publishing and the opposition.

I did not know what to expect on October 28. Would the Czechs take a page out of the East German handbook? What seemed to be driving the East German revolt, however, was the desire of the East Germans to reunite with West Germany, whether through exile or through political change. The motivation among the majority was certainly economic as much as political. An additional cause was that the East German regime was so obviously an artificial creation. Not all of these considerations applied to the Czech situation, which left me wondering how the people, and how the regime, would react to the October 28 national day. I later learned that the university students in Prague were debating whether or not to participate in the expected demonstration. Their teachers were urging caution, arguing that those of them who were reform-minded would be weeded out as part of an easily predictable reaction on the part of the regime. This time around, the students listened to their mentors.

Pierre and I went down to Wenceslas Square at the appointed hour. It was a grey and bitterly cold autumn day. Like clockwork, a few thousand people came off the sidewalks and out of side streets and gathered in front of the statue of King Wenceslas on horseback. Once again, the square would become a symbolic and literal battleground for the hearts and minds of a nation. There was a short speech by someone I did not recognize from one of the smaller opposition groups. Then this crowd and the thousands of onlookers standing on the sidewalks began singing the national anthem. Suddenly, hundreds and hundreds of riot police marched from the metro station entrances and lined up across the top and bottom of the square. They were wearing white helmets with visors and they were carrying large shields and long white truncheons. It was a frightening, overwhelming show of force. The onlookers along the sidewalks, who had been singing the national anthem only moments before, started fleeing down side streets.

From the top and the bottom of the square the lines of riot police advanced in lock step on the crowd of protesters in the middle. Their heavy boots clapped against the pavement as they marched and they held their truncheons with both hands in front. Cold-blooded and determined, they simply walked into the crowd and hit at random. Many protesters now tried to escape, but a few hundred refused to be intimidated and just stood there defiantly. The police beat these brave men and women as they stood. They were boxed in on all sides and there was now no escape. They were dragged by their clothes and by their hair and thrown into ten or twelve waiting paddy wagons. About 350 would spend the next few days in jail until they were processed and charged. If the recent past was a guide, some could expect to be held without charge or trial for six months or even a year. Except that this time their stay in jail would be cut short.

But despite the bravery of the few, I could not escape the conclusion that this protest was a desultory affair compared to the East German demonstrations. Perhaps about 5,000 people had come out. Havel and other opposition leaders had been arrested the day before. With these pre-emptive arrests and the deployment of a huge number of riot police, the regime wanted to prevent what was happening in East Germany from spreading here. Later that evening the TV news proudly showed Wenceslas Square completely empty, except for barricades and riot police. It was an odd display of the regime's special sense of patriotism. Moreover, the spectacle of the regime beating up its people was now an anachronism in the eyes of its neighbouring bloc allies.

What I did not know on the day of this demonstration was that the riot police were about to use a technique that they would perfect a few weeks later, on November 17. They created a box around the protesters by closing off the square above and below. By lining up shoulder to shoulder, they then proceeded to make the box smaller and smaller. On October 28, the riot police left one corner of the box open, where the faint-hearted could escape if they chose. I did not grasp my predicament on October 28 until, inside the box, I decided that I was a little too close to the action. I tried to get out of the box through the police lines, but they refused, despite the fact I showed them my diplomatic credentials. These are normally supposed to provide some form of immunity from the local justice system, in this case the riot police. Immunity supposedly prevents diplomats from being hindered during the legitimate pursuit of their diplomatic duties. Part of my job was to monitor the regime's compliance with internationally agreed human rights obligations. It appeared my monitoring, on occasion, had certain risks.

Blocked from getting out of the box by the nearest line of riot police, and now aware of what was going to happen when the riot police closed in, I made my way up the square towards the other line of riot police. There was a small hole at a side street that led from Wenceslas Square, which was left open by the police until the last moment. I managed to slip through this hole, with some relief, just as the riot police closed it off. They then proceeded to tighten the noose and moved in on the few hundred demonstrators remaining. These few hundred were beaten up randomly and thrown to the ground before being herded into paddy wagons. The same technique would be deployed on November 17 against the students, but with a bloody twist. It would provide the spark that ignited a revolution.

I felt literally sick at heart after the demonstration on October 28. It was as if I had an almost physical reaction to the violence as we returned home in the car. I was disgusted and depressed at what some so-called civilized humans could do to other civilized humans. As chargé d'affaires, I made an official protest at the Ministry of Foreign Affairs. The government of Canada condemned this flagrant and violent denial of the freedom of assembly. What made it worse was that the regime's brutal attack had obviously been premeditated.

I had recently confirmed permission from headquarters to protest the denial of freedom of expression. The regime had of late taken aim at underground publishers of opposition reviews, newspapers, and *samizdat* books. They had all been found guilty of "incitement" and jailed. Incitement was defined in the criminal code as the action of anyone who, out of hostility to the socialist system, incited at least two other people to adopt the same views, or used media to do so. The penalty was one to five years. I said that this provision was inconsistent with the regime's signature of the Vienna human rights document under the Helsinki Accords, and demanded that the regime take immediate action to rectify the discrepancy. I then handed over a list of 27 people charged and convicted of incitement, requesting their release. As expected, the protest of the government of Canada was vehemently rejected by the regime's spokesperson in the ministry. But the point was to keep on pushing, and to convey to the regime that we were never going to let up on this fundamental violation of international law. Canadians, and their government, were adamant.

I was getting used to this pattern of dissent, repression, and diplomatic démarche. I did not exactly pull any punches and went toe-to-toe with senior communist officials, berating them over the regime's mistreatment of the most basic rights. But there was more to it this time. East Germany had erupted in mass demonstrations. I could not help being disillusioned by the feeble protest in Prague. The most striking thing on October 28 was the total absence of young people, especially students. After the demonstration, I stopped on the street to talk with a couple I knew. He was a Czech baptist minister and she was an American. I admitted to a feeling of disappointment that more people had not demonstrated. I shook my head with incomprehension at the fact that the university students had once again refused to be in the forefront of change. No revolt would ever carry the day without the energy and creativity of the young. Of course this was easy to say for someone who had diplomatic immunity. But I was convinced, and had been since the first sizeable demonstrations in January of that year, that the regime had clay feet and would crumble if given a shove.

16

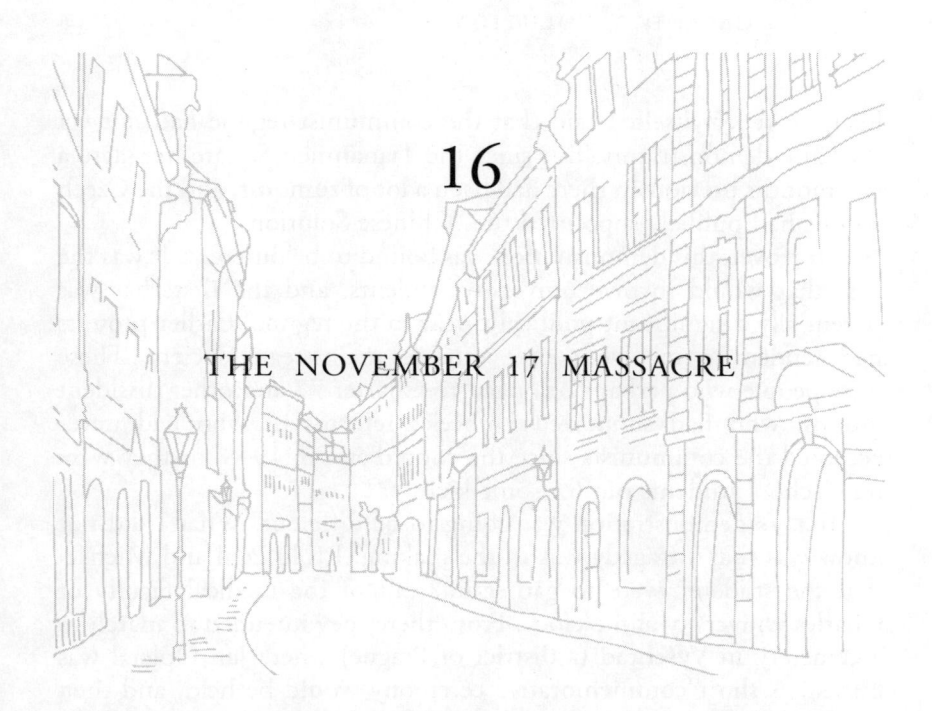

THE NOVEMBER 17 MASSACRE

NOVEMBER 17, the day of the "massacre," began innocently enough. It was a Friday morning and two Canadian journalists came to see me at the Embassy. Paul Koring of the *Globe and Mail* and Michael Hanlon of the *Toronto Star* had been covering the collapse of the Berlin Wall. Like many other Western journalists, they had travelled to Prague overnight by train, fully expecting that Czechoslovakia would be the next domino to fall. I was not so sure. I had been dealing with the communist regime for almost a year and a half, and had seen demonstration after demonstration put down violently by riot police. A number of my Czech friends and acquaintances had been thrown in jail without trial, even without being charged. Unfurling an "anti-socialist" banner at May Day, or reading "anti-socialist" pamphlets, was enough to get the person responsible arrested and locked up. Undeterred by my scepticism, these travel-weary journalists were intrigued by the fact that there was going to be a demonstration that very afternoon.

Friday, November 17 was the 50th anniversary of International Students' Day. The British had named it after a Czech student, Jan Opletal, who had organized a demonstration on this very day in Prague, in 1939, against the Nazi occupiers. Opletal had been shot and killed at the demonstration, and other Czech student leaders were later executed. Michael Hanlon asked, only half in jest, if history was likely to repeat itself. I said that the communist regime had not yet shot any demonstrators. But since the Tiananmen Square massacre a few months previously, there had been a lot of rumours, and the Czech regime had publicly supported the "Chinese Solution."

Moreover, this demonstration was bound to be different. It was the first that would involve university students, and the first that was potentially a significant political threat to the regime. Earlier protests had tended to involve people outside mainstream society. These were people who perhaps belonged to Charter 77 and other dissident groups, who had supported Dubček's reforms or who had never accepted the communists since the coup d'état in 1948, or they were high school students out for some kicks.

Today's demonstration was going to be different. What I did not know was that a tragedy was in the making. I told Paul and Michael that the students were to gather in front of the medical faculty of Charles University at 4 o'clock. From there they intended to march to a cemetery in Vyšehrad (a district of Prague) where Jan Opletal was buried. A short commemorative ceremony would be held, and then everyone was supposed to go home. I found it strange that the local communist authorities had agreed to the march, though permission had come only after much negotiation. The past year and a half had witnessed increasingly large protests against the regime. In fact this series of demonstrations constituted the first significant public opposition to the regime in twenty years. The authorities must have expected that any "legitimate," peaceful march, especially by young people, was likely to give them trouble. This implies that the terrible violence that was to be unleashed on the students was premeditated.

It all began when a few students asked the communist rector of Charles University for permission to hold the commemorative procession. It was a legitimate request, because Opletal's anti-Nazi demonstration was years later praised by the communist regime. It was praised only years later because, in 1939, due to the Hitler-Stalin pact, the demonstration was regarded by the communists as "premature anti-fascism." Now, fifty years later, the rector simply relayed the students' request to the local municipal committee, or communist "narodní výbor," which refused. The students reacted by setting up their own independent students' council, outside the Communist Union of Youth, in order to drum up support for the march. The Communist Union of Youth, seeing its influence leak away, joined the new students' council in pressing the authorities to permit the march.

This self-organization of the students over a relatively trivial issue turned out to be the undoing of the regime.

Over the past year, the students of Prague had failed to participate in any demonstrations against the regime. What had to be remembered was that permission to study at university was to some extent determined by the political "reliability" of the parents. The parents of many students were either Communist Party members or, at a minimum, in good standing with the regime. The march that was planned was legitimate enough, to mark International Students' Day and to remember Jan Opletal's death at the hands of the Nazis. The students agreed with the local communist municipal committee that the march would not proceed to the heart of the city, towards Wenceslas Square, where earlier protests had been staged. They were to march from the medical faculty of Charles University to Vyšehrad cemetery, a little further out of the city. I suppose the regime finally agreed to the march because there was no choice: there would be a march anyway.

I sensed there was going to be something different about this event when I talked that morning to a language teacher associated with the Embassy. We had planned to read through some Czech newspapers that afternoon. I was about to telephone him to cancel our appointment, when he phoned to say he would not be able to make it either. He said simply, "I must be with my Czech students today." I agreed and added that I would be there too. Then he said, over a telephone line we knew was tapped, "perhaps we will both learn something today. Perhaps the government also." It occurred to me that he had been an increasingly outspoken critic of the regime in recent months. To talk this way over the telephone was a reckless invitation to a session with the StB. In retrospect, it is apparent he knew better than I what was going to happen.

The rallying point for the start of the student march was a long narrow street between cream-coloured baroque buildings that housed the medical faculty of Charles University. By the time Lynn and I arrived there was already a surprisingly large crowd of students. They were holding banners and chanting slogans. I had never seen this number of students involved in any kind of demonstration in Prague before. Because we were packed closely in the street I could not see the full extent of the crowd. But what really surprised me was the volume of slogans shouted. These could be heard blocks away, and as you approached you knew there was a large, active group of young people who might have been, in other circumstances, marching to a university football game, perhaps a championship. There was also a fair number of foreign journalists and TV cameramen about. It seemed as if everyone had left the Berlin Wall to come to Prague.

I thought at the time that the journalists' expectation of mass protests along the lines of what had been witnessed in East Germany was a naive and superficial judgment. They knew virtually nothing about the struggle of the last year and a half, or about the nature of the regime. How odd, with this simple perspective, that they turned out to be right. Aside from the journalists, I did not see many of my diplomatic colleagues at the march. The Brits and Americans were there, as usual. The Canadian, American, and British Embassies seemed to be the only visible presences at these demonstrations, though others no doubt watched occasionally from a distance.

The timing of the journalists' interest was, in retrospect, perfect. This demonstration *was* different. The protesters were virtually all students, they were energized, and they were loud. They were also having fun and there was a lot of laughter and joking about. It was a relaxed laughter that came from the sudden release of constraint. Some of the banners said, "Democracy, Freedom, Free Elections," "Freedom for Christmas!," and "The Soviet Union Our Example, at Last." Before long, I detected "anti-socialist" slogans being shouted, the words "Charter 77," and "Havel." And then they began to shout "It's already here," as if recognizing that, yes, a corner had been turned. I looked around and saw that there were no uniformed police, nor the riot police that would have been expected if the demonstration had been taking place in Wenceslas Square. Earlier I had noticed, at the bottom of the street where you could turn away from or towards the city centre, that there was one VB (police) car parked. The officer inside was talking into a radio microphone. I assumed his job was to alert other units if the crowd headed downtown, towards the square.

I had seen enough demonstrations at this point to know that there were plain-clothes police officers in the heart of the crowd itself. These undercover agents seemed to have two functions at previous protests. They tried to lead the crowd down side streets so that it could be more easily broken up by police, or they tried to provoke the crowd by shouting anti-Russian slogans, so as to create the rationale for brutal intervention by the riot police. When the riot police attacked, they would grab demonstrators in the centre of the crowd and arrest them, often throwing them to the ground. During all of the demonstrations, which were peaceful protests, I never saw the crowd attack any of these undercover StB agents.

The march finally began and made its way down in front of the medical faculty. The crowd was well-organized. At its head were students carrying the Czechoslovak flag, and then a row of students carrying candles. The candles were to become symbolic, in light of subsequent events. Scattered amidst the crowd and the banners were placards with the Czech lion, except that the red star inserted by the communists over the lion's head had been removed. The demonstration, which was larger and louder than any I had seen before, turned away from the centre of the city and marched towards Vyšehrad cemetery. This was what had been agreed with the communist authorities. There were well over 10,000 students marching. It seemed the significance of the 50th anniversary of Jan Opletal's death had a certain resonance today.

At this point Lynn and I, unluckily, or luckily as it turned out, had to attend a social function at the American Embassy. I was chargé d'affaires during the absence of my Ambassador, Barry Mawhinney. Ambassador Shirley Temple Black and I were co-hosting an American and Canadian reception. From the frantic phone calls I received from journalists at home after the reception, I pieced together what happened after we left. The crowd made its way to Vyšehrad cemetery. Alexander Dubček, who was supposed to address the crowd there, had been detained by police earlier in the day and was being held. At the cemetery there was a ceremony to mark the death of the students in 1939. The crowd had grown to perhaps 20,000, as large as, or larger than, any of the previous demonstrations. There were a lot of anti-regime slogans. Then, in what can only be described as a fateful moment, the protesters turned toward the river and marched down along the Vltava river toward the city centre. They thereby broke the agreement with the communists. The goal, at least for some of the young people, was to reach Wenceslas Square and the statue of the King on horseback: the patron saint of Bohemia.

The police were just as determined to prevent it. They had recently perfected a new technique for intimidating public protesters, and they were eager to use it. The idea was to escalate the violence to such an extent that those foolish enough to have come out once would not be inclined to do so again. We had had a taste of this on October 28 when the riot police boxed in the crowd, leaving only one narrow opening for escape. It was the opening I had used to get away. But once it was felt that a sufficient time had elapsed for those who wanted to get away, the hole was closed off.

It was this police tactic that was awaiting the students when they turned toward the city, but with a new, and bloody, twist. The crowd now stretched out along the Vltava River for a kilometre or more. They marched in the fading half-light of early evening. The Castle and Saint Vitus Cathedral were already lit up on the other side of the river. The flickering lights along Charles Bridge, linking the old town with the lesser town, were barely visible. The lead group of students, perhaps not more than a couple of thousand, then turned away from the river on to Narodní Street, and marched toward Wenceslas Square. They were in high spirits, intoxicated by the freedom of speaking out, of shouting to the roof tops what they knew almost everyone in this godforsaken country felt in their hearts.

But the trap had been laid and they walked straight into it. Half way down Narodní, near the Reduta Jazz Club, the riot police halted the march by forming a line across the street. At the same time, another line of riot police formed across the street behind them. The lead group were caught in a box, while the riot police blocked the other protesters from entering Narodní street. The trap was not completely shut. For the next hour of so, individual students were permitted to leave the box. But not many did.

The students in the box sat down on the pavement, many holding candles wavering in the now blackened night. They sat down right in front of the helmeted riot police, who stood shoulder to shoulder, long white truncheons at the ready, their visors down, their shields held firmly in front. The visors had an odd way of distorting their faces so that you could not see them clearly. They looked tense and removed, ignoring what was going on in front of them. The students sat, still holding their banners. Sometimes they sang songs. A few tried to put flowers on the shields of the riot police, or spread flowers in front of their boots.

Police loudspeakers told the students to go home. The students shouted back, "Wenceslas Square is our home." The loudspeakers told them they were breaking the law. The students shouted back, "But whose law do you serve?" Then the long, excruciating wait began. It was a stand-off, of sorts. One hour, then another passed. Suddenly, the riot police let no one leave the box any more. The waiting continued and the tension began mounting. Some of the young women students were crying, their boyfriends quiet and grave. Obviously something was being planned, something prepared for them. This was all the more unsettling given their false sense of security earlier in the evening. The police, also young, looked hard and angry, almost beside themselves, as if drugged or psyched out. There were lined up behind them some soldiers with red berets. This was the army's anti-terrorist squad of trained killers.

Hundreds of candles now burned on the pavement. There was interminable waiting. There was tension that suffocated speech and an unreal nightmare of streets, street lamps, and motionless, steaming riot police. They ignored the flowers, the banners, the entreaties, as if blinded. They did not seem to see at all. And then, almost imperceptibly, they were given a signal, because they just started walking into the sitting students in front of them, clubbing them across the heads and shoulders. Many of the protesters just fell over unconscious and bleeding. There was no charge, the riot police just walked into the young people swinging, with deliberation, the long white truncheons. They knew there was no way out. The plan was to beat them all without exception. Some young women screamed and everyone tried to move back but there was no escape. And then the riot police started grabbing some people and pushing them down and hitting them, and then running after others. Here and there several riot policemen would beat a prone student, already unconscious.

In the slow motion world of real-time violence, there was terror-stricken screaming and scuffling. The banners lay twisted on the pavement, the candles broken and squashed. The red beret soldiers, the terrorist squad, also took part, beating the students. There were a number of journalists caught in the box, including TV cameramen. The police grabbed their cameras and smashed them on the pavement. They grabbed anything held by the journalists, even their notebooks, and then the journalists were beaten too. One cameraman was so severely beaten he lost consciousness. They beat him across the kidneys and later he was flown to Paris for emergency medical treatment for kidney damage. A woman journalist from a newspaper in Chicago was hit across the head and needed sixteen stitches. Others were knocked out and had to be carried away by their colleagues. But the students had it worse, much worse.

Young people lay unconscious on the black pavement, blood oozing from their heads, and still they were beaten. Others were caught in street doors, cornered, and beaten by two or three policemen at a time. The women students were beaten as badly as the men. Many suffered permanent injury. Upwards of a thousand required hospitalization. Finally the police opened a narrow corridor of escape at one end of Narodní street. More riot police lined up on each side, and as students and journalists limped through or carried their friends, they were hit again with truncheons. Many others still lay unconscious on the streets and sirens filled the night air.

Afterwards, the independent students' council was to call this a massacre. And it was. Not with rifles and bullets, but with truncheons and boots. Late that night my phone rang repeatedly. These were calls from Canadian and American journalists who had been at the demonstration. There was a Canadian journalist who had been there and had not been seen since, and there were fears for his life. Another phoned who was with an American journalist who had been badly beaten. I gave advice and contacted the American Embassy. As the night wore on, I could hear the sirens downtown from my house in Dejvice. What would I do if a Canadian had been killed? Then, sometime after 2 A.M., another call, the Canadian had been found, still groggy and badly beaten but otherwise all right. I finally went to bed thinking this had been the worst demonstration so far, though one in a series of brutal confrontations over more than a year. How far would the regime go? But with the students now playing a role, things had changed.

17

THE STUDENT STRIKE

THE NEXT DAY was bright and cold, a Saturday. There was something unreal about the normal activity of the city. People drove in their cars, the state radio played the usual happy Czech muzak. Everyone seemed to be going about their business as usual, though it looked to me artificial, like normality in a prison camp. But there was something else in the air too, something I had not felt before. There was the feeling that a line had been crossed. There was the premonition that something was going to happen, perhaps something worse than had already happened. I went to Wenceslas Square at 3 P.M., since this was the usual time for demonstrations, especially on Saturdays.

In front of the statue of King Wenceslas on horseback, a small group gathered, several hundred at most. A young man stood up and said he was a representative of the independent students' council. He said that in response to the brutality of the previous evening, the council was calling for a students' strike to begin in two days, on Monday, November 20. The council was also calling for a general strike by all workers one week later, on Monday, November 27, between 12 and 2 P.M. The council also wanted a full investigation of the massacre and the responsible people brought to justice. This seemed to me a strange program, especially the two-hour general strike. But further reflection revealed its brilliance. The people in Czechoslovakia had been terrified into submission. The smallest sign of discontent brought StB investigation, loss of job, and the end of schooling for one's children. A two-hour general strike at lunch time might be just enough to attract real support from a timid people while sending an unmistakable signal to the regime. There would be a small amount of real economic disruption.

As soon as the student read out the announcement there was a scattering of applause and then the meeting broke up. No police intervened. Indeed, there were no police to be seen anywhere. It was as if someone somewhere had realized what had happened the previous night, its implications. Life went on as usual, but now something had started, fate was beginning to weave its web. There was a palpable expectation that something would happen, and already bedsheets made into makeshift banners and calling for a students strike started to appear here and there on walls and from window to window. Then the banners appeared draped over the base of the statue of King Wenceslas. Finally, with my phone ringing all day long on Sunday, and with foreign journalists seemingly everywhere in Prague like bees to honey, a rumour swept the city that a student had been killed on Friday night. At least one student. All we knew was that his name might be Šmid, perhaps Martin Šmid.

It was later widely believed that this rumour had been started by reformist elements within the regime, although a parliamentary commission never confirmed it. The goal in starting this rumour was evidently to accelerate change in the direction of Gorbachov's reforms. A woman, "Martin Šmid's sister," had been found, or blackmailed, along with a doctor at some hospital. Peter Uhl, whose task in life as a dissident had been to verify who was being held, who was in prison, and who was charged, spent the better part of the day checking the information. When an independent witness, the doctor, had verified it, Uhl released the information, though still with a caveat. Of course, the Western press seized on it. What Uhl and the rest of us did not understand was why anyone in the government would want to start such a rumour. But then a few days later, "Martin Šmid" appeared on TV, denied the rumour, and Uhl was arrested. The conservatives in the regime took up the rumour and its falsehood to discredit the opposition and shift attention away from what had happened Friday night to the spurious issue of Martin Šmid and the opposition's credibility.

This had been a risky, not to say foolhardy, gambit by some "closet" reform communists. The rumour was all too believable in terms of what had happened. Many people were seriously, permanently, disabled by the beating, and one or more could easily have died. Western journalists, eyewitnesses to the massacre, reported the rumour as unconfirmed. But it was at the same time possible, and the tenor of their articles implied this. Meanwhile, all that weekend, with stories of the massacre and the rumour of death spreading across the country, a new resolve gripped the people of this nation. It was hard to put your finger on, or to see in any visible way, but it was there.

A line had been crossed by the regime. The students, university students mostly, were by definition the children of well-behaved parents, mostly Communist Party card carriers who had absolutely unblemished records. They had acquiesced in the "normalization" process begun by the neo-Stalinist regime installed after the Warsaw Pact invasion of Czechoslovakia in 1968. The unwritten pact these parents had entered into with this despicable regime was something like this: we will obey you and stay out of "real" politics and play the charade in exchange for a career, a reasonable standard of living, and education and opportunity for our children. When the regime started beating their children, for most the important part of the equation, the pact collapsed.

The social pact had in any event been shaky for some time now. With the rise of Gorbachov had come a push from the East for more openness, if not "restructuring." Like other conservative communist regimes in the region, the Czechoslovak regime had felt obliged (after much resistance) to loosen up travel to the West and to stop jamming Radio Free Europe. Even the shameless communist collaborators could see how badly they had fallen behind the West in terms of quality of life. The show of obedience had come to look and feel perversely hollow. And when the regime began to beat up the children of those willing to play along, the pointlessness of this silent acquiescence was just too apparent.

By Sunday, November 19, significant supports for the communist house of cards were beginning to collapse. The students began organizing themselves, creating a network led by the independent students' council. They set up strike committees at universities across the country. Private videotapes and photos of the massacre were spreading through the underground to the average citizen. The rumour of a death or deaths shook the silent majority. Late Sunday afternoon about 10,000 people, mostly students, gathered in Wenceslas Square shouting anti-government slogans. As on Saturday, no police were visible. The crowd then marched from the square down Narodní street, where they stopped to commemorate briefly the victims of the massacre. Hundreds of candles were lit and a makeshift shrine was erected.

A hand-painted sign said, "here the government killed a student." The crowd marched down along the Vltava River and crossed one of the bridges which led in the direction of Prague Castle, where President Husák lived and worked. On the other side of the bridge, as the crowd poured into a narrow street, riot police appeared suddenly with white truncheons at the ready.

The riot police formed a line across the narrow street and blocked further progress. Then another line of riot police formed behind the first several thousand demonstrators, cutting them off from the rest of the crowd behind. This was the same tactic that had been used Friday night on Narodní Street. The group thus caught, mostly students, decided to sit down. One could not help wondering if the brutality was about to be repeated. There was a difference, however. There were thousands of people on the other side of the second line of riot police, so that this line of police was itself effectively surrounded by the crowd, a crowd which could easily have overwhelmed them. The stand-off lasted some time, and then, perhaps recognizing their untenable position, this second line of police withdrew.

The students, for their part, seeing that the way to the Castle remained blocked by the first line of police, returned back across the Vltava, loudly shouting anti-government slogans all the way. Though it was true that the riot police had blocked the way to the Castle, it was also true that the demonstrators had faced the police down and won. At least that was how it felt. There had been no beatings and no arrests. Momentum was now with the crowd, and the enthusiasm of the young reflected this. They knew they were in the right, and they felt that Friday night was the end of something, and the beginning of something else: the nascent whiff of democracy and the democratic spirit.

18

THE BIRTH OF CIVIC FORUM

AT THE SAME MOMENT on this Sunday evening when the students were confronting the police, an impromptu meeting of opposition groups was taking place, led by Václav Havel. It was at this meeting that Havel founded the political movement known as Civic Forum. It would act as an umbrella for all opposition groups, uniting them behind agreed objectives. In fact Forum would become the lever that would topple a dictatorship. For the first time the meeting on Sunday night brought together representatives of the ousted reform group from 1968, and from the two co-opted parties still officially part of the National Front coalition with the communists. The two co-opted parties were the Socialist Party and the People's Party. Since the communist coup d'état in 1948 they had of course been only the shells of parties, totally controlled by the communists and permitted to exist solely to give the impression of a united coalition government devoted to the national interest. The two parties were also useful in deflecting the criticism that the Czechoslovak Socialist Republic was a one-party state. But by late 1989 even some figures in these parties could understand what Gorbachov meant for Central Europe. And this conclusion was only reinforced by the domestic political implications of a falling standard of living. They could see that totalitarian communism had a limited shelf-life.

Jan Škodas of the Socialist Party was present at the formation of Civic Forum on that Sunday evening. He had been a school chum of both Ivan and Václav Havel. But he did not officially commit his party to the coalition that was to become Civic Forum, saying he had to consult the membership. Still, he was sympathetic to Civic Forum's goals, and to the declaration that emerged from this historic meeting. Representatives of the People's Party were also at Havel's meeting, at least those who represented the "revival wing" of the party. These people were already trying to overthrow the current co-opted leadership of their party. They wanted to return the party to its religious roots. Hence, they signed on to the Civic Forum Declaration, without caring what the leadership of their party thought.

But there were many other individuals present too, influential in their own way, from across the whole range of society. These were actors, singers, priests, philosophers, scientists, writers, and so on. The gathering included the whole of the Charter 77 crowd, plus the Independent Peace Initiative, and the other independent opposition groups, as well as the Jazz Section, Obroda (the purged group of 1968 reformers who had surrounded Dubček), and naturally the independent students' council. It must be remembered that Civic Forum was created as an initiative—not with the immediate objective of planning and carrying out a revolution, or of forming a government. It was an initiative intended to chip away at the regime's powers. And the regime, as of Sunday, November 19, was still very much in power, with all the repressive and violent tools that it wanted at its disposal. It was natural that Václav Havel should become the head of Civic Forum, virtually by acclamation. His moral authority was a unifying factor among the diverse points of view now huddled under Forum's umbrella. A simple declaration was drafted setting out Forum's raison d'être.

The declaration was not unlike Charter 77 initiatives in the past. The call for respect of human rights and the restoration of democratic process was reminiscent of earlier Charter demands. But this time there was the addition of a condemnation of the police brutality meted out on Friday night, and the reference to broad support from other official and unofficial groups, and from the two small political parties, the Socialist Party and the People's Party. The Socialist Party had its own newspaper, called *Svobodno Slovo*, which meant "the free word." This paper, like the party itself, had simply mouthed Communist Party propaganda over the past forty years. But in recent months it had begun, ever so tentatively, to adopt a slightly different line from that expressed in the Communist Party daily newspaper, *Rudé Právo* (which meant, "the red truth"). And on this particular night, Sunday, November 19, *Svobodno Slovo* printed Civic Forum's declaration on the front page of Monday's edition.

It is difficult now to describe how daring that act was. Individuals who were caught with any opposition pamphlets at their workplace or in the privacy of their home were fired, prosecuted for anti-socialist acts, fined, and jailed. Their careers, their spouses' careers, their relationships with their friends and neighbours, and the educational prospects of their children, were forever changed. And now here was a declaration, whose drafting was led by public enemy number one, appearing on the front page of an official newspaper. It took one's breath away. During the night Jan Škoda had received a call from his newspaper's office, saying four men from the StB were there. Škoda went down to the newspaper offices located on Wenceslas Square. He told the StB to get out. They did, surprisingly, but took with them many of the copies already printed. Moreover, the edition for the countryside was intercepted on the trains and removed by the StB. For all that, when *Svobodno Slovo* appeared next morning, heralding the birth of Civic Forum, Czechoslovakia entered another era. It was as if King Wenceslas had suddenly appeared on the battlefield, emerging from the early morning mists, ready to engage the forces of evil.

19

DON'T START THE REVOLUTION WITHOUT ME

THERE WAS AN AIR OF EXPECTANCY that first morning of the revolution. The sheer violence of the attack on the students was beginning to sink in. There were countless critical injuries, and there was the rumour of at least one death. Public outrage, spreading across the country, seemed to crystallize. Václav decided to hold a press conference in his apartment to announce the formation of Civic Forum. Pierre and I caught wind of it and showed up. Of course no one there, among the few of us present, could predict what would happen later that day. It was Monday morning, November 20, 1989. I found myself sitting in a chair on the other side of the desk at which Václav Havel would soon announce the creation of Civic Forum.

It had been a long road to that moment: over twenty years since the Warsaw Pact invasion of Czechoslovakia and the crushing of Dubček's Prague Spring. And over ten years since Havel, the so-called dissident playwright, had founded Charter 77 with a few other defenders of human rights. Havel had spent five of those years in prison for his efforts. Now it was a year and a half since the first sizeable demonstrations against the regime began. That was in the summer of 1988, the summer in which we arrived in this hardline communist state. I discovered that Havel and the ragged band of Charter signatories were a controversial lot both for their countrymen and for the diplomatic community. Many in both camps wondered what possible impact this small group of dissidents could possibly have on a totalitarian state. Within days of our arrival, Havel had responded in an opposition journal by arguing that he could theoretically imagine a situation where a series of events might turn even Charter 77 into a definable and visible movement with a large following. But the point was that Charter's strength derived from the truth it articulated. The importance of the mirror's existence far exceeded the number of people holding it.

Now, as I waited in the Havels' apartment, we were on the verge of that transformation. Thousands, even hundreds of thousands of people would rush forward to hold that mirror so all would see the regime for what it was, without equivocation. And this had come about because the need to live in truth, experienced by a growing number of people, was converted into the courage to do so. In his article Havel had articulated the commitment that inspired a revolution. "I base my actions on a fairly simple human philosophy: namely, that I have to say what I think. I have to speak the truth. I have to fight for the things I know to be right." The brutality unleashed by the regime on the students of Prague clarified the mind of an entire nation along the same lines.

The desk was in a corner of the room. Havel came through a door behind the desk. First, he announced that he would not go to Sweden to receive the Olaf Palme Award, which had just been awarded to him, even if he was given a passport by the regime. Havel said that, in the current circumstances, he had to stay in Czechoslovakia. It was as if he knew already what the day would bring.

Then Havel announced the formation of Civic Forum. The cameras of foreign journalists whirred and microphones were thrust forward. There were lights and TV cameras from American networks. Everything started moving quickly now, and I think Václav sensed it was about to take off. I expected the police to burst in and break up the meeting. Havel laughed lightly, saying it was his first press conference. He talked about Civic Forum's declaration, the need for political change and the need to find out who was responsible for Friday night's brutality. The photographers shot and whirred, and the journalists wrote. We all felt something new in that apartment: incredible hope tinged with foreboding. This was still the regime that had applauded the Chinese "solution" of last June, the Tiananmen massacre.

As I sat listening to Václav, I did not know what the regime or the people would do. The pattern of the past had not been encouraging. Very small groups had risked showing their displeasure with the regime, and had paid an inordinately high price for it. All Czechs and Slovaks grumbled, of course, and there was a constant stream of jokes about the uneducated, boorish leadership. But violence and intimidation had worked in the past, and the beating dealt out on Friday night was no doubt intended to teach the students a lesson.

As remarked earlier, in January, 1989, I had sent a telegram to headquarters arguing that the story of that year would be the decline, perhaps precipitous, of the regime's public authority. This prediction had been inspired by the week of demonstrations in January marking the 20th anniversary of Jan Palach's suicide. I had argued that the fall of the regime would come as the result of some miscalculation, an overreaction to dissent. Perhaps that was what had occurred on Friday night. Perhaps a corner had been turned after all.

Nonetheless, as Havel joked about his first press conference, I knew he half expected, as I did, that the regime would intervene sooner or later, that he would be arrested once again, like so many times in the past. Yet he was cheerful and determined, flying without instruments in a storm. As we sat there, my mind drifted back over the past year, remembering his trial in February, and before that, the time when I first met him. It seemed like a very long road to me, but only the last mile to him. It had already been more than a year of tremendous highs and lows, of enthusiasm and disillusionment. In the midst of these confusing signals, Havel grasped immediately, sooner than any of us, the significance of Civic Forum. For the first time, all of the opposition groups would be brought together under one umbrella. Even more important, a number of groups from the "grey zone," the zone of those sympathetic to the opposition but outwardly obedient, would also join.

Rita Klimova was sitting beside Havel interpreting. She had been brought up in Brooklyn as a child by Czech parents before returning with them to Czechoslovakia. It was wonderful to hear Havel's very precise and highly charged pronouncements being rendered in a Brooklyn accent. Rita would become Havel's ambassador to the United States two months later. Also present was Michael Žantovský, who had studied at McGill University. He would become the President's spokesman, and then succeed Rita in Washington as ambassador. Ivan Havel and his wife Dáša, a Slovak, stood behind Havel, barely able to contain their excitement. Havel himself wore no tie or suit jacket, of course, simply an open white shirt with the sleeves rolled up. The business of opposition was about to start in earnest.

When asked whether the regime was in contact with him Havel said that there had been indirect contact from Prime Minister Adamec. Adamec would play an important role in the days ahead. And then Zdeněk Urbánek's grandson, David, rushed in with information about a demonstration on Narodní Street, and most of the journalists left hurriedly, camera lights and all. Everyone seemed to be rushing everywhere at that point. Unbelievably, the frenetic pace would continue unabated and culminate in Havel's election as President six weeks later. There was a sense that the old rules no longer applied to anything, an assumption that was soon taken for granted.

When Havel's first ever press conference ended, I waved goodbye and went into the streets. Already, all over town, there were university buildings draped with banners proclaiming the strike. The buildings were barricaded and students were occupying them, often sitting defiantly in the windows a few floors up. It brought back to me the excitement of the 1960s and the feeling that sometimes people had to do the right thing regardless of the consequences. I was given a copy of the student demands, surprised momentarily to see that it was a computer printout. They were establishing strike committees at all of the universities and high schools across the country. They had resources and organizational talent, two important ingredients that the opposition groups had not always possessed.

I went back to the Embassy and wrote my report on Havel's initiative and on what was happening in the streets. I had earlier arranged to meet the Canadian journalists Paul Koring and Michael Hanlon at the Hotel Jalta, just before the four o'clock demonstration called for in the Civic Forum declaration. The Jalta was located just about halfway up Wenceslas Square. Paul and Michael had rented a room at the hotel four floors up, with a balcony over the square. I arrived early, a half hour before the time, in case the police chose to close off the square, as they had done in the past.

As we gathered on the balcony at the appointed hour there were already more than 10,000 people in the square, more than I had ever seen at any previous demonstration. The atmosphere was electric as dusk fell and turned into twilight. People kept streaming into the square. There were thousands of students, but there were thousands of ordinary men and women too. Seen from the balcony, they seemed to swarm in from all sides, noisy and shouting and carrying Czechoslovak flags. This was no meek gathering of the morally pure. It was not at all like the Gandhi-inspired demonstrations of the past. This was a surging crowd that had a life of its own and was looking for action.

Some portable loudspeakers had been set up at the foot of King Wenceslas. The voices were almost impossible to understand because they echoed off the buildings. It did not matter at all to the crowd.

"It's all over." Demonstrators fill Wenceslas Square on November 20, 1989

This huge square filled up. There was a dense moving mass of people over its whole length of half a kilometre. The sound of a crowd of 200,000 people is both moving and frightening. It is pure power, the power of the general will made manifest and irresistible, both spiritually and materially. The roar from this mass deafened the handful of us perched a few floors up.

The last daylight died away and the lights in the square glowed softly. The crowd throbbed and moved like the sea, chants starting in one corner and moving down the square in a wave, breaking and echoing off the buildings. I stood there with the journalists, hardly able to believe my eyes—or conceal my excitement. I was seeing this through the lens of a year and a half of repression and brutality. Finally, I could not contain myself any longer, and exclaimed, "Well, that's it. It's all over." In my mind, the regime was finished. I knew that the resentment against the regime, against communism, was so deep, that once the door was opened the whole nation would rush through. The elaborate construction of lies, backed up by fear, would collapse. Living the lie for fear of falling into the abyss was the essence of the regime. The people massing in the square below were not afraid any more.

Those who were not afraid any more would show others and then no one would be afraid of the communist bullies any more. Those fearless people in the opposition had tried to show the way during their years in the wilderness. Now, in that crowd below, I saw the whole process multiplied and condensed. I saw that it would not be stopped, unless massive force was used to block it. And I did not believe that force was an option for the communists, not after what had happened only weeks before in East Germany; not after Gorbachov had signalled that the days were over when Warsaw Pact armies were used for internal policing. This was not to say that the regime's leadership might not have wanted to use force. They simply realized at one point that week that without the help of the Soviet troops stationed in Czechoslovakia, they could not be sure of crushing a revolution.

"It's all over." It was quoted by the group of journalists on that balcony, journalists from the *New York Times*, the *Washington Post*, the *Globe and Mail*, and the *Toronto Star*. What I meant was that the repression would stop. Innocent people would be released from jail. Decent, blameless people would have their rightful jobs back. Their children would be able to go to school like any normal child.

In that huge jubilant crowd there were the students and there were people from all walks of life and of all ages, including the proverbial little old ladies. Many held candles as a symbol and memory of the Friday night massacre. As the minutes went by and people began realizing what was happening, the crowd began to feel its strength. Slogans were chanted that must have been heard all over Prague. They shouted "down with! ..." followed by the names of various regime figures, including the General Secretary of the Communist Party, Milan Jakeš. The statue of King Wenceslas, sitting nobly on his horse, was covered with Czechoslovak flags and signs that called for free elections and pluralism. As the night wore on, the crowd took out their keys and began shaking them, making a loud cacophony. Unable to hear clearly what had been said to inspire this odd gesture, I asked one of the Czechs with us what this was all about. "They are tolling the death of communism," he said.

Although people tried to speak to the large crowd through the improvised loudspeakers, they could not be heard. The crowd had its own life, the slogans rising and falling, or drifting down the length of the square and disappearing in a far corner. Then someone shouted, "to the Castle!" This was where the office of communist President Husák was located. It was also the closest thing to a traditional, if geographical, location of Czechoslovak sovereignty. The entire crowd poured out through the bottom of the square into several streets, but mostly on to Narodní Street, and headed toward the Vltava River. We marched along Narodní and then turned down along the Vltava river to Charles Bridge. Charles Bridge spanned the river just below the Castle, which nestled on a hill.

I recognized several people in the crowd. There was a lady to whom I said hello who was an underground Catholic activist. She had ten children at home and she was carrying a candle. I was walking along with these people when suddenly the part of the crowd in which I found myself moved on to Charles Bridge, while the rest moved on to other bridges up and down the river below the Castle. I saw armed personnel carriers move on to the bridge from the other side. They had large metal screens mounted on the front to push back the crowd. They came halfway across the bridge and stopped, the dull metal dimly lit by the soft lights on the bridge. The effect of confronting these small tanks on a fourteenth century bridge was eerie to say the least. I felt a little anxious, even claustrophobic, because I was in the front of the crowd and was facing these army vehicles with a huge crowd at my back. The black water of the river moved swiftly below the thick stone walls. I wondered whether I would be capable of jumping from the bridge into the river if push came to shove, or bullets started flying. I had stupidly broken my own cardinal rule for all demonstrations, which was to ensure an escape route was handy.

The armed personnel carriers blocked the crowd. We were packed on to the bridge like sardines. Looking behind, all I could see was a river of people that stretched back through the streets into town. The armed personnel carriers had six wheels and each had a turret mounted with a large gun and a couple of heavy machine-guns below. There were shouts from the crowd to sit down and we all sat down. I guess the idea was, once again, to wait out the confrontation. This tactic had not always worked well in the past. It was the same tactic that had been used on Friday night, when the police attacked the crowd after waiting for two hours. I knew damn well that we were sitting ducks on that bridge and swore at myself again for letting myself get into this situation. The minutes passed, each minute feeling like an hour. Then there were other shouts, some close to me, that called out for a return to Wenceslas Square, and to the Old Town Square. I could tell by the looks of the agitators close to me that these were from StB agents that had infiltrated the crowd.

The result was confusion. Some people sat. Others stood up and turned, wanting to retrace their steps. No doubt because most did not like the idea of confronting military vehicles on a bridge, everyone eventually stood up and walked back towards town. The StB strategy of divide, if not conquer, worked. A part of the crowd headed in the direction of the Old Town Square, while the rest headed for Wenceslas Square. I followed the group heading for the Old Town Square.

Groups of protesters roamed about, mostly young people, relishing their freedom, calling for an end to communism and carrying Czechoslovak flags draped over their shoulders. In the Old Town Square a crowd of perhaps 50,000 to 100,000 gathered. Some climbed the statue of Jan Hus. They were cheering and shouting slogans. The statue was covered with homemade banners, made from bedsheets, demanding free elections. Jan Hus would have been proud. Other young people were dancing Czech folk dances in the middle of this huge crowd that filled the square like a sea. It seemed that no one was particularly disappointed that we had not made it to the Castle. They all knew that sovereignty, the spirit of the Czech people, was with them here, now. It was wonderful to let oneself be carried away by the exhilaration of that evening. Still, the old hands in the opposition, and the Stalinists in the regime, were well aware that the this popular uprising had yet to become a revolution.

20

A KINGDOM FOR A BALCONY

VÁCLAV HAVEL and Civic Forum became revolutionaries the next day, on Tuesday. They did this, among other things, by getting their logistics right. Civic Forum produced a stadium-quality public address system, spotlights, and a balcony on Wenceslas Square that could be used as a speakers' platform. In doing so Václav Havel had come up with the means to channel the power of the crowd, the revolt, into effective pressure on the regime. The speakers' platform, with lights and sound, could engage the attention of 300,000 people. Havel would use that direct link with the people to obtain support for specific political demands. A journalist standing beside me that Tuesday night, witnessing this dramatic development in crowd management, commented wryly that the dissidents were hijacking the revolution. Perhaps he was right, but I felt there was no other option. A seething crowd chanting slogans was the ultimate sanction, but its power had to be directed if there were to be any results. And results there were. In almost any other scenario the crowd was vulnerable to StB provocation, which would have provided the excuse for the regime's use of armed intervention.

Nor was it true that the dissidents were operating in isolation, like some sort of revolutionary elite. Civic Forum was a true umbrella, and incorporated not only the opposition groups, but also the reformers of 1968, writers and intellectuals, the independent students' council, actors and theatre managers, some union representatives, people from the two co-opted parties, and even some disenchanted communists. It was already a broad coalition of interests, and the only legitimate counterpart in any future negotiation with the regime. It was safe to say that there would not have been any negotiations if the opposition had been splintered. Moreover Civic Forum demanded what most Czechs and Slovaks wanted: the resignation of the Party leaders associated with the humiliating 1968 Warsaw Pact invasion, and with the period of repressive "normalization" that followed. These leaders were regarded quite simply as traitors. Many were still in prominent positions, including General Secretary Jakeš and President Husák, and others in the Communist Party politburo.

Civic Forum, echoing the slogans in Wenceslas Square, also demanded the resignation of the Prague Communist Party boss, Miroslav Štěpán. Štěpán was widely thought to have been responsible for the terrible violence that had been unleashed on the students. He was also known to have been behind the brutal repression of demonstrations in Prague going back to the summer of 1988. Strangely, in the fall of 1988, long before it was imagined that communist regimes might fall in our lifetime, Štěpán was thought by some to be a potential reformer. Shortly after Alexander Yakovlev's visit to Prague in November of that year, Štěpán had given a long interview to *Rudé Právo* that implied he was sympathetic to Gorbachov's reforms. Štěpán was young and considered to be a future regime leader. As described earlier, I saw Štěpán on several occasions, including the communist May Day celebrations in 1989, where he gave the "keynote" address. But now there were a lot of complaints within the Party about Štěpán's newspaper interview, most claiming that he was speaking out of two sides of his mouth. The criticism of unprincipled opportunism had the effect of stalling his rise within the Party at the December central committee meeting. From that point on he tried to out-Stalin the Stalinists, which was no mean feat. He ended by getting deep into the mechanics of repression. It was exactly what his rivals in the Party intended.

On that Tuesday, November 21, the day after the first big demonstration in Wenceslas Square, the government showed no sign of biting. There was no reaction to Civic Forum's demands. Havel only admitted that he had "feelers" from Prime Minister Adamec. Adamec was not a heavyweight in the communist politburo, but neither was he tainted with traitorous deeds from 1968. He was the only member of the politburo that had even marginally supported Gorbachov's economic reforms. On the other hand, he had just completed an official visit to Austria during which he had called Havel and the other dissidents a "bunch of nobodies." It was a sign of the times that, despite these comments, he was considered by most of the dissidents to be a potential interlocutor for Havel. Dialogue with just about anyone else in the hardline politburo was unthinkable. But on that first day after the first massive demonstration, the government was not moving. The politburo issued a statement saying simply that there would be no dialogue with anti-socialist agitators.

This was clear enough. But it was also code language directed at reformers within the Party, and within the two co-opted parties, the Socialist and the People's Parties. The real message was that there would be no negotiations with those who did not recognize the leading role of the Communist Party. The statement issued by the politburo also emphasized that it would not permit laws to be broken. The implication was that force might be used against the crowd, which raised the spectre of the "Chinese solution" witnessed only a few months before. On day two of the revolution it was impossible to predict what the regime would do. There had been a lot of tough talk over the last year, and those in power had raised the ante on Friday night. But to deal with a crowd of 200,000 shots would have to be fired.

Even during the course of the first big demonstration it was clear to me that the Communist Party would replace General Secretary Jakeš. The Party leadership must have been in a state of shock. The leadership had seemed to believe that it was genuinely popular. Even the relatively small demonstrations in January had come as a surprise to the Party stalwarts. I had reliable information to the effect that the Stalinist ideology chief, Jan Fojtík, had been thrown off guard by that week of protest. Now that a demonstration had brought out a sizeable part of the population of Prague, the leadership must have been reeling. The easiest decision would have been to wait and see what happened the next day (which is more or less what they did) while making a not-so-veiled threat about dealing with any future protest. The hesitation could be explained in two ways. The numbers involved in any demonstration would not necessarily impress the regime unless the workers were there. For Marxist-Leninists, sovereignty was invested in the workers, and in the regime as their vanguard. It was fully expected that the remnants of the bourgeoisie would engage periodically in counter-revolutionary acts. That remnant would continue to require stern measures until it disappeared sometime in the future, at the dawn of true socialism.

The involvement of the workers would put a very different complexion on the revolt, at least for the regime leaders. The students were now on strike, which was not in itself a major difficulty for the regime. The ringleaders would be dealt with at the proper moment. But the students had called for a general strike, and this was subsequently backed by Civic Forum. The general strike was to be staged the following week, on Monday. By calling for a strike that had to include workers, the opposition had drawn a line. That line would turn out to be a political Rubicon, after which nothing would hold back the march of the revolution. The other reason for the regime's hesitation was what must have been tense communication with Moscow, and with Warsaw Pact commanders located within Czechoslovakia. "Fraternal assistance" would have been one of the options the regime considered in the early stages of revolt.

The next big demonstration in Wenceslas Square, on Tuesday evening, was totally different from the first. The rally was called for 4 P.M. and it was scheduled to finish an hour later. Everyone was expected to go home afterward. This was to minimize the possibility that random acts committed by roving groups, once the demonstration broke up, might create the excuse for intervention by the police or the army. Dispersal into smaller groups, as had happened on Monday night, would also have provided easier targets for the riot police. There were other changes too. The Socialist Party, though a co-opted Party under the communist regime, permitted the balcony of its newspaper office to be used as the speakers' platform. The office of *Svobodno Slovo* was conveniently located about halfway up Wenceslas Square. The huge sound system turned the square into a stadium and spotlights lit up the revolutionaries as they spoke from the balcony.

By 4 P.M. there was a huge crowd, at least the 200,000 that had come out the day before, if not more. I had wondered if the massive turnout would be repeated, and was pleasantly surprised. The one-hour event offered an organized program of speakers. Havel spoke, but so did students, actors, workers, and formerly banned singers. Václav Malý, the underground Catholic priest, was in effect the master of ceremonies. Malý was an active member of various independent groups and, like Ivan Havel, Martin Palouš, and Zdeněk Urbánek, was one of the people in the opposition I knew best. I understood why he was chosen for this role. The clear round tones of his voice carried marvellously down the whole length of the square. As I stood shoulder to shoulder in the huge crowd, he was a pleasure to hear.

The effect of the logistical changes was dramatic. The mass protest of the night before had been transformed into a political rally. Great care was taken by all of the speakers to maintain a calm, responsible attitude toward their common objectives. There was, in fact, a dialogue between the balcony and the square, with words and slogans being picked up by one side and then by the other. There was a genuine spirit of generosity and confidence and determination. The speakers and the crowd remained open and receptive to each other. At 5 P.M. everyone was thanked for coming out and asked to go home peacefully. Which they did. Each demonstration was brought to a close that week by a moving rendition of the Czechoslovak national anthem. It was led from the balcony by the unaccompanied and incomparable voice of Marta Kubisova, a legendary pop singer. She had been banned by the communists from performing for over twenty years.

I had not wanted to be on the balcony with the journalists this night. I wanted to be right in the middle of the crowd, to be submerged in the space-time continuum of revolutionary history. Lights lit up the speakers above us in unnatural white light as twilight faded into darkness. The person who was possibly the most important on that Tuesday was not there. This was Cardinal Tomášek, the ninety-year-old Archbishop of Prague. A message from Tomášek was read out by Václav Malý. The Archbishop exhorted the people to seize democracy now. The crowd went wild and shouted, "Tomášek, Tomášek, Tomášek!" Tomášek's gesture was revolutionary, perhaps more than he realized. But it was a sign that society as a whole, civil society, was prepared to emerge from the underground, from the privacy of conscience, to confront the regime in the open. The psychological transition was breathtaking. Tomášek had not minced his words, had not tried to maintain his bridges to the regime through elliptical platitudes and equivocations. He went straight to the heart of the matter, seizing the main chance to throw off the yoke of communist repression. He was a source of authority in society that the communists had to some extent successfully marginalized, but he put all of his weight behind the revolt on that Tuesday night. The demonstrations provided the opportunity for—and in fact forced—the polarization of political forces that was necessary to overcome the regime.

21

THE RETURN OF HISTORY

ON THAT TUESDAY NIGHT, looking at the newspaper offices of *Svobodno Slovo* where the speakers' balcony was located, I wondered how the Socialist Party newspaper had got so involved so quickly. It was ironic to see the dissidents on the balcony just below the sign on the building, which in English translated as "Free Speech." How appropriate. The Socialist Party was trying to break free from forty years of communist tutelage. The Ambassador, Barry Mawhinney, and I decided the next day to go and see the leader of the Party, Jan Škoda, to find out exactly what was happening. The Party's newspaper had not only provided crucial logistical support on the very day it was required; it had also been publishing Civic Forum demands daily since Sunday night.

I had known Škoda on and off over the past year. He was a big man with a diffident, intelligent approach to politics. Under the regime he was known to be something of a reformer within the Socialist Party. But he must have made his compromises with the communists in order to have survived in politics at all. During the period when I knew him he did not appear to harbour any affection for the regime. Still, after the revolution, he would be forced to retire from political life for having been active in official circles. The steps he took in agreeing to put the newspaper of the Socialist Party, and its offices, at the disposal of Civic Forum were not enough. A page would be turned and he would be seen as part of the old story. Still, I rather liked

Škoda. We laughed at one point during the revolution over the fact that only a few weeks before we had both picked Štěpán, the relatively young and ruthless Prague party boss, to become the communist General Secretary in May, 1990. We had also agreed that Štěpán would likely introduce slow but steady changes. In fact Štěpán was arrested shortly after the revolution. He was found responsible for approving the violence meted out to demonstrators.

The Socialist Party and its newspaper had been trying to distance themselves from the Communist Party since the summer of 1989. In the months leading up to the revolution the Socialists had been increasingly critical of human rights abuses. Their offices were rather well-situated on Revoluční Boulevard, just down the road from the art nouveau masterpiece, the Municipal House. I was struck by the fact that "The Socialist Party" was written in blue neon lights in the window, making it look for all the world like a rather inviting restaurant. The impression was not broken when we were greeted by a nice old lady in slippers who took us through some dark panelled hallways to an equally dark office in which loomed the large leader of the Socialist Party. After the ritual of being offered and accepting an expresso and a glass of mineral water, we questioned Škoda about the problems that lay ahead for the revolution. Our thinking was that, having one foot in the regime and one foot in Civic Forum, Škoda was in a good position to predict what the Communist Party might do and what the revolution might accomplish.

On the positive side of the ledger, Škoda felt that the mass protests were a reflection of the deep democratic traditions of Czechoslovakia. These traditions dated from the interwar period, 1918-1938, during which President Masaryk had set high moral goals for political life. The communist system, said Škoda, was an alien political model that had been imposed from the outside. But that broad dislike of the communists could in the future be fractured. The political landscape in Czechoslovakia could once again resemble the fragmented terrain that was typical before the communist coup d'état in 1948. With regard to the immediate survival of the revolution, Škoda said that Civic Forum would have to work hard on the differences that split town and country, and develop a strategy to prevent economic change from negatively affecting political stability.

There would have to be a concerted effort to build democratic traditions in the new parliament. Škoda said that the Socialist Party, if it was to resume its interwar role, would need to broaden its support. But the wholesale incorporation of all democratic forces within a single political party would not be the best solution in terms of strengthening a new parliament. Škoda added that the Socialist Party had its own political traditions, and these would not appeal to everyone. What was more important was offering the electorate a choice. This was how political experience was acquired. There was in Škoda's assessment an implicit criticism of Civic Forum, which was taking shape as a broad-based movement. Škoda thought that the offer of an umbrella to all democratic opposition groups would create a confusion of standpoints within any party. Then he smiled and threw up his hands and said that the only sure thing about the future was that political pluralism would return to Czechoslovakia, though many still in the bureaucracy and the Communist Party would try to resist.

Returning to the present, and the mass demonstrations of Monday and Tuesday nights, Škoda emphasized that it would be important to see how the workers in the factories reacted in the next few days. The Communist Party's paramilitary force, the People's Militia, was still strong in the factories. It was the armed People's Militia that had been sent into the streets by the Communist Party to secure the takeover in 1948. Still, workers in the big towns and cities, and in the polluted areas of the country, were sympathetic to the students' demands. In small towns and villages workers and the population generally were more tightly controlled by the Communist Party, and the revolution would find it heavy going. Škoda also thought that the influence of Cardinal Tomášek was important. The communists, on the other hand, were in total disarray. The mass protests had seemingly changed everything.

Later that same day, Wednesday, we heard that the Communist Party was calling for an emergency plenum of its highest ranking officials. It would take place two days later, on Friday. I thought this was a rather lackadaisical approach, given what was happening on the streets. I was also able to confirm that the People's Militia, the paramilitary arm of the Communist Party, had in fact been brought in from across the country. Its members were massing in football stadiums on the outskirts of Prague. What we did not know was that special units in the army had been put on alert. These units had been trained to intervene in the event of a public uprising. All of these steps were entirely credible, given the fact that the Communist Party could hardly permit the general strike to take place next Monday. It was surmised that the general strike would show that the workers, too, were against the regime. The People's Militia and at least a part of the army were prepared to move against the uprising, and would have, if the Communist Party's central committee had not been in disarray. It was a very close thing.

I heard through my network of contacts that General Secretary Jakeš would resign at Friday's Communist Party plenum. Prime Minister Adamec meanwhile was playing the reformer, and publicly rejected the Party's condemnation of the demonstrations. He also refused to interfere with the logistical support that the newspaper *Svobodno Slovo* was providing for Civic Forum and the protests. Adamec then made the leap and met with Civic Forum representatives and guaranteed that there would be no police intervention. According to my contacts he did this without consulting General Secretary Jakeš. The helpless, not to say witless, Jakeš was by this time a lame duck. A power vacuum had opened up which provided Adamec with just enough room to manoeuvre. It seemed that he was in regular contact with Moscow to ensure that the lines were clear in terms of Soviet support for his strategy.

Without trying to assign any particular merit I felt that, so far, three individuals had been crucial to advancing the objectives of the revolution. These were Havel, Cardinal Tomášek, and Adamec. An honourable mention was due to *Svobodno Slovo*. Somehow, the mass protests had combined with moral leadership and party politics to make for a political breakthrough. In retrospect, it might seem as if all of this had to be. But it did not. The risk of social upheaval and armed intervention was real. It was as close as the outskirts of Prague. The ensuing violence would have made 1968 look like a family feud. One of the reasons for the political success of this week was the paralysis of the Communist Party. The central committee of the Party was old, orthodox, and undemocratic. It was unable to react creatively to a direct and apparently unexpected assault on its power and authority.

On Wednesday night, at another demonstration of over 200,000 in Wenceslas Square, Havel announced that revolutionary strike committees were being set up in factories and schools across the country. This was in preparation for the general strike called for Monday. Then he said, "history is coming back to our country," an allusion to the fact that communism had succeeded in freezing the natural evolution of both people and nation for over forty years. He added that he had sent letters to Bush and Gorbachov about the events of 1968. "Now those who drowned our wishes in blood are afraid of us. Now our time has come." Václav Malý read out a letter from Dubček, who was still in Bratislava. Dubček greeted the crowd and called for the resignations of all those connected with 1968, including President Husák and General Secretary Jakeš. The crowd roared its approval. Dubček added that he hoped to join the protesters in Prague in the next few days. But his first priority was to attend the trial of the Slovak opposition figure Ján Čarnogursky in Bratislava. The fact that Dubček was not prevented from doing so was another sign of how fast the political landscape was changing.

On this third night of mass protest much of the focus in remarks made by Civic Forum leaders was on statements received from other opposition groups in Central and Eastern European countries. There was also a lot of effort devoted to messages being sent to these groups and to governments in the West and the East. The strategy was to "internationalize" this nascent mass movement, to create a web of contacts that gave it both recognition and international legitimacy. But the support for Dubček coming from the crowd that night was also remarkable. A huge roar went up when his name was first read out.

Though a Slovak, Dubček was immensely popular across the whole country, and popular with those who had not yet heard of Václav Havel. It is hard to convey the tremendous personal standing which this leader of the Prague Spring had at that time with Czechs and Slovaks. In the minds of many he was a tragic figure, struck down in his prime as he was leading the nation to freedom. This sense of tragedy was only amplified by Dubček's charisma, itself imbued with a sense of the decency and tolerance that he had brought to public life. Hence his intervention in support of the revolution was another decisive step forward.

22

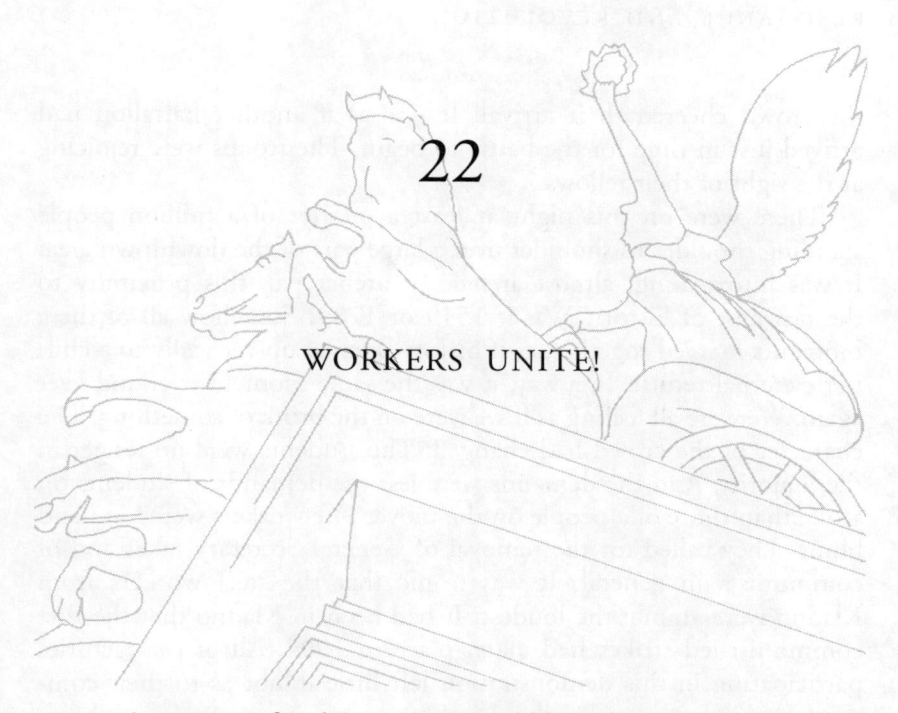

WORKERS UNITE!

DUBČEK'S SUPPORT for the uprising would have had very little impact on the regime itself. It was still the workers who mattered from a Marxist standpoint, especially those in the large state factories that were the traditional power base of the communists. The regime must have been worried about the workers, even more so on Wednesday when Prague party boss Štěpán was booed at CKD, a large factory on the city's outskirts. Nonetheless, the communists would have noted that the people in the mass rallies were fairly mixed in terms of occupation. There was a significant number of students. I did not see any groups that were obviously from factories, nor many who were wearing the usual blue overalls of factory workers. The regime's leaders must still have been hedging their bets on Wednesday night.

By Thursday night, all bets were off. I found myself packed tightly in the middle of the huge crowd in Wenceslas Square, just in front of the *Svobodno Slovo* newspaper office. At 4 P.M., when the crowd was already overflowing down the side streets, a long line of workers from the CKD factory came marching noisily into the square. CKD was the biggest factory in Prague. The workers were carrying a banner marked with its initials and were shouting out their support for the revolution. This scene was repeated in other parts of the square as workers from other large factories streamed in. The chanting of slogans by these factory men was loud and raucous and it echoed everywhere as the rest of the crowd cheered their arrival. It was as if another battalion had arrived just in time for the battle to begin. The troops were rejoicing at the sight of their fellows.

There were on this night at least a quarter of a million people standing shoulder to shoulder over a large part of the downtown area. It was intoxicating, almost archaic or archetypal, this proximity to the nearness of history. Was it 1519 or 1789? Somehow all of these moments merged together, as if history opened up vertically to a chiliastic eternal return. In a way, it was the same moment over and over again. We were all feeling as if we were on the brink of something. The character of the crowd had changed. The students were no longer in the majority. And the demands were less the demands of students on strike than those of a people on the move. The workers were loud and blunt. They called for the removal of General Secretary Jakeš and of communists in general. It was ironic that the steel workers from Kladno were among the loudest. It had been in Kladno that the first communist-led strikes had taken place in 1904. All of the factories participating in this demonstration left little doubt as to their commitment to the general strike slated for Monday.

Havel spoke to the crowd, his voice now hoarse and almost unrecognizable. But the words were Havel's all right. He said the country was at a crossroads. It was a decisive moment for both Czechs and Slovaks. Civic Forum was ready to begin negotiations with the communist authorities. He said simply, "we want a free, democratic, prosperous Czechoslovakia." Everyone knew what he meant because they felt so deeply what the communists had denied them. He then appealed to all workers to support Civic Forum's demands with a general strike. The churches in every town and village would ring their bells to signal its start. "The success of the strike will decide whether our country starts down the road to democracy." Both Civic Forum and the regime leaders understood fully what the strike meant. Havel made it clear to the people that they must choose.

Perhaps at least as crucial as the call to the workers was Havel's next appeal, to the army. I had not yet heard the information about special units of the army having been put on alert. These were the units trained to deal with "public insurrection." They would secure the downtown core, evict the students from the universities and take control of the radio and TV stations. The special units were waiting for a signal from the Communist Party leaders. It turned out that the leadership was split. This would become evident at the Party's central committee meeting the next day. A power struggle was taking place, related to the ouster of Jakeš. There were a number of would-be contenders who were jousting to replace him. And none of these were prepared to give the army a signal to do anything, at least until the succession was agreed. By the time the new General Secretary of the Communist Party was chosen, during the course of the weekend, the demonstrations would swell to 600,000 people on the Letná plain. The option to use force, if it ever existed, was simply superseded by events.

But on that Thursday night I, like most people, did not know what was going on in the army. Havel was surely tipped off. After he asked the workers to support the general strike, he made a dramatic appeal to the army to side with the people and, if necessary, to defend them. I thought that this sounded rather ominous, and that there must be something going on. The day before, the army chief of staff had made a statement on TV. He said that the armed forces fully supported the Communist Party and would defend socialism. This alone would have been enough to focus a few minds at Civic Forum. Havel's appeal to the army to defend the people was a brilliant counter. It was likely to create uncertainty in the minds of the generals about the reliability of their young conscripts. It was also likely to raise the spectre of civil war at a time when it was increasingly clear that no fraternal assistance was likely to come from Warsaw Pact allies. To make this possibility clear to both Moscow and Washington, Havel went on to say that many wars had started in Czechoslovakia. He added, "not only our future is at stake, but all of Europe's."

Havel then confirmed what was evident to the crowd, that the huge CKD factory had decided to support the general strike. The crowd roared its approval. Václav Malý spoke, announcing the full support of the church. The crowd roared again. Then Jan Škoda spoke. He told the crowd that, in the last forty years, the Socialist Party had been free only for the last few days. It had been a real political party under the Austrian monarchy and in the interwar period during the time of President Masaryk. And now again, said Škoda, it wanted to build on the traditions of Hus and Masaryk to work for free elections. He said that he had told the communist leadership that only democratic means should be used to overcome the crisis—and that this was the last chance to do so. Implicit in his remarks was the risk of the crowd turning against communists in a spirit of revenge. It reminded me of the account I had picked up of Gorbachov's meeting with Jakeš a few months before. Apparently Gorbachov had asked Jakeš what would happen if the Soviet Union publicly admitted that the 1968 invasion had been a mistake. There were some in the Soviet Union who believed that such an admission would usefully underline the Soviet commitment to glasnost. Jakeš replied that communists in Prague would be found hanging from the lampposts.

Škoda was well received, if not enthusiastically. But he was a reminder of how the parliamentary traditions of the First Republic (1918-1938) had reemerged so quickly and so strongly. The non-communist political parties, though emasculated by the communists since 1948, had been quick to reorganize and to reaffirm their traditions. The Socialist Party's support of Civic Forum was just one sign of this. The way that the demand for free elections surfaced early and insistently at the demonstrations was another. The memory of Czechoslovak democracy was close to the surface, and this gave the opposition that week a real sense of self-confidence. People felt that they knew what they wanted and had a fairly precise idea of what it would look like. This brought with it practical difficulties when the new political system was created a few months later.

On this Thursday night, Havel had put in place some key building blocks necessary to the success of the general strike scheduled for Monday. The most important element was the active engagement of the traditional heavy-industry workers. The strike would be greatly weakened without them. Nor was it clear that the regime would permit the strike to take place. No one could predict whether or not it would rule out military intervention over the next three days. This was why the appeal to the military was so vitally important. Every day that passed without intervention strengthened the opposition and made a military response increasingly unlikely. Every day was another nail in the regime's coffin.

23

A COMMUNIST INTERMEZZO

BY FRIDAY, November 24, I was convinced that what I was witnessing was not a process of reform but a revolution. I also believed that the course of the revolution had to follow its own internal logic. I was familiar with the Communist Party and I had met a number of its senior figures. I knew it was sclerotic and incapable of real change. It would not be able to finesse the desire for something new. And it would no longer be able to steal the revolution through dramatic offers of reform. The revolution had to work itself out, and it would do this with or without bloodshed.

I was aware of the risk that the whole thing might turn out badly, but I never believed it would. I pushed the danger to the back of my mind. I did this on the basis of my feel for the divisions inside the Communist Party, on a guess as to the likely attitude of Moscow, and on my knowledge of the considerable political skills of people like Václav Havel, Václav Malý, Ivan Havel, Martin Palouš, Saša Vondra, Michael Žantovský, Jan Urban, and so on. Despite the water cannons, the riot police and the armed personnel carriers, I was convinced I was not risking life and limb, at least not yet.

Events began to move at an incredible speed. It became obvious that the Communist Party was not only in disarray, but in a state of rapid decay. The Party leaders met first on Friday to try to sort things out. This led to the announcement Friday night that the politburo had resigned, which was accompanied by spontaneous celebration among young people downtown. There was a lot of flag waving, dancing and singing. By Saturday morning, however, it was announced that virtually the same politburo had been reappointed. Either the Party had an extremely low estimation of the intelligence of most people, or it was incredibly stupid. I concluded that it was the latter.

Anger suddenly gripped the people of Prague, even many Communist Party members, over this sop from the regime's aging leaders. It was only after more mass protests on the weekend that we saw, on Sunday, the resignations of General Secretary Jakeš and most of the politburo. My prediction last Monday night that the communists would not look with kindness on a leader who had put them in this mess turned out to be right. The new communist leader would be Karel Urbánek, a relatively young 48. But appearances were deceptive. Despite his youth, he had been supported within the party over the past year by the faction of neo-Stalinists.

The resignations obtained on Sunday included the now infamous Prague party chief Miroslav Štěpán. Stories had circulated for some time about how he had supervised the police intervention against protesters from the rooftops around Wenceslas Square. Such was the fate of opportunists. He had given his liberal-sounding interviews in 1988 only to find out that Moscow would not engineer his leadership bid. His subsequent attempts to please the dinosaurs in Prague led to his downfall. The worst of it was that he had actually done their dirty work, and was tried and went to prison after the revolution.

The problem for the communists, in terms of the changes in the politburo announced on Sunday, was that the reshuffle did not convey the impression that a reform wing within the Party was emerging. There was no identifiable figure, no Gorbachov protégé, within the group. The message on this eve of the general strike was that there would be no fundamental change: this, despite the fact that the grass roots in the party were pushing for it, and that hundreds of thousands of people in the streets were calling for the Party's immediate removal from power. The Party just could not come up with anyone to fill the bill. Such was the price it paid for the enforced conformity that its leaders demanded from the rank and file following the Warsaw Pact invasion in 1968.

The new General Secretary, Karel Urbánek, though relatively young, was a Party hack without a reformist bone in his body. Urbánek went on TV Sunday night to say that there should be a coalition government that would include non-communists. But the existing government already conformed to this model, since there were a couple of ministers from the co-opted Socialist and People's Parties. Urbánek's proposal was taken for what it was: a bit of not so smart sleight of hand. He said nothing about the constitutionally mandated leading role of the Communist Party, or about free elections. I thought that Urbánek must have spent the weekend at his cottage.

Civic Forum was relentless in keeping the pressure up. The demonstrations seemed to be getting bigger every night, if that was possible. The momentum had been building as we went into the weekend; the demands were now loud and clear for free elections and a market economy. There was every reason to believe that support for the general strike set for Monday would be massive. I noticed that the speeches at the rallies were becoming more precise in terms of the contributions they made to the political platform of Civic Forum. By the time of the strike, there was no doubt about the basic goal of elections or about the market orientation of Forum's leaders. The economic policy platform of Civic Forum was strong and consistent from the beginning. This was because right-of-centre economists from the Forecasting Institute of the Academy of Sciences had become involved in the movement over the past week.

The most prominent was Václav Klaus, who had attended the Chicago School of Economics, and was an ardent admirer of Mrs. Thatcher. Klaus would take over the key job of finance minister after the revolution and became the principal architect of economic reform in Czechoslovakia. He became Prime Minister of the Czech Lands after the 1992 elections and began negotiations with Slovak Prime Minister Mečiar that would eventually lead to the division of the country. Ironically, Ivan Havel told me he was the one who had first introduced Klaus to Civic Forum. Ivan had promoted Klaus as an economic theorist to be taken seriously. We had to laugh about that later, given the fact that Klaus's party would trounce the party dominated by the former dissidents in the 1992 elections.

In sum, the political and economic policies that emerged rather quickly in Forum this week were both clear and sophisticated expressions of liberal democratic politics. The Communist Party's attempts to transform its policies into reform communism were both bogus and confused. The option of a *transition* from communism to pluralism, if there ever was one, was now gone. Revolution would be the order of the day. The communists had let the "correlation of forces" get out of control.

24

ALEXANDER DUBČEK

DUBČEK APPEARED at the demonstrations in Wenceslas Square for the first time on Friday night. He spoke again at the huge rallies on Saturday and Sunday on the Letná plain. But on that first night, in the twilight, the crowd roared long and loud when he was introduced. They had been waiting twenty years for this moment. History had finally come back to Czechoslovakia, as Havel had said. In the form of Alexander Dubček, it was now standing on that balcony. We could not believe our eyes. It was as if everything since 1968 had been a bad dream, and now it was put right again.

Alexander Dubček stood there, a slight man with sloping shoulders, looking just as he had so long ago. His hair was now grey, but he had that same happy/sad look, the look of destiny and of a nation's soul. To the continuing cheers and shouts that must have been heard all over Prague, he stepped forward and opened his arms wide as if to embrace the crowd, and said simply, "you know I love you ..." The crowd went wild. For a few moments, I lost my interpreter, who was helping decipher the shouts and calls, as she burst into tears. She smiled up at me helplessly. The tears rolled down her cheeks.

We were standing on a balcony with some journalists across the square from the speakers. My interpreter was in her sixties, smartly dressed in a style from long ago. Without speaking, she took from her lapel a piece of red, white and blue ribbon, the colours of the

Czechoslovak flag, and pinned it on the lapel of my trench coat. This tricolour, like the Czechoslovak flags, had become the proud symbols of the revolution. She straightened the ribbon on my lapel for a moment, like a conscientious grandmother, and we just smiled at each other as the crowd roared on. She said simply, "Dubček!," and smiled and lifted her hands and started crying again.

Dubček said that people were once again lifting their voices in search for a better society. "Already, once, we witnessed a new dawn. Let us act now so that dawn becomes day." The crowd began shouting, "Dubček to the Castle, Dubček to the Castle!" meaning to the President's office. He replied simply, "that depends on you." Husák, the tottering architect of "normalization," was still very much in power. It was both wild and perversely exhilarating to even think of Dubček becoming President. Speaking on this Friday night, he referred to the changes announced in the politburo as insufficient.

He then became quite specific as to who should be removed, including those whom he, and everyone else in the square, regarded as the traitors of 1968. These were the ones who had either actively sought the Warsaw Pact invasion or actively cooperated with the occupiers afterward. People like Jakeš and Bilak were widely assumed to fall into the former category, Husák and others into the latter. The odd thing was that, after their removal, and after the revolution, none of these people, with the exception of Štěpán, would actually spend any time in jail. But an enormous parliamentary effort would be devoted to weeding out from government those further down the ladder who had been thought to have cooperated too actively with the occupiers.

Havel said on Friday night that Civic Forum was ready for negotiations. In fact, by Sunday, he would be sitting at a table across from Prime Minister Adamec. As on Thursday night, he said that the general strike would be a referendum on "the leading role of the Communist Party." This could be translated as the "illegal rule of the Communist Party." He asked that all strike committees remain in place for the indefinite future. The point was to communicate to the regime that more strikes were likely if the government did not react to Forum's demands. Then Havel defined the role of Civic Forum for the first time, as a bridge from totalitarianism to democracy and free elections.

At the huge demonstration on Sunday afternoon, Havel and Dubček introduced Prime Minister Adamec to the crowd. The reception was polite but cool. When Adamec said that the next day's general strike should be only symbolic, and only for a few minutes, he was

Alexander Dubček just before the Warsaw pact invasion of Czechoslovakia in 1968, convinced he had an agreement with Brezhnev to let the Prague Spring be

widely and loudly booed. He then told Havel privately that he could not negotiate under this kind of pressure. Havel left Adamec in no doubt that Civic Forum would call for mass protests when it saw the need to do so. Months later, when Barry and I were talking to Dubček, he was surprisingly apologetic about this tactic. He explained at length that he would never normally condone mass protests. They were innately undemocratic, he said. Sometimes, however, they were necessary as part of the fight for democracy. His own involvement in the demonstrations clearly bothered him. I admired Dubček for the fine precision of his conscience, but the demonstrations taking place as they did within the broader context of communist lawlessness, did not bother me. I did not see how Civic Forum could act as a bridge without this entirely non-violent sanction.

Dubček's appearance at the demonstrations was yet another emotional high point of the revolution. On this night, though Havel was respected and admired, Dubček was loved. He too returned history to Czechoslovakia by symbolizing the reality of the democratic aspirations he promoted in the riveting months of 1968. I think Dubček also found a place in people's hearts because they saw him as a modern-day Don Quixote, a tragic figure whose failure and punishment only enhanced his nobility. Alas, both his fate, and the fate of those who had participated in the Prague Spring over twenty years before, were to remain controversial in post-revolutionary Czechoslovakia.

25

THE GENERAL STRIKE

THE WEEKEND PROTESTS were remarkable for their sheer size. Foreseeing this likelihood Civic Forum organizers changed the location of the demonstrations scheduled for Saturday and Sunday to Letná Park. This was a vast plateau overlooking the Vltava River and the Old Town. Armies used to do battle on the Letná Plain, just as now Civic Forum and the armies of its followers were prepared to seize the country by force. Though it may have been a velvet revolution, there was no doubt in my mind that it was a revolution. And revolutions overturn existing orders through force embodied usually in overwhelming numbers of people mobilized for a cause.

To accommodate the numbers Civic Forum constructed a huge stage on the plain, with another state-of-the-art sound system. As I watched it go up, my mind went back to the rock festivals of the 1960s. Civic Forum was convinced that if they built it people would come. They were right, and 600,000 people came out on to the Letná Plain on Saturday and again on Sunday afternoon. This was no longer a crowd. It was a city, in fact exactly half the city of Prague. Linked to similar demonstrations all over Czechoslovakia, it was a nation. This was a nation of convinced democrats who were prepared at that precise moment to be revolutionaries.

Though there were demonstrations in towns and cities all over the country, Prague and Bratislava were the focal points. The fact that these cities were the seats of government for the Czech and Slovak Republics partly explained the phenomenon. They were also media centres, and the media were starting to magnify the dramatic events taking place in the capitals. The TV stations had been pretty well converted to the cause of revolution by midweek. It was odd, by the weekend, to catch all of this on TV as it was happening. The revolution was hot, and TV brought the revolution into your living room. This fact alone was sufficient evidence, if any was needed, that the Communist Party, which had seemed so formidable only a week before, was now in chaos. The threat of military intervention was no longer believable. As the threat of force faded, the Party itself seemed to wither away. Looked at from another angle, it suddenly became less important in the scheme of things. It was widely assumed that its so-called leading role was about to be abolished by the very government that was supposed to be its puppet.

There were other signs, too, of the Party's rapid eclipse. Civic Forum was about to come out with a detailed political program on the very day of the general strike. It would contain proposals for free elections, a market economy, legal reform, social policy, and so on. The national TV network actively supported these initiatives by carrying live coverage of the demonstrations all over the country. It set up and televised debates and discussions virtually around the clock. I noticed that almost everybody on the TV screen had either been banned since 1968 or had been imprisoned. They appeared in the TV studios with the tricolour pinned to their chests, in clothes well-worn from long years of penury. My friend Miroslav Galuška, the Minister of Culture in 1968, made a big hit on his return to TV. He had been a popular Minister in Dubček's government: urbane, charming, and a democrat. All of these qualities had made him an early target of the Stalinists soon after the Warsaw Pact invasion. People were mesmerized by his eloquent account of the events of those days, and of the whole Prague Spring. Any talk of the period had been strictly banned for twenty years. There was an incredible thirst, not least among the young, to learn more about the true history of Czechoslovakia since the communist coup d'état in 1948 and before. Miroslav joked about how people now stopped him on the street to shake his hand, but I could tell that he was deeply touched by this. He was almost seventy now. I imagined that it was fairly important to know that it had not all been for nothing—that people thought that what he had done was important—and so it was.

The meeting between Havel and Prime Minister Adamec on Sunday, the day before the general strike, was strange to say the least. Nothing was discussed. But the fact of the meeting, and Havel's presence, was itself significant. Adamec had at first refused to meet with Havel, preferring instead representatives from Civic Forum who had not been dissidents. A change of heart came after Adamec made a lightning visit to Moscow. Havel and Adamec agreed that the next meeting should be on Tuesday, the day after the general strike. Perhaps Adamec wanted to see what kind of hand Havel was holding.

There was soon little doubt about that. The general strike brought the entire country to a standstill. Virtually everyone took what in effect was an extended lunch hour and marched around their towns and factories carrying Czechoslovak flags. The TV scrupulously carried it all live. In Prague, workers streamed out of their offices and marched downtown, congregating in Wenceslas Square. There were banners and songs, as if a great victory was being celebrated. I suppose it was what May Day was meant to be. The strike was kicked off with the ringing of church bells all over town. In the Embassy I could hear them tolling in every direction. I was now convinced by the claims of tour operators that this was the city of a thousand spires. Even our locally-engaged Czech staff walked off the job. Given Canada's political support for Civic Forum, we could hardly complain.

November 27 was also the day that Paul Wilson finally managed to get back into Czechoslovakia. We had been pushing the Foreign Ministry on this for the past week. Paul had lived in Czechoslovakia from 1967 to 1977 and had become involved in the almost legendary origins of Charter. It began during his last few years in Prague, when he was a singer with a rock band called Plastic People of the Universe. The lyrics of the band's songs got it into trouble with the regime. Plastic People and other bands were eventually charged and put on trial. It was in reaction to this development that Patočka, Havel, and Hájek formed Charter 77. As a foreigner, Paul was thrown out of the country and barred from coming back. He settled in Toronto. But in what can only be described as the proverbial twist of fate, he became the most accomplished translator of Havel's works, thereby bringing Havel's dissection of totalitarianism to the English-speaking world. Now, with revolution in the streets and the regime's power structures collapsing, the Foreign Ministry finally relented and Paul was back.

The general strike clearly impressed Adamec and others in the Party. In the talks on Tuesday, Adamec was the spokesman for the communist government, and Havel led the Civic Forum delegation. Havel and the rest of Forum were as shocked as I was by the outcome of the meeting. After barely two hours of discussion, Civic Forum emerged with virtually all of its initial demands accepted. Adamec said that he would propose, before next Sunday, a new coalition government. It would include not only representatives from non-communist parties, such as the Socialist Party, but people belonging to no party at all. This was a tactic to reassure Forum that the Communist Party would not be pulling the government's strings. Adamec also agreed to introduce a bill in the federal assembly the next day that would amend the constitution so as to rescind the clause affirming the "leading role of the Communist Party." The National Front, which was the ruling coalition made up of the communists plus the co-opted parties, would be opened to other new parties or groups. Adamec also agreed that school curricula would no longer include indoctrination into Marxism-Leninism. Lastly, all political prisoners would be released that day.

Civic Forum moved quickly to back up these agreements with a threat. If the measures were not implemented immediately, or if the new coalition government was not acceptable, Civic Forum would seek the removal of Prime Minister Adamec from power. Another general strike would be called if necessary. Furthermore, at the meeting, Havel had made a new demand. He called for the resignation of President Husák by December 10. According to what Václav Malý told me afterward, Adamec bristled at this and turned red in the face. He resented the demands and he was losing his patience. But it was obvious that his brief visit to Moscow had set him straight on a few things. He had to deal directly with Havel, because the Soviet Union was not in any way about to retrieve the position of their Czechoslovak comrades. Civic Forum was not particularly grateful to Gorbachov, however. It sent him an open letter demanding that he come clean on the events of 1968.

One of the most remarkable phenomena during those days was the way in which the underground civic society of independent groups rapidly made the transition into the open, forming the first building blocks of a market economy. A former underground newspaper, *Lidové Noviny*, had finally been put out of circulation by the StB only the week before. When it was still publishing, I had obtained copies of the newspaper from Miroslav Galuška. Now, *Lidové Noviny* became an official daily carried openly in the streets the same day on which the leading role of the Communist Party was abolished. Even to have possessed a copy a few days before would have been reason enough to get fired and go to jail. Had it only been a week? The irony was that although the federal assembly was full of communists, it really was a rubber stamp. It calmly voted for the measures that destroyed one-party rule.

26

THE REGIME STRIKES BACK

FOLLOWING Prime Minister Adamec's promise to Havel there was a lot of guessing about the eventual makeup of the new government. Valtr Komárek, the head of the Forecasting Institute at the Academy of Sciences, was holding press conferences in government offices promoting himself as a future prime minister. After attending one of these events at a palace downtown I concluded that anything was possible. The Social Democratic Party, banned since the communist coup d'état in 1948, was reestablished. A Green Party was founded too. Later it was discovered to have been infiltrated by StB agents. Despite all of this activity, I knew that the Communist Party was well-entrenched in the bureaucracy and in the countryside. I wondered how it would react to the fact that Adamec had sold the store. These thoughts were soon pushed to the margins by the growing discussion about who would replace Husák as President. Though Dubček's name had been bandied around by just about everyone, already by November 28 there was a growing number of people who spoke to me about Havel. At the time we all regarded this as somehow unbelievable, even as we spoke of it.

The very possibility of Havel's presidency brought back a discussion I had with Václav Malý and Martin Palouš in June, 1989, during the bad old days. We were having a beer at a pub, U Flekou. We were sitting outside in the courtyard, so that it would be more difficult for the StB to pick up our conversation. We were reflecting on how well things had gone in Poland, and the importance of a unifying personality like Walesa, who seemed able to bring intellectuals and working people together for a common cause. We also reflected on the situation in Czechoslovakia where, up to that time, at most 10,000 people had come out to demonstrate. We knew that there was a potentially large number of people who were sympathetic to the opposition. But no charismatic figure, like Walesa, had emerged to mobilize them. I told Martin and Václav that I did not see anyone in the opposition who fitted that bill. Václav Malý, to his credit, said that Václav Havel did. I doubted it and said that Havel was a very nice and very intelligent man and that I liked him very much. But he was extremely, even painfully, shy, and very intellectual. So much for foresight.

On Wednesday, November 29, the communist federal assembly convened in its usual locale, a building that had been the stock exchange prior to the communist coup d'état in 1948. With pro forma debate, the assembly duly approved the demands put to Adamec by Havel. Adamec also called for a public reassessment of 1968, which had been a key Forum demand. But the resistance of the communist nomenclature, as I had feared, began to stiffen. The new General Secretary of the Communist Party, Karel Urbánek, gave an old style speech to party functionaries. He talked of how "our opponents" had taken the initiative. He called for communists to take a more active role in the media. And he refused to disband either the Communist Party's paramilitary force, the People's Militia, or the network of Party cells in the factories.

Barry and I decided to go around and talk to newspaper editors that week to get a feel for the fluid political situation. We spoke with Bohumil Mašek, the editor of *Svobodno Slovo*, the Socialist Party's newspaper. Mašek predicted that the formation of the new government would be difficult for Adamec. Nonetheless, meetings that had already taken place tended to confirm that it would be a genuine coalition. He thought that free elections were a real likelihood in the next six months. What Mašek did not know at the time was that the Communist Party central committee would not agree to a real coalition government. Worse, Adamec did not have the support of the Party leadership.

And so the new government announced by Adamec on Sunday, December 3, was a major setback. There were a few token non-communists in unimportant posts, while sixteen of the twenty-one positions were filled by communists. Even the individuals brought in from the co-opted parties, like the Socialist and the People's Parties, were totally unknown. None of the proposed ministers were associated in any way with Civic Forum. To add insult to injury, not one of Civic Forum's specific demands regarding the nomination of ministers had been accepted. Forum had asked that a civilian be named defence minister, that a non-communist be named interior minister, and that there be a new foreign minister. In sum, the Communist Party simply failed to respond to the last two weeks of mass demonstrations and the general strike.

Civic Forum reacted swiftly. It called for a protest in Wenceslas Square for the next day, Monday, December 4. There was even talk of another general strike, perhaps for the following Monday. Forum had already said that it would seek Adamec's resignation, and I wondered how Adamec could stay on after this fiasco. Nor could I square the new communist-dominated cabinet with the fact that parliament had already rescinded the leading role of the Communist Party. It was as if the left hand did not know what the right hand was doing. My sense was that Adamec might have been able to rush a few things through parliament, but the communist politburo had finally overruled him.

I had heard that he had been upset when the politburo insisted on approving the nominations for the new government. On the other hand, Civic Forum had not been exactly helpful. It had refused to provide Adamec the names of those people it would have liked to see in the new cabinet. This strategy had only weakened Adamec's leverage in dealing with the conservative politburo. It coincidentally left Forum free to criticize the result. Forum must have decided that the freedom to oppose was of paramount importance, so long as it was not going to have total control over the nominations.

I had found Forum oddly quiescent during the days following the general strike and before the announcement of the new government. There had been no more demonstrations while the negotiations were on. Forum seemed to be sitting back and waiting for Adamec to name his government. People went about their work as usual and life went on. I wondered if the week of demonstrations had only been a dream. It suddenly seemed unreal, as the traffic and taxis returned to Wenceslas Square. Where was the change? Millions had come into the streets, but to what effect? The Party, if the new government was any indication, had not been moved. I began to wonder whether Civic Forum could bring people out again, whether it had lost its momentum. It had been a brilliant start, certainly. This had in part been due to the students, who had called for the demonstrations and for the general strike. Now, without any visible sign, I wondered whether the network of organizers and the popular support was still there. The protest slated for December 4 was meant to prove to the communists that Civic Forum could fill the streets at will. My feeling was that this one simply had to be a success.

With the announcement of the regime's excuse for a cabinet on Sunday, the machinery for Monday's demonstration had to be jump-started at short notice. I was worried by the report that Václav Malý, who had acted as a master of ceremonies at the previous demonstrations, had suddenly returned to his priestly vocation. The student strike, now well over two weeks old, had started to look shaky. A lot of students seemed to be back in class. The memory of the student protest on November 17, and the beating, was fading. With the announcement of the communist government, and its many unknown if anodyne faces, the balance of forces between the communists and Civic Forum gave the appearance of greater equilibrium. And the regime still had all of the levers of power at its disposal.

There was no longer any particular, explosive, issue that might spark protest, such as the earlier rumour of a student death at the hands of the police. This had proved to be incorrect, but only after the country had been rocked by mass demonstrations. If people came out again it would not be as spontaneous. It would be a rational decision based on a generalized and deep dissatisfaction with the regime. The mood would likely be less euphoric than it had been a week ago, and it would have to be resolute. But even if people did come out, what would be the result? In the present context, any new government would have a limited shelf-life if it lacked the confidence of the people. But then again, what would replace it? At least as far as public opinion was concerned, it was now increasingly clear that the communists had lost their one chance to compromise. There simply could be no meaningful role for the Communist Party in any future government.

As it turned out, and to my relief, Civic Forum did fill Wenceslas Square again on the evening of Monday, December 4. It did not rank with the biggest demonstrations of the past two weeks, but there were over 250,000 people protesting in Prague alone. This number was matched by similar crowds in cities and towns across the country. The difference this time was the feeling that the whole community had come out. It was the children's demonstration, and they seemed to be everywhere, perched on their parents' shoulders or holding their hands. Flags fluttered in the floodlights and there was an air of winter festival. Still, it was a demonstration, and the crowd ridiculed the new government of Prime Minister Adamec.

Civic Forum representatives let it be known that if there was not a new government by the following weekend, another general strike would be called for Monday, December 11. They pointed out that the abolition of the leading role of the Communist Party was meaningless if the party still dominated the government. In short, this was not the coalition that had been promised. Strike committees in the workplaces were to be put on alert so as to prepare for the next strike. These committees would also take over the official trade union organizations. A number of speakers directed their criticism at the federal assembly. They ridiculed the party hacks, such as the neo-Stalinists Bilak, Indra, and so on, who sat as duly "elected" members of parliament.

Even the Party's attempt to look into the events of 1968 was criticized by Forum. Ladislav Lis noted that there had been as yet no admission of treason by those in the Party who had actively sought the invasion of their own country in 1968. Nor did the Party allude to the moral and physical devastation of the nation that resulted. Hundreds of thousands of people had lost their jobs or had been forced into exile. It is difficult for us now to appreciate the full extent of the trauma that this country suffered. It was on a par with the Munich betrayal of 1938. Lis said that the people were still waiting for the list of names of those who had "invited the tanks."

To my surprise, Václav Malý then made an appearance on the speakers' balcony. Not only did he appear, but he gave the keynote political speech of the evening. Malý had become an extremely effective orator at these events, and once again that wonderful voice of his wafted clearly over our heads. I knew from discussions with Malý during the past year that he was also one of the people in the opposition with genuine political smarts. I, and others, put him on a level with the best in the opposition, although I knew he would deny it. On this evening, Malý announced that the basic political goal of Civic Forum was free elections by June, 1990. This was barely six months away.

Malý said that the neo-Stalinists were becoming active and would try preserve the old system under a new guise. These people had misused the state in the past. The goal of free elections could only be assured, said Malý, if Civic Forum became the umbrella for all of the democratic forces in society. Hence Forum would enter the elections with a single list of candidates. The political affiliation of each candidate could still be given. No doubt, after the elections, some political parties would separate from Forum. But the basic idea was that Civic Forum would offer itself as a political organization even after the elections to those independent candidates not associated with any party. According to Malý,

Civic Forum's role was to act as a bridge to a democratic state by contributing to grass roots democracy. He then appealed to the crowd, saying simply, "we need your support now, more than ever."

He then described for the first time how Forum would deal with the elections. It would enter the elections as a political force representing "all circles of the republic." Coordination would take place through Civic Forum strike committees in towns and villages. Looking forward to the next few weeks, Malý said he hoped for a peaceful transition. To be sure, the communists had drawn a line with the nomination of the government, and no one could predict how they would react to more mass protest. Malý was absolutely right about how crucial support was, now that the Party had demonstrated its reluctance to give up the reigns of power.

The protests in Prague and across the country on this day were again carried live on TV. At one point during the rally I entered a hotel lobby to get warm. There, on television, I watched the demonstration as it was happening outside the window. I was sure that Marshall McLuhan would have had something pithy to say about revolution in the age of mass media but, just then, I could not think what it would be. I was too preoccupied by the revolution.

After the success of the demonstrations on Monday, negotiations with Prime Minister Adamec began in earnest the next day. Civic Forum had proved that it could mobilize the country at will. No more protests were announced for the moment, but the proposed general strike for a week hence hung over Adamec's head like the sword of Damocles. Another general strike, or any attempt to prevent one, would have put the nation on the road to crisis. In the meantime, the regime resorted to tried and true methods to deal with subversion. A leaked secret Party document, sent to all basic Party organizations, revealed that Communist Party members were instructed to infiltrate the group of former Party members who had been expelled from the Party in 1968. This opposition group was called Obroda, or "revival," and it had joined Civic Forum at the beginning. It contained many figures from Dubček's government. Once inside Obroda, the communists were to create dissension within Forum by establishing left-wing groups. These basic Party organizations were also to try to limit the spread of Civic Forum in the towns and villages. They were instructed to get into the strike committees and split the students away from Civic Forum by sowing discord. All in all, it was a dirty tricks campaign, and it was aimed at Forum's weakest link, the countryside.

Then, in a surprising move, Prime Minister Adamec went on national TV on Wednesday night to denounce Civic Forum's pressure tactics. Forum had given Adamec until Sunday to come up with a government or face a general strike the next day. Adamec pleaded that he was "in favour of holding democratic elections, as soon as possible. But I cannot agree with talks under time pressure, under threats of strikes and demonstrations." Adamec presented his new government (the sequel) to the ruling national front coalition the next day, on Thursday, and then resigned. He had been unable to find a compromise between Forum's demands and the insistence of the Stalinists within the communist central committee that the Party retain control of key ministries. At about the same time Havel met with the new General Secretary of the Communist Party, Karel Urbánek. Urbánek reassured Havel that the Party's paramilitary unit, the People's Militia, would be incorporated into the army. He also claimed that the StB would no longer be involved with internal affairs. This was a euphemism for the suppression of freedom of speech and assembly.

In light of these confusing developments, Barry and I decided to call on Bohumil Kučera. Kučera was the long-standing chairman of the co-opted Socialist Party. But he also chaired the so-called governing coalition of the national front. The national front was just that, a front for the Communist Party. Hence Kučera had long-time links with the regime. He would soon be ousted from the Socialist Party once the revolution removed the communists. But at this moment we thought that Kučera might be able to give us another view of the backstage manoeuvring. Kučera began by saying that he had hoped that Adamec and Forum could have come up with a compromise, but this was not to be. He said he thought Forum was reluctant to participate in any new government because that government would have difficult decisions to make. It could end up being very unpopular. This was a key consideration, given the coming elections. On this point Kučera was definite: there would be elections. It was now obvious that there was "no other solution."

Kučera went on to explain what he thought were the implications. New electoral laws would be required, and the process for delivering them would make June the earliest possible date. Civic Forum had originally wanted a longer time frame in order to consolidate. It was now pushing for the first open window. Kučera thought that Forum would pick up a lot of support from the non-communist parties, but that the communists would retain some support, just as they had between the wars. It was something of a tradition in Czechoslovakia.

Finally, Kučera smiled and said, "of course the democratic process is complicated and difficult, but sometimes in its first stage what is really needed are demonstrations."

What struck us again in these comments from those who, like Kučera, had spent their careers in the company of the regime was the conviction that the communist gambit would fail and that elections were on the agenda. In retrospect, this seems obvious. But at the time, we were discussing the possibility of the first free democratic elections in Czechoslovakia since 1947, over forty years before. It all seemed unreal even as we spoke of it.

27

THE GOVERNMENT OF NATIONAL UNDERSTANDING

THE WEEK OF THREATS, demands, dirty tricks, and euphoria ended on Sunday, December 10. Departing Prime Minister Adamec asked Marian Čalfa, the Minister responsible for Constitutional Affairs in the previous communist government, to take over from him and to try his luck at forming a new government. Čalfa did just this. He came up with a government of ten communist ministers and eleven non-communists. But what convinced Civic Forum to give it a chance was that many of the communists, such as Valtr Komárek from the Forecasting Institute of the Academy of Sciences, were communist in name only. More to the point, several Civic Forum leaders became ministers.

One of the big surprises, and it seemed absolutely unbelievable at the time, was the nomination of Jiří Dienstbier as Foreign Minister. Dienstbier had been a typical dissident. Though a foreign correspondent in the 1960s, he supported Dubček and was thrown out of his job. He later signed Charter 77 and became one of its most prominent figures. He spent time in jail with the likes of Havel. I got to know him during the bad old days as one of the rumpled intellectuals whose human rights stand was a permanent thorn in the side of the regime. When I heard the news of the appointment I told one of my colleagues from the American Embassy. Though this colleague was a strong supporter of the opposition, his reaction was typical, I think, of many. He laughed out loud in disbelief. I had to admit that it was hard to see Jiří, with his dissident garb and his bohemian lifestyle, as Foreign Minister. The wife of a deceased member of the opposition loaned Dienstbier the dead man's suit for the swearing in ceremony. It improved his image only marginally. For all that, Dienstbier turned out to be one of the great success stories of the first Havel government.

Prime Minister Čalfa proposed the new government, Civic Forum representatives and all, to President Husák. Husák swore them in on Sunday, December 10, and then resigned. This had been one of Forum's demands. Among the four Deputy Prime Ministers named was Ján Čarnogursky, a Slovak dissident. Carnogursky had been serving a jail term when he was told that he would be released so that he could be sworn in as Deputy Prime Minister. He told me afterwards that the ceremony involving Husák had been unreal. President Husák, now well into his seventies and very frail, was somewhat out of touch with his surroundings. It was difficult to know if he was fully aware of what was happening on the political front. According to Carnogursky, Husák revealed not a whit of remorse or regret. He demonstrated the good humour of someone who had just lost a friendly game of cards. At one point during the swearing-in, he asked Carnogursky how long he had been in prison. When Carnogursky said that it had been about eight months, Husák laughed and said that it was nothing compared with the years he had spent in prison in the 1950s. From what Carnogursky and others told me, being sworn in by Husák was something like being sworn in by the Mad Hatter. In fact it was easy to have the impression that the whole country had gone through the looking glass.

Husák's resignation was a key step in loosening the communists' hold on power. Although the president's role was somewhat undefined, he nonetheless possessed authority on paper to appoint a new prime minister, and to have him form a government. Over the years following the coup d'état, the communists had succeeded in restricting the role of the president. Its occupant became a figurehead, without even the power to name a prime minister. The real decisions were made by the General Secretary of the Communist Party. Nonetheless, many of the powers still existed in the constitution, although they had not been exercised in a long time. The right person could do much to further the course of the revolution. The wrong person would be fatal to its success. The challenge would be to resist communist pressures.

President Beneš had failed to do just that in 1947-48, with catastrophic consequences. Of course Dubček's name had been on everyone's mind since the first days of the revolution. He was the symbol of the Prague Spring. Now in his seventies, he would have no difficulty giving back to the office its honour and its respect in the eyes of the people. Also important was the fact that Dubček was one of the few Czechoslovaks who were known outside the country. The international image of Czechoslovakia would be key to obtaining Western political and economic support during the move to democracy and the free market.

Civic Forum now gave the issue its undivided attention. Husák's resignation meant that the federal assembly would be expected to elect a new president in the next few weeks. The new government agreed that this vote would take place on December 29, in order to permit a new president to take power by January 1. Those in Forum who insisted on the importance of strong leadership in a time of uncertainty started to talk about Václav Havel. There was absolutely no question that Havel's moral stand over long difficult years, and his time in prison, demonstrated that he would never compromise with the communists. Dubček was better known and at that time more popular. But there was a lingering doubt about Dubček within Charter 77. Some of the former dissidents were critical of him for his silence during the period of repression. These same people argued that he had wavered in 1968, that he had not stood up to the Russians. They said that he did not have the necessary stamina when the going got tough. The final argument was that Dubček was now a man of the past, at a time when "socialism with a human face" was no longer the goal. A new figure was needed to symbolize the aspirations of a whole new generation. Civic Forum soon decided that Václav Havel was their man. The problem was that he was almost unknown outside opposition or literary circles. And if he was known at all, it was from the rather unflattering portraits offered up in scurrilous articles published over the years by the communist press.

The Czechoslovak constitutional system, even before the communist takeover, was geared to provide a delicate balance between Czechs and Slovaks in the state's higher offices. Prime Minister Čalfa was a Slovak. This normally meant that the President would be a Czech. The principle both worked against Dubček's candidacy and gave the Havel camp an incentive to keep Čalfa on. Nonetheless the Slovaks in the opposition pushed hard for Dubček, and in the end Dubček agreed to run for president too. He made it clear, however, that he was not running against Havel, but "alongside him."

The fact that we were deep into a debate over Havel or Dubček for the presidency less than a month after the student's demonstration left my head spinning. Surely someone would pinch me and I would wake up to the dreary perambulations of "normalization." But no, there was a poster with Havel's face on it. He was running for President. He was wearing the same corduroy suit that he wore at our Pen International lunch in October. I could remember vividly standing in the courthouse in Žižkov the previous February, watching him marched by in manacles to his trial. As for Dubček, twenty years ago he had suffered a foreign invasion and been ousted from power. A political comeback after that would be a case of dialectics at its weirdest. It seemed that the world had been turned instantly and completely upside down.

Prime Minister Čalfa was the right man in the right job at the right moment. It was difficult, however, to know how long that moment would last. He had, after all, been proposed by the communists to lead the government of "national understanding." On the other hand, he had provided the doorway through which Civic Forum had entered the government. Marian Čalfa was a technocrat with no real reputation for reform or anything else. He had been an executive assistant to Prime Minister Štrougal in the 1970s, a lawyer, and apparently a good administrator. His political instincts proved to be good, too. When Barry and I called on him on December 14, four days after his appointment, he laughed at his predicament. He said history had thrown him into this job completely by accident. He personally did not expect to stay there very long. Čalfa impressed us as being sincere and friendly. One could not help liking him. Both Dienstbier and Havel would have the same reaction.

As to why his instincts were good, Čalfa demonstrated from the beginning that he was a Havel loyalist. He would do nothing without clearing it first with the president. Although many of Havel's advisors wanted to get rid of Čalfa because he had come up through the regime, Havel resisted and kept him on, over their objections. I think that the reason for this was fairly evident: aside from the question of personal rapport Čalfa had no personal constituency, at least not one with any influence. Rather than taking on the role of a true prime minister Čalfa became a cabinet chairman. He left the initiation of policy to others, particularly to Havel, Dienstbier, and Finance Minister Klaus. The result was that Havel became embroiled in many day-to-day issues that he might better have avoided.

The second, more serious, result was that a split developed in cabinet over the pace of economic reform. Čalfa did not have the political weight to resolve the differences, and this delayed the implementation of the economic reform package. In fact it was not resolved until Havel finally entered the debate. This was, paradoxically, the one issue on which he had refused to intervene because he believed he did not have the expertise. He finally came out supporting Klaus, but only after six months had been lost.

Where Prime Minister Čalfa was particularly successful in his first few months was in preparing for the elections. It was decided that these must be in June, in order to provide the country with a truly legitimate government as quickly as possible. Čalfa moved swiftly in preparing legislation on political parties, elections, and basic freedoms. He was helped with this aspect of the government's mandate by Ján Čarnogursky. Both Carnogursky and Čalfa were lawyers, and had known each other in law school, although their subsequent careers had taken very different turns. During this same period, in the early months of 1990, Carnogursky founded the Christian Democratic Movement in Slovakia. The movement was moderately nationalistic and, at that time, was in direct competition with the Civic Forum counterpart in Slovakia, Public Against Violence.

The Christian Democratic Movement was closely associated with the Catholic Church in Slovakia and its very conservative teachings. Religion and nationalism was the political mix that had animated the Slovak fascist state during the war. Many Slovaks both at home and in exile regarded this one-time independence of Slovakia as a kind of golden age. My own impression was that the Slovak state did indeed enjoy a degree of popularity during the war, despite the fact that its priestly leader, Tiso, was executed as a war criminal afterward. In conversations with Carnogursky about this he told me that there was in fact a very thin line that could not be crossed in the months ahead. His goal was to preserve what was of value in Slovak traditions without falling backwards into demagogy and prejudice. Carnogursky would learn that trying to resurrect only the *good* traditions was a tall order, and that others would be less discerning than he.

Valtr Komárek was the Deputy Prime Minister in charge of the government's other main preoccupation, economic reform. He had been head of the Forecasting Institute of the Academy of Sciences under the communist regime. Though he was a member of the Party, he had managed to turn the Institute into something of a refuge for non-communists. Václav Klaus had been on staff there. The Institute produced economic and social forecasts which the regime ignored, largely because they demonstrated that virtually every aspect of society was in a state of increasingly rapid decay. During the period of uncertainty in early December, when Adamec seemed incapable of putting a government together, Komarek had made a bizarre attempt to launch himself as a potential prime minister. He held a press conference and invited foreign journalists and just about anybody else who would come. In the curriculum vitae which he handed out there he started off by emphasizing that he was born illegitimate. He went on to describe how, despite the fact he had been in the Party, he had really been shunned by it for his progressive ideas. There was a grain of truth in this, but he had hardly lived the life of a dissident.

I had met Komarek a number of times in the past year. He was a strange fellow, with long, curly white hair shooting out in all directions, rather like a caricature of Einstein. Yet I was never convinced by his plans for a painless transition to a market economy. There would have to be the pain of adjustment, at least in the short run; and there was. Komarek's theories had more to do with wishful thinking than with economics. Klaus was also critical of Komarek's ideas, and this conflict would lead to stalemate on economic reform until Havel intervened. Komarek eventually resigned. He resurfaced a year later as head of a small social democratic party.

The real economic brains of the new government belonged to Václav Klaus, the Finance Minister, and Vladimír Dlouhý, who had become Chairman of the State Planning Commission. The latter had been one of the big jobs under the communists, since the minister in question set the price, wage, and investment levels for the entire economy. Two days after their appointment to the cabinet I visited Dlouhy and Klaus in Dlouhy's apartment. It was Tuesday, December 12. I brought along a bottle of Moet & Chandon champagne. Dlouhy lived in a rather modest flat on a busy street in downtown Prague. He had been Deputy Director of the Forecasting Institute, under Komarek. The apartment was typical of state accommodation for many mid-level bureaucrats. Though it was cold outside, the windows were wide open because it was too hot inside. There was no thermostat to regulate the heat. There were no thermostats anywhere in Czechoslovakia. If the radiators were too hot one just opened the window. It was this kind of economic insanity that Klaus and Dlouhy set out to cure. When I met them that evening they were still uncertain about what they were getting themselves into. Klaus had yet to develop fully the magisterial persona that would mark his political life and that of the nation. But it was there in nascent form. I remember, about this time, talking with an old colleague of his, who joked that even twenty years ago Klaus could be counted on to push himself forward to the front of the line. That tenacity would ensure that Czechoslovakia would take the most direct route to a market economy. But its effect on the constitutional debate propelled the country into high-risk negotiations over its future.

Klaus was not the only minister with an angular personality, of course. I had not known Dienstbier as well as some of the others in Charter 77. He had the appearance of someone who had endured hardship both in prison and afterward. His physical and mental stamina flagged occasionally, and during his dissident days he was not easy to approach. After his appointment as Foreign Minister his humane and humorous qualities flourished and his foreign policy was truly one of the bright lights of the early months. At the time of his appointment I took a perverse pleasure in trying to imagine how he would be received in the Foreign Ministry. There were more than a few there whose careers had accelerated after 1968, when many of their colleagues were fired for supporting Dubček. By December 1989, the hardliners in the Ministry must have thought that their worst nightmare had come true. First Deputy Minister Sadovský was promptly sent off to Bucharest as Ambassador; not a plumb posting. Lagos was reserved for Deputy Minister Vacek, who seemed to have had close ties to the StB. Former Foreign Minister Johanes was sent to Ankara, but as a counsellor rather than an ambassador. And this was before the real vetting started of those officials who had had regular contacts with the StB.

Dienstbier's first priority, however, was the negotiation of the withdrawal of Soviet troops from Czechoslovak territory. There were somewhere between 75,000 and 100,000 Soviet troops in what was regarded as a front-line country. Dienstbier vigorously pursued these talks with the Russians and in a matter of weeks a basic framework had been agreed upon that would see the troops out by June 1991. Soviet Foreign Minister Shevardnadze was key to these talks. He was able to overcome the resistance of the Soviet military establishment. In February, I talked with both Dienstbier and his new Deputy Minister Matejka about the negotiations. Dienstbier was absolutely uncompromising in his position and quite aggressive whenever the Russians were mentioned. There was going to be no flexibility in the Czechoslovak negotiating mandate. Czechoslovakia was now the most determined among the former Warsaw Pact allies to get the Russians out. As an example of what the Czechs were up against, Matejka described the attitude of the Russian generals around the table. He said they resented giving up Central and Eastern Europe and did not bother hiding their resentment even when Gorbachov was present. This only spurred Dienstbier and Matejka to move as fast as they could to secure a withdrawal. They had the distinct impression that the window would not be open for long.

All of these issues, whether economic reform or the withdrawal of Russian troops, quickly became bound up in political calculations as the new ministers focused on the fact that elections were only six months away. For example, some of them argued there could be no sweeping economic changes before a new government, and a new assembly, had been elected on the basis of a political program. Hence the economic reform package was not agreed until after the June elections. In one respect, this delay may not have been such a bad thing. Václav Malý told me that he believed both Civic Forum and the people had a lot to learn in the six months between the revolution and the elections. There had to be genuine political debate. Everyone would have to work hard to make themselves conversant with a whole range of new questions. And then each prospective voter would have to identify those candidates who reflected his or her views. Virtually the entire electorate would be going through this process for the first time, despite the fact Czechoslovakia was a fully-fledged democracy during the interwar period. The price for this learning curve was lost momentum. Right after the revolution, everyone would have accepted difficult economic decisions without a second thought. Six months later, when the thrill of revolution had started to fade, vested interests would seek to slow the pace of change, and Havel would begin talking of the need for a second revolution.

28

THOMAS BATA'S HOMECOMING

IN DECEMBER 1989 and in the first months of 1990, however, the thrill of revolution changed people's lives. These were exhilarating days. We could not have been any closer to the very lifeblood of history. Being Canadian was an additional advantage. Many Czechs and Slovaks had fled communist Czechoslovakia over the years, and a lot of them ended up in Canada. Now they were coming back. For most it was the first time back in twenty or even forty years, and they were ecstatic. But in those first days, one return stood out. It was the homecoming of Thomas Bata, then seventy-five years old. He had not been back since just after the war, in 1946. Incredibly, that was now almost forty-five years ago.

Bata's father, Thomas Bata Sr., had been a hero of the First Republic, between the wars. He had introduced modern manufacturing techniques and created a huge export industry. More importantly, he had introduced programs to set up hospitals and schools for his workers and their families. He even introduced a savings plan to permit them to buy their own homes. Those who had worked for Bata Sr. had regarded themselves as privileged, as part of a Bata family. Virtually from the start of the revolution there were excited rumours that Thomas Bata Jr. would come back. The name alone had mythic proportions in a nation that looked back wistfully to its golden age under President Masaryk.

As it turned out, Bata's return was to play a significant role in Havel's campaign for the presidency. And I was to have a small part in it. Two of Bata's advisors, Jiří Sedlacek and Otto Daičar, called on me at the Embassy on Monday, December 11, since I was chargé d'affaires in the ambassador's absence. The new government, under Prime Minister Čalfa, had been named the day before. Havel, Dubček, and another candidate were running for president. Sedlacek and Daicar wanted to know what Mr. Bata could do to help. When should he think of visiting? As Canadians of Czech origin, they knew the impact the visit would have on the political scene. I said to them that the only person who could answer their question was Václav Havel.

I went to Civic Forum headquarters to meet with Jan Urban. Urban, the former dissident journalist, was now in Forum's executive. When I told him Bata's people were in town and related the questions they had posed, he became increasingly excited about the prospect of Bata's return. He told me to wait where I was. We were in some sort of media control centre in the basement, and there were people constantly rushing in and out. Civic Forum headquarters was the beating heart of the revolution. Jan came back in a hurry and slightly out of breath. He said that a meeting had been set up between me and Havel for the next morning. I was to bring Sedlacek and Daicar. I went to the Esplanade Hotel, near Wenceslas Square, to relay the message to Jiří and Otto. Jiří asked me what they should say to Havel. I said they should be as frank as possible. They should simply ask when Mr. Bata should come.

We returned to Forum headquarters the next morning. It was like the middle of a storm. Young men and women from a karate club provided security and bodyguards for Havel. People came and went in a hurry, telephones rang, and impromptu meetings took place on stair landings. The building was located at the bottom corner of Wenceslas Square. Ironically, it had previously housed the Czechoslovak-Soviet Friendship Society. It was consequently in quite good repair. I said hello to Ivan Havel and Martin Palouš. They rushed by with worried looks on their faces. The revolution was still very much in the making. Reports were coming in from the provinces about the latest successes of Forum and the dastardly deeds of the communists.

I felt as if I had suddenly travelled back two hundred years to 1789. There was the same unshaven bohemian look, the men wearing ponytails and ear-rings, the women in long flowing gowns. Then we were ushered in to see Havel. He recognized me and said a brief hello. He looked as if he had not slept in weeks, and probably had not. He sat in a chair in the middle of the room while others clustered around taking notes, answering the telephone, or just listening. Havel was the man at the eye of the storm, the beating heart of the revolution. He sat in this chair leaning forward most of the time, looking down, totally concentrated. He rubbed the arm of the chair compulsively and smoked and drank beer. He listened quietly to a brief description of the reason for our visit. He then began what can only be described as a monologue, focused totally on his thoughts, that described the current political situation and the present dangers. He rocked back and forth, stroking the arm of the chair as he spoke slowly and carefully. If his analysis had not been brilliant, I might have wondered about his mental state.

It is hard to exaggerate how creative Civic Forum was at that time. The means were always unorthodox, but there was a surplus of political intuition. The posters put together by the graphic arts students, and the more experienced professionals who had crossed over to Forum, were sophisticated models of communication. There was one that was particularly striking. It was a black and white photograph of the statue of King Wenceslas on horseback rising above the crowds in Wenceslas Square. On his standard was the red, white, and blue Czechoslovak flag. Underneath was written rather prominently "Free Elections," and in small letters at the bottom of the poster "Civic Forum." It was impossible, of course, for Civic Forum headquarters to control what was going on, or even coordinate it. A lot of activity in Prague and in the countryside was simply spontaneous, in the best traditions of the 1960s. There were humorous graffiti everywhere. People were speaking up and finding themselves. They felt free, and free to laugh. This was the perfect environment for creativity of every kind, from political strategy to posters to civic initiatives.

Thomas Bata had written a letter of political support for Havel. Jiří Sedlacek handed it to him during our meeting. Havel read it on the spot. Then Jiří popped the question. When should Mr. Bata come back to Czechoslovakia? Havel replied simply and instinctively: as soon as possible and definitely within the next week. I think I saw Jiří and Otto pale visibly. They said they would speak with Mr. Bata that very day. As I took leave of Havel, I asked myself how he could keep up his twenty-four hour workdays. I truly wondered if he would survive it all, given his sometimes fragile health. He was by then well into his campaign for the presidency. Mr. Bata's return would be a definite help in winning over public opinion. There was no question that the Bata name was associated with the pride and prosperity of the First

Republic. Civic Forum had a lot of work to do, and Thomas Bata was going to help do it.

It was my turn to pale when I talked with Jiří Sedlacek after he had spoken with the Bata family. Mr. Bata would do what Havel asked. My first meeting with Bata's representatives had been on Monday. I found out on Tuesday night that Mr. Bata and his wife Sonja would arrive on Thursday. How could I possibly organize the visit in twenty-four hours? My first step was to call Barry Mawhinney, the Ambassador, who was in Brussels. He was at an important meeting and would not get back to Prague before the morning of the Batas' arrival. I was on my own. It turned out to be easier than I expected. The Bata name in Czechoslovakia was legendary. The loyalty to Thomas Bata Sr., which survived forty years of communism, is beyond our grasp today. In the 1920s and 1930s, over 100,000 people proudly called themselves part of the Bata family. When I started organizing the visit it seemed as if everyone I talked to had a relative who had once worked for the Batas. And everyone had their own Bata story to tell, always with a heavy dose of nostalgia and a genuine feeling of attachment.

Of course, some of the positive recollections were amplified by comparison with the horrible period of communism that followed. President Masaryk and Bata were the symbols of a lost golden age. That golden age was cut short by the deaths of both Masaryk and Bata Sr. in the 1930s. It was succeeded by the Munich debacle, the Nazi invasion, and the communist takeover in 1948. The revolution suddenly unleashed the pent-up longing for this stolen youth. The Bata name represented what had been and what many wanted the country to become again. I found that the name opened all doors. On the Tuesday night when I met with Dlouhy and Klaus after their appointment as ministers, I mentioned that Mr. Bata was arriving on Thursday. He would meet first with Havel as a way of signalling his unqualified support. The next day he would meet with Prime Minister Čalfa, Komarek, and Dienstbier. Klaus and Dlouhy wanted to meet him too. Bata's return symbolized the return of Western business interest. Not a bad program for a day's work.

Civic Forum assumed, correctly, that Mr. Bata would want to visit his home town, Zlín, in the region of Moravia. This was where the headquarters of the firm had been located. In fact Mr. Bata wanted to lay a wreath at his father's grave. Thomas Bata Sr. had died tragically in a plane crash. After their takeover in 1948, the communists changed the name of the town to Gottwaldov, to honour Klement Gottwald, the first communist President of the Czechoslovak Socialist Republic.

The local Civic Forum now wanted to change the name back to Zlín on the first day of Mr. Bata's visit there. A nice touch, I thought. In the day or so before Mr. Bata's arrival the press caught wind of the visit. Newspapers and TV were swept up in Batamania. The communists had confiscated the Bata holdings without any compensation. He was coming back, taking one step at a time. He would support Havel and Civic Forum. He would see his country of origin, and his countrymen, after 45 years of exile. But the question of the return of any properties would be long and complicated.

I had seen a lot of strange and wonderful events in the last few weeks. One was the jingling of car keys by 300,000 people to toll the end of communism. Another would be Mr. Bata's arrival by private jet at the airport. We knew the press had been playing up the visit, and we expected a certain amount of press interest in the arrival. To be on the safe side I decided to alert the Foreign Ministry that we might need some airport security staff to ensure that Mr. Bata could escape the press after a few questions. They put a couple of policemen at the door of the airport building to restrict access to the VIP lounge. A half hour before the arrival of the jet, 10,000 people jammed the building, crowded together on the roof, and many more lined the street that led from the airport to downtown. There were banners and flags everywhere, and sporadic cheers.

Dlouhy was on hand to provide the official welcome. With flowers for Mrs. Bata under his arm, he was clearly as nervous as we were about the huge crowd that had come out. We, and the government, had totally underestimated the Bata myth in Czechoslovakia. I was still chargé d'affaires and, together with Pierre I walked out on to the tarmac as the plane touched down. This seemed to be the signal the crowd was waiting for. Everyone rushed out on to the runway. We found ourselves propelled forward by the crowd as the plane came to a stop. Thousands of people pushed forward, trying to get close, as the hatch popped open. We leaned back with all of our might trying to make room so that the Batas could step down from the plane. Our shoes slid on the asphalt as we tried desperately to maintain the minimum of official decorum.

Out stepped Mrs. Sonja Bata and then Mr. Thomas Bata Jr. The crowd surged forward and the TV cameras jostled. They were covering it live on TV. Dlouhy tried to stay on his feet while presenting flowers to Mrs. Bata. The Batas smiled and waved graciously as people cheered. At this point I was genuinely concerned that they were going to be overwhelmed by the crowd. There was a real danger that someone was going to be crushed or trampled under foot. The situation was becoming completely out of control as thousands of people scrambled forward. Pierre and I put ourselves in front of the Batas and made a wedge as we pushed the crowd out of the way and edged inch by inch toward the terminal. We were on our own in what was a mob scene. The two policemen remained at their stations by the door to the terminal. That doorway seemed a lifetime away, as people reached out to shake Mr. Bata's hand or to shout their own names, the names of people who had worked long ago for the legendary firm.

We finally made it to the terminal and squeezed through the doorway into the relative tranquillity of the arrival hall. All of us, including the Batas, just stood there for a moment, left breathless by the reception we had just experienced. But Mr. Bata was clearly on top of the world, and his incredible personal energy did not flag for an instant. We walked into the VIP lounge and were immediately swamped by another mob, the journalists. Flash bulbs popped, TV lights blazed, and a forest of microphones were pushed toward Mr. Bata. Since the nice chap from Protocol was not prepared to intervene, I appointed myself press secretary and directed the questions one at a time to Mr. Bata. He handled them extremely well, in both Czech and English. He said simply that he had come back to see what he could do to help. He would be meeting Havel and Prime Minister Čalfa and other ministers. Yes, he was interested in the fate of the family properties after all these years, but that was not his immediate concern. When I felt that the journalists had got all they needed, we ended the press conference and headed for the waiting limousines. The crowd outside cheered as we emerged from the airport and then we pulled away in our motorcade on our way to meet with Havel. The streets were lined with well-wishers waving at us. None of us had seen anything like this before.

As a politician, Dlouhy could not have hoped for a better public relations event. He told me, while we were waiting for the Batas' plane to arrive, that his mother had thought it nice he had been made a Minister. But what had really impressed her was that he was going to welcome Mr. Bata. That seemed to sum it up. It was the kind of homage that followed us everywhere we went in Czechoslovakia. The motorcade stopped near Civic Forum headquarters and we decided to walk a bit in Wenceslas Square before going in to meet Havel. Suddenly people recognized Mr. Bata and an instant crowd formed around us. There were questions and handshakes and Mr. Bata laughed and made others laugh.

We were in need of crowd control again just to walk the twenty yards to Civic Forum. We made it at last and went straight in to see Havel. He was wearing a black sweatshirt and black jeans. Havel and Bata sat side by side at the end of a table while the cameras whirred and the TV lights lit up the whole room. The seventy-five year-old Mr. Bata was as neat as a pin in a well-tailored suit. Havel looked slightly weary, chain-smoking. You could hardly imagine two more different people: the elderly capitalist and the bohemian writer. But at that moment they represented not only considerable personal accomplishment. They were living symbols for their compatriots. Now they were thrown together in the fight for a free and democratic Czechoslovakia.

As the cameras whirred, Havel quipped that Mr. Bata's father, Thomas Bata Sr., would have insisted that he put out his cigarette. In the 1920s and 1930s, the Bata company had provided the first non-smoking workplace in Czechoslovakia. This was due to the flammable properties of shoe-making material, including glue. Mr. Bata laughed. He then got down to the business at hand. He stated his clear and unequivocal support for Havel. In strictly electoral terms, this was exactly what Havel needed from the meeting. They then talked about the political situation. Each displayed such deference to the other that the conversation was a little formal. Mr. Bata did not mention it at the time, but he had once dated Havel's mother as a very young man. Fate was strange indeed. But I suppose this was not the moment to talk of personal matters. Then Havel winced and massaged his foot. He said the Czech footwear industry urgently needed Mr. Bata's help. A fact to which he could personally testify. Everyone laughed. And then before we knew it, the meeting was over. Everyone was shaking hands again and even the cameramen wanted to shake Mr. Bata's hand.

We headed down the stairs past piles of about thirty or forty fax machines. Mr. Bata had brought them with him on the plane, piled on seats. He thought that the revolution could benefit from the latest communications equipment, unknown in Czechoslovakia at the time. The fax machines would create a country-wide communications network for Civic Forum. Perhaps someday someone will write a doctoral thesis about the impact of fax machines on the revolution. As we headed out of Civic Forum Mr. Bata decided that he wanted to see the equestrian statue of King Wenceslas at the top of the square. The last time he had seen it had been just after the war, but had memories as a child playing between the horse's hoofs. A Civic Forum representative was at the steps of the statue talking through the sound system to a crowd that filled most of the square, a crowd of perhaps 150,000.

People recognized Mr. Bata standing at the edge of the square. They pushed him up the steps between the hoofs and handed him a microphone. Where once he played in the shadow of his father, now he encouraged his compatriots to follow the path to freedom that they had chosen. The period of transition would be less difficult if they consolidated democracy and a market economy quickly. The crowd roared its approval and we were off once again.

We met the next morning with the new economic team of Komarek, Klaus, and Dlouhy. Though they had been ministers for only a few days, the message they delivered was that they wanted to proceed rapidly to a market economy. There would be no halfway house. Klaus said that the goal was to get the country back into the international financial community and into the group of countries with a free market orientation. Hence there would be no attempt at all to reform the communist system. It would simply be thrown out. First the central planning system would be dismantled. This would be followed by quick privatization of the entire economy.

Klaus argued, correctly, that the government would have to take these steps as soon as possible in order to build on the enthusiasm of the revolution. He said that a slow approach would risk losing the support of the people as the economy adapted to market mechanisms. All of this sounded impressively decisive from the standpoint of broad political goals. Especially when the team had been in place only a few days. I think Mr. Bata was impressed, too. But given the distance to those goals from the existing system, the proof of the pudding would definitely be in the eating. And the eating, as we were to find out, would come only six months later.

More impressive was the fact that Klaus went on to describe exactly how he would obtain these goals. He had it all worked out. He had been thinking about this day for a long time. Incredibly, he would stick to the basic outline of his plan over the next two years, and achieve the most successful transition to a market economy in Eastern Europe. When we talked to him, he said that the key was the proper sequence of economic changes. Any mistake would lead to economic collapse. The principal components of the plan were privatization, a restrictive monetary policy to keep inflation under control, and a structural shift away from heavy industry to light industry and the service sector.

In other words, mere decentralization of the economy would create chaos. There had to be macro-economic control, using economic levers. This was the role of monetary policy. Dlouhy joked that, unlike his predecessors, he faced the immediate task, as Chairman of the State Planning Commission, of abolishing state planning. Komarek then reminded everyone that the priority for the next six months in the run-up to the elections would be a stable political environment. And that meant no economic disruption. The first warning shot had been fired in a battle that would split the cabinet.

So there it was, the lines were drawn in a government only days old. Klaus and Dlouhy wanted to get on with the task of economic change. Komarek wanted to keep a steady hand on the tiller. This did not bode well for the future. In a sense, I suppose, Komarek would end up having it his way, at least until the elections. The deadlock in the cabinet ensured nothing would be implemented. And this served his strategy just as well as a victory. But the conflicting signals from this government would also be typical of the way it tried to deal with Thomas Bata's expropriated property. Again, Klaus and Dlouhy thought that some sort of agreement could be reached, even if an exception had to be made. It would turn out that these were the tentative speculations of new ministers. The Bata case was soon to become a complicated and long-suffering negotiation. I think that the main difficulty was the attempt to satisfy Mr. Bata's claim without opening the door to compensation for the thousands of Sudeten Germans that had been expelled from Czechoslovakia after the war. Havel himself would question the morality of that expulsion in the first days of his presidency.

When Mr. Bata went to see Jiří Dienstbier at the Czernin Palace, ghosts from the past almost crowded us out of the room. Dienstbier had only been Foreign Minister for a few days, and there was palpable shock and dismay among the apparatchiks. Many must already have felt like walking ghosts. When he sank into an armchair, cognac in hand, in a reception room impeccably restored to its 1668 grandeur, Dienstbier conveyed the impression of a man very much in charge, with a clear idea of his priorities. He talked about the importance of getting the Soviet troops out and of getting into Western institutions. This talk inevitably turned to the current inhabitants of the building. It led Dienstbier to decide on the spur of the moment to take us on a little tour.

It seemed that Edvard Beneš, who had been Foreign Minister to President Masaryk, had actually set up an apartment in the palace. I could see why Dienstbier wanted to show it to us. All of the legs of the tables and chairs had been sawed off. Apparently Beneš had been rather short. The furniture looked like the kind of thing IKEA might have produced for children in the 1920s. I wondered if there was any connection between the furniture and the fact that Beneš had caved in to the Nazis in 1938, and again to the communists in 1948. No doubt this was another doctoral thesis waiting to be written.

Dienstbier then took us into the infamous bathroom of the apartment. Jan Masaryk, the son of President Masaryk, had succeeded Beneš as Foreign Minister and had lived on and off in the flat. In 1948, when he was the only non-communist in a new communist government, he had fallen from the window of the bathroom to his death five stories below. The question was whether he jumped or had been pushed by communist agents. Dienstbier tended to the latter theory. The window was rather high and small, not the sort of thing that easily presented itself as a place from which to jump. The pale blue bathroom was unchanged since 1948, and as we stood there I noticed that Mr. Bata was uncharacteristically quiet. He said that he had known Jan Masaryk well in the 1930s. They had been at many of the same parties, the sons of two famous fathers. Jan was an accomplished composer and pianist, and would inevitably end the evening playing the piano, to everyone's delight. Mr. Bata had kept in touch with Jan Masaryk during the latter's World War II exile in London. In fact Bata had been talking with him over the phone at the time of the communist takeover. Jan had been very depressed. It was not the first time. Sadly, Mr. Bata had concluded that Jan Masaryk might well have jumped.

When we went to see Cardinal Tomášek in the Archbishop's Palace, located just outside the Prague Castle gates, I began to understand how closely Mr. Bata, and his father, had been involved with the main figures of Czechoslovak history in the twentieth century. Cardinal Tomášek had turned ninety years old the previous June. Mr. Bata spoke slowly. There were long pauses before the Cardinal replied. We sat around a table on large, ancient wooden chairs. Tomášek said he remembered Mr. Bata as a boy. The Cardinal had been a parish priest in Moravia. Mr. Bata was about five years old at the time, running around in shorts, and usually making trouble. We all laughed. Mr. Bata was seventy-five now, and he was not used to being treated as an upstart.

The events Tomášek was describing happened just after World War I, in the first years of Czechoslovakia's existence as a country. Given what had happened since, it seemed a very long time ago to Tomášek, and to Mr. Bata. Tomášek spoke a little about the communist years. He was very bitter about what had been done to the church and to people generally. He was not very optimistic about the future of religious belief in Czechoslovakia. Tomášek lamented what had happened to Christian traditions under the regime. He was sceptical that they could be revived at a time when most people's interest would be spurred by the new world of free enterprise. As we prepared to leave, he gave each of us a ballpoint pen with his photo on it. He offered a blessing to speed us on our way.

29

THE CAMPAIGN FOR PRESIDENT

IN MID-DECEMBER, CIVIC FORUM was throwing itself into the campaign to get Havel elected. This had never been a direct election, even before the communists. The President was elected by a majority in the Federal Assembly. The real objective this time around was slightly different. Civic Forum had to increase and consolidate Havel's popularity in order to deter the communists from trying to play games. The Assembly was still dominated by communists who had been "voted in" under the old regime in elections where there was only one candidate. There was no question that the massive demonstrations in Prague had helped to spread Havel's fame. But he built on this in succeeding weeks by travelling across the country and speaking at meetings and rallies everywhere. This rather shy, and yet charismatic, man became the nation's favourite.

Havel was both a hero and an anti-hero. This odd combination made it possible for people to look up to him, to admire his intellectual and moral prestige, without feeling that he was condescending to them in any way. His popularity in towns and in the countryside increased dramatically. Havel was not a very good public speaker in the usual sense, and he was clearly uncomfortable on a stage. His appearance could hardly be described as slick. But the rumpled look of this chain-smoking heroic anti-hero, and his beautifully crafted words, caught everybody's fancy. He did not hurl thunderbolts from some

"Havel to the Castle!" A campaign poster from December, 1989

moral height. He talked about "our" compromises with the regime, and with human decency, over the years. And he conveyed a vision of the future that struck a collective chord. Havel had started time again, he had opened the door to possibility, and he was a hit.

By the week before Christmas I think just about every Czech and every Slovak counted himself and herself among the most ardent revolutionaries. The Communist Party correctly concluded there was no point playing games. An agreement was reached, with all of the political parties, that a new president would be elected on Friday, December 29. The actual vote would not take place in the Federal Assembly building, the former stock exchange. It would be held instead in the historic Vladislav Hall of the Prague Castle. It was here that Czech kings had been crowned in medieval times. No doubt many saw Havel's prospective election in the same light. The irony was that the parliament was filled with Communist Party appointees. If ever there was a rubber-stamp legislature, this was it. The communist representatives would soon be expected to rubber-stamp Havel and seal their own fate. Another deal, shortly after Havel's election, would replace most of the deputies with a new group nominated by Civic Forum and other parties. This would create an interim parliament to rule during the six months prior to the elections.

Admittedly, this was a very rough equivalent of democracy. But what else could be done until the various political parties and movements had had time to organize, and new electoral laws had been discussed and passed? The communist parliament it had replaced had been even less representative. I suddenly found that many of my friends from the opposition had become deputies, with real constituencies to represent. Though hardly approximating the image of the politician in the West these former dissidents were of course a vast improvement on the communist ciphers they replaced. And I would venture to suggest that a few Western politicians could have learned a thing or two from them in terms of intellectual debate and moral commitment to a set of ideals. Still, we laughed about it when we ran into each other. The transition from the counterculture of dissent to the established halls of power left us all a little giddy. It remained to be seen whether the total, almost physical commitment to dissent could be transformed into leadership and adapted to the imperatives of building consensus.

In the highly charged days prior to Havel's election, spontaneous public events seemed to be driving the political process. A train began travelling from the far reaches of eastern Slovakia towards Prague, picking up students from across the country along the way. There was a virtually round the clock demonstration in front of the Federal Assembly proclaiming support for Havel's candidacy. The point of this was to remind the communist deputies that they were expected to "do the right thing." But what emerged most clearly in these few days was the extent to which Havel's friendly competitor, Alexander Dubček, was suddenly regarded as a man of the past. This was not to minimize the respect that all Czechs and Slovaks felt for him. It was simply that Havel had become the hero of a new generation, and that socialism with or without a human face was deeply suspect. Dubček picked up on these sentiments and emphasized again that he was not running against Havel, but with him. Havel dealt with the potentially delicate situation by offering Dubček the job of President of the Federal Assembly. This was a traditionally prestigious position, normally ranked in protocol terms after the President of the Republic and the Prime Minister. The offer would also help placate Slovak nationalist sentiment: the Prime Minister, Čalfa, was a Slovak, as was Dubček.

For all of these constitutional niceties, Havel was at this time quite popular in Slovakia too. Nor did he shy away, during this period, from difficult meetings with discontented groups anywhere in the country. This included those Slovaks who were seeking greater autonomy. He also talked with the workers in heavy industry, for example at the steel mills in Kladno, who would soon be affected by economic change. Whole towns had been built around a single industry under the communists. These towns had been previously regarded as well-organized Party strongholds. During the revolution, the workers in these towns had been convinced to come out in favour of Civic Forum. Yet they hardly knew Havel, and they suspected that economic change would mean lost jobs. They were right, of course.

Havel took on the difficult task, in the thick of his campaign, of convincing them that a better economy, a market economy, would eventually be to everyone's benefit, even theirs. Remarkably, Havel was well-received in Kladno and at other similar sessions across the country. Havel's grass-roots meetings were classic exercises in town hall democracy. This effort to go directly to the people, to encourage participation outside the usual political channels, was an early plank in the Civic Forum platform. It responded well to the disenchantment with party politics that was felt by many. But it would not survive long after the June elections.

In the midst of all of this worthy boosterism I decided to catch up with Václav Malý and seek his views on the political scene. My conversations with Malý were always a welcome antidote to the manic politics of those days. He lived in a small bare flat in Smichov, a working class district in Prague. There were always a few philosophy and politics books on a rough wooden table. I could not quite decide whether these spartan living conditions were totally appropriate or totally inappropriate to the role he had played in the opposition and during the revolution itself. Though he was ready to laugh at the drop of a hat (as was Havel), he was also like Havel in his utter seriousness when discussing politics. It seemed that only the two Vaclavs were keeping their heads during those intoxicating days. And during those days Malý was just about as well known as Havel. This was because of his prominent role at the demonstrations. But what I admired most was his uncanny ability to understand what made other people tick.

Malý said that Havel really had no choice but to accept the presidency at this delicate stage. He did not think that Havel was particularly eager to take it on, because of his low regard for title and position. In fact, Havel had said that he only wanted to stay on until the elections. Malý feared that Havel would be forced by popular demand to remain as president beyond this first six months. Of course this was exactly what happened. At that point in time neither Malý nor I could see anyone who might emerge in the intervening period to succeed Havel.

The problem, for Malý, was that he did not think a longer term commitment by Havel to the presidency was a good thing. He fully understood why it was necessary now. But it was only by distancing himself from day-to-day politics that Havel could retain his moral leadership. Malý thought that Havel was already making political compromises which, while necessary, did not accord with his personal beliefs. He felt that the principled and often difficult stands taken by Havel as a dissident were even more important now when society was in flux, when people felt a profound sense of political vertigo. He was afraid that Havel's "pure moral vision" would be diluted by the demands of the presidency.

For his part, Malý said that he would offer his support to Civic Forum, but he would no longer continue as one of its leading figures. The Church would soon give him a small parish of his own. There was an abandoned church called St. Gabriel's. How appropriate for someone who had heralded the revolution from on high (a balcony). Maly was going to restore it and open it to the people again. He felt that the compromises and cynicism induced by the communist regime had left people without a spiritual life. The worst thing was that they could not even put it into words. The vocabulary, the very concepts, that make up an inner life had been flattened out and deadened. Ethical issues had to be discussed at the most basic level because people had to relearn everything. So, instead of devoting himself to the machinations of politics at the top, he would try to revitalize spiritual life from the bottom. Some journalists had portrayed this decision as a sign of conflict within Civic Forum. It was not. But I felt that it might also have had something to do with the church's reluctance to have one of its priests too directly involved in politics, and too well known.

Malý's point was that, despite sweeping political change, even revolution, it was difficult to overcome the impact of forty years of communism on the way people thought. I found his argument compelling. No less compelling, though surprising, was his apparent lack of political ambition. He had, after all, been one of the more interesting figures in the opposition, and a leader at the mass demonstrations. Everyone knew him, in Prague and in the countryside. I had no doubt that if he had not been committed to pastoral work, if he had not been a priest, he too would have occupied a high political office. Or would he? But I also detected in his comments a note of nostalgia as he watched Havel on the campaign trail.

Malý frequently referred with admiration to Havel's plays, and particularly to his political writings. Of course, even Malý's gentle misgivings were conveyed with good humour. And he could hardly contain his enthusiasm at finally getting his own church. He had, after all, been forbidden by the communists to celebrate mass in public. For my part, I wondered whether he would be able to stay out of politics. He had become a household commodity at a time when the nation desperately needed heroes. I noticed that he now had a telephone in his flat (it was bright orange). He had not had one before, and now it never stopped ringing. Everyone seemed to want his advice about something. I hoped one of the callers was Václav Havel. Malý's advice was always fit for a president.

30

THE DECONSTRUCTION OF COMMUNISM

THE COMMUNISTS held a Party Congress in late December and no one took any notice. How the world had changed in six weeks! Former Prime Minister Adamec took over as chairman of the Party, and the former head of the communist youth organization, Vasil Mohorita, was made General Secretary. The aging faction of neo-Stalinists was gone and the new leadership was untainted by the worst abuses of the past. What was more important was that they would ensure stability in the run-up to the elections. There would be no games. This was crucial, given the numbers of former StB officers and People's Militia who were kicking around looking for revenge.

In fact the Communist Party under its new leadership adopted a strategy of hunkering down and keeping a low profile. It tried to offer as small a target as possible during the anti-communist backlash. The Party's hope was that the collapse of support might be reversed years down the road when economic change brought tough times. What they could not foresee was the depth and breadth of the backlash. It would lead to the return of private property (nationalized in 1948) to the original owners and the vetting of all government officials for links to the former StB. (But the backlash would go beyond this and include highly-publicized attacks, by right-of-centre parties, on people who had once been Communist Party members under Dubček.) The strategy adopted by the Party at this stage permitted Civic Forum to get on with major initiatives without having to fight off a fifth column on the left. The Communist Party Congress also made an apology to the nation for its abuse of power for over forty years. With Havel waiting in the wings to become president, this seemed either totally irrelevant or simply pitiful.

The new government quickly demonstrated that it did not particularly care what the Communist Party thought about anything. Prime Minister Čalfa delivered a program to the Federal Assembly that made a clear break with the recent past. Czechoslovakia would become a liberal democracy, as it had been between the wars. The main goal for the government was the general election scheduled for June, 1990. But getting there was going to be half the fun. New laws were required on everything, not least to separate the legislative, executive, and judicial powers. Even basic laws on freedom of assembly, freedom of the press and freedom of speech, and laws on political parties and on the electoral system itself would have to be drafted. The citizens and lawmakers of this country were about to rediscover that pluralism was a complicated, intricate affair, with checks and balances where one least expected them.

With this daunting political agenda the government decided to leave the drafting of a new constitution until after the elections in June. This may have been, in retrospect, a big mistake. As difficult as it would have been to negotiate a new constitution, there was still at this time a common loyalty to the revolution and to its principal heroes. The stirrings of Slovak nationalism, aided by groups of exiles, was still a thing of the future. Nor had economic reform yet produced that unequal effect in the two republics that was to heighten the sense of Slovak injury. There was still, at this stage, enough shared experience and shared commitment to have made a constitution at least negotiable. Perhaps, in any case, it would have unravelled later on. But this was the last best chance to pull it off. None of us knew that, of course. Logic suggested that only a government with a mandate from the people should begin constitutional change. Although this was true in one sense, the momentum of the revolution would lose sufficient velocity by the time of the elections to make a new constitution impossible.

The practical day-to-day measures that the government took had an immediate and sensible effect. Religious orders were given the green light to reestablish themselves. For the first time in decades priests, nuns, and monks could be seen on the streets of Prague again. The traditional black and white garb came as a shock of differentiation in the post-totalitarian world of greys and browns. The government also turned its attention to the former StB, the state security service: thousands of its agents were let go, its files were quarantined, and the surveillance of otherwise law-abiding citizens was halted. And of course Marxist ideology was purged from the schools and workplaces, and Party cells were outlawed in factories and in the army.

It was difficult to predict where the government would act next, or how much debate might be inspired in the Federal Assembly. I felt sometimes as if the government was acting on a very long wish list, crossing off its priorities as it went. But the people seemed to be totally behind its leaders in this respect. Both wanted to recreate a "normal" Western society again as soon as possible. There was a degree of hit and miss, but a remarkable success rate too. The deputies of the Federal Assembly were putting in eighteen-hour days, virtually seven days a week. But their determination to seize the main chance kept them going, well beyond the physical limits of fatigue.

Prime Minister Čalfa, though he had emerged from the communist bureaucracy, somehow attuned himself to this new atmosphere. He quit the Communist Party about the time the Ambassador and I met him in the second week of December. He told us of his admiration for the golden age of the First Republic between the wars, when Czechoslovakia was democratic and capitalist. He was shy, and surprised by the twist of fate that had put him into this job. But he stated forcefully that the credo of his government would be to open doors, everywhere. The days of closed doors and delay were over. Čalfa noted that a change of attitude was necessary. People would have to begin to think differently about private property and material incentives. I thought that the change would come quickly. The Czechs still had all of the attributes of the quiet, industrious burgers of Central Europe for which they had once been famous. But I also thought of the change in thinking that Václav Malý sought. I wondered how a spiritual revolution could succeed at the very time when the attractions of material life suddenly beckoned. Perhaps Tomášek would be proved right after all.

A few days before Christmas, the whole country nestled down into a comfortable reverie. There were still sporadic student demonstrations in favour of this or that, but these were mostly celebrations and healthy exuberance. The Canadian journalist Paul Koring, from the Toronto *Globe and Mail*, finally decided that he had to go home to his fiancée. Paul had been through the revolution from that first day on November 17. With his departure, a phase of the revolution seemed to come to a close. Havel's election was only a formality now: a hoped-for Christmas present, waiting its proper moment.

31

PRESIDENT HAVEL

THE DAY OF VÁCLAV HAVEL'S ELECTION to the presidency was clear and cold. The Ambassador was invited to attend the ceremony on December 29 in the historic Vladislav Hall of the Prague Castle, where the Federal Assembly would vote. With everything I had been through over the last year, including Havel's trial in February, I decided that I could hardly sit back and watch the event on television. I went down to the Castle and found a huge crowd jamming the square in front of the large iron gates. There were parents with children on their shoulders, couples arm in arm, and flags and banners that gave the event a festive atmosphere. The cold provided the usually smiling Czech faces with some particularly rosy cheeks. I made my way slowly through the crowd and finally managed to squeeze in through the main gate. Loudspeakers outside broadcast the ceremony to the crowd. It would be followed by a mass in St. Vitus Cathedral, located within the walls of the Castle itself.

The Castle grounds consisted of a series of courtyards opening on to one another. They led to the Cathedral and to the main entrance of the Castle itself. The crowd outside the gates and in the courtyards was standing shoulder to shoulder. I made it as far as the second courtyard. There were banners and the red, white, and blue Czechoslovak flags everywhere. Some people were standing precariously on the rim of a large baroque fountain in the middle of the courtyard, waving a sheet that said "Havel for President." The courtyard itself was a soft white and beige colour, its architecture a monument to the Habsburg baroque style. Yet somehow Prague Castle was more gentle and whimsical, as if purged of its German, northern baroque antecedents.

I gave up trying to get to the inner courtyard and the Cathedral. There were just too many people. I was a little concerned that the crush on the inside would become intolerable as more and more people tried to move forward. As at the demonstrations in the bad old days, I was still looking instinctively for a quick exit if needed. I contented myself with staying amidst this jubilant Czech crowd in the second courtyard. They were out to witness the culmination of their struggles over long years, a victory over the forces that had sought to humiliate the basic sense of decency in every single one of them. Now that was over, like a bad dream, and they were filled with irrepressible joy.

The election in Vladislav Hall went off without a hitch. First, the Federal Assembly, under Dubček's chairmanship, voted for Havel. The many communist deputies voted for him too and it was unanimous. The next step was part of an old tradition. An official of the Federal Assembly was dispatched to bring Havel to the hall. He had been watching the proceedings on TV in an adjoining room. When he saw he was elected, he decided it was finally time to put on a tie. As he was escorted by the parliamentary official down a long corridor I wondered if Havel was thinking about the many times he had previously been escorted to a police station for interrogation. When he arrived at the entrance of the hall Dubček in his capacity as President of the Federal Assembly accompanied him down the centre aisle. Havel was wearing a new navy blue suit. He made a short speech. I noticed he looked a little uncomfortable in his new suit, but even this was refreshing. I do not think any of us could believe that what we were witnessing was actually happening. Then Havel made his way to the main balcony of the Castle to say a few words to the crowd outside. This was followed by the mass in St. Vitus Cathedral celebrated, appropriately enough, by Cardinal Tomášek.

For the first time it suddenly dawned on me and on the crowd around me that this magnificent Prague Castle, the seat of Czech kings, belonged to them again. It had been the domain of the Nazis during the war, and then of the communists after 1948. The people who had suffered both had been forbidden to enter its grounds. Husák had turned the Castle gardens into his own private domain. The communist army guards posted everywhere had only served as a reminder that some communists were more equal than others, and that communists in general were more equal than anyone. Now the sun shone in a clear sky. I think at least some of the people standing in that courtyard were relishing the moment when they had finally thrown out the impostors. Havel was a worthy successor to the line going back to Masaryk.

It was clear from the start that he did not regard position and power as an end in itself. I think that there was also a populist element in him, reflected, for example, in the way Civic Forum identified itself as a movement rather than a party. One of the first things that Havel did as President was to throw open the doors of the Castle to the citizens of the country, a populist touch reminiscent of U.S. President Andrew Jackson. On January 1, children from the neighbourhood were running up and down the long halls of Prague Castle, while their parents gawked at the huge glass chandeliers and paintings. None of them had seen any of this before. The Spanish Hall took one's breath away with its rococo cherubs and scintillating cut glass reflecting a white and gold panorama. It was just too sensuous for words.

As Havel came out on to the balcony on the day of his election, a roar of approval burst from the inner courtyard and spread to each successive courtyard, echoing off the walls. It swept by me and there were cheers and the muffled sound of mitts and gloves clapping. He spoke briefly from the balcony. I thought to myself that somehow the fairy tale had come true. Everything now seemed so easy and so light. There was no problem too great that could not be overcome. I looked at the children, thinking how lucky they were to have escaped the idiocy of the past forty years, to have escaped the subterfuge, and the psychological and the real violence perpetuated by dictatorship. Now freedom lit up their future like the warm rays of this December sun. These children, at least, would be whole and undamaged. As I stood in that courtyard, I inwardly rejoiced for them and for their parents.

New Year's Eve fell on the Sunday. It was two days after Havel's election. I went down to the Old Town Square with Ole Mikkelsen, my friend from the Danish Embassy. We imagined, rightly, that there might be some special festivities to mark the beginning of this New Year. Lynn and I had known Ole and Anne-Marie from the first days of our arrival in Prague. Our children were in school together, and we had shared some adventures and some good times during this amazing period in our lives. Ole had been with Pierre and me, and a friend from the American Embassy, Cliff Bond, on our ill-fated trip to Jan Palach's grave in January, 1989. I think that, following that escapade, Ole's Ambassador was none too happy about the notorious company he was keeping.

Soon after that confrontation with the StB, the executive assistant to the communist Foreign Minister Johanes had asked me if NATO had chosen Canada to give communist Czechoslovakia a hard time. Or did it just come naturally? I said it was the latter. In any event, as Ole and I came into the Old Town Square on New Year's Eve in that remarkable revolutionary year, we found that people were literally dancing in the streets. A giant Christmas tree lit with winding strings of white lights towered above the crowd in the middle of the square. Young people danced around it to the sound of traditional Czech folk music. A hot air balloon moored by a rope rose and fell, bobbing just above the songs and laughter of the crowd.

There were a lot of young people. They were dancing what looked like Czech reels, spinning around arm in arm. Czechoslovak flags were draped over the black statue of Jan Hus. There were some hand-painted sheets that called for free elections and the end of the Communist Party. Hus seemed to be supportive. Candles were burning everywhere, and some of the young people put them on the cobblestones and danced around the flickering flames. The flames lit up the flushed faces of others sitting around in a circle, clapping their hands. It was cold, but this was a celebration, and it was a celebration about being young and alive and being totally and fantastically free. Not that they, or I, understood what that meant. But they definitely felt it here and now and it would be seared into our memories no matter what happened after. They danced all night until they dropped.

Havel's New Year's Day address in his new role as President of the Republic was unlike any by a politician, ever, anywhere. It was by turns sobering, philosophical, and determined. It was called "For a Humane Republic." Havel began by saying that he had not been elected to lie to people. He then went on to describe how the country was not flourishing, how in fact the economy, the educational system, and the environment were all in an advanced state of decay. He added, "But this isn't the most important thing. The worst is that we are living in a contaminated moral environment. We have become morally sick because we have got used to saying one thing and thinking another. We've grown accustomed not to believe in anything, not to notice one another, to look out for ourselves only." Havel described how the regime had exploited and demeaned both human being and nature. He said that everyone had got used to a totalitarian system, accepted it as a fact, and thereby kept it going. "In other words, all of us—each to a different degree, naturally—are responsible for the functioning of the totalitarian machinery; none of us are just its victims, but all of us are at the same time its co-creators."

This was a tough lesson to deliver at the height of the revolution. Yet I think people were sufficiently big-hearted then to accept it. The admission was, for a time, liberating. But it did not quench the thirst for justice and for revenge, which would resurface barely six months later when the search for collaborators would begin in earnest. Nonetheless, at this moment, Havel was asking everyone to shoulder their part of the responsibility for the horrors of the past, and to participate in the making of the future. He said he was encouraged by two things brought to light by the revolution: the totalitarian system had not been able to erase human striving for something higher; and the humanist and democratic traditions of Czechoslovakia were seemingly only asleep.

Havel emphasized that, at last, "both our nations have straightened their backs by themselves" without the help of, or dependency on, a larger power. He referred to the fact that Masaryk based politics on morality and hoped that this approach, at the crossroads of Europe, might constitute a specifically Czechoslovak contribution to international politics. He then set out his main priorities. The first was, of course, free elections. But the second, significantly, concerned Czech and Slovak relations. Here Havel said that his task was "to see to it that we go into the elections as two genuinely autonomous nations which mutually respect each other's interests, national integrity, religious traditions and their symbols." He added that he felt a special obligation to ensure that the interests of the Slovak nation be respected. Havel emphasized the need to improve the lot of the disadvantaged and minorities. And he wanted to humanize the army, while strengthening the role of Czechoslovakia internationally as a country of peace and tolerance.

But his most controversial initiative was the declaration of a relatively broad amnesty for prisoners. His argument was that the system of justice had been less than perfect under the regime. He wanted to give the people who had been subjected to it a second chance. This gesture made sense against the background of Havel's own five years in prison, and it recalled the amnesties granted by kings at the time of their coronation. However the rise in crime during the first year of his presidency, due to many factors, would in the public mind be associated with Havel's amnesty. In fact people were going to find it difficult, generally, to live up to his demands for tolerance and understanding, at a time when political and economic change was sensitizing them to their vulnerability in the new order.

32

THE CANADIAN CONNECTION

TWO WEEKS into January, I caught wind of a possible visit by Havel to the United States. He had been to West and East Germany, Poland, and Hungary within days of his election. These were all neighbouring countries and their fates in the near term would be bound together, though in each case for differing reasons. For obvious symbolic reasons Havel had no desire to go too soon to Moscow, the other neighbour. He decided not to despite the fact that the withdrawal of Soviet troops from Czechoslovakia had already been raised both publicly and privately with Soviet officials. One might have also argued for a visit for the simple reason that the only pipeline providing oil to Czechoslovakia came from the USSR, and that the largest single market for Czechoslovak goods was still the USSR.

But the days of satellite diplomacy were definitely over, and the importance of symbolism at the beginning of Havel's term often overrode the more usual political calculations. What seems not to have been considered at all in the first few days of January was the symbolic importance of going first, as the new President, to Bratislava, in Slovakia. Unfortunately this symbolism would outlast all the rest and come back to haunt Havel in the months and years ahead. As for the possible visit to the U.S., I was convinced that if Havel went to the States, he would simply have to come to Canada on the same visit. I doubted that, given the distance and the government's agenda, there would be another opportunity. We sought and obtained quickly approval from headquarters to approach Havel with our offer.

I telephoned Saša Vondra, Havel's principal foreign policy advisor. I had known Saša from the days he was in the opposition. He had been a Charter 77 spokesperson in 1989 and had been a key figure that year in launching the petition "A Few Sentences." In part because of that effort, he was thrown into jail by the regime. When I had attended Havel's trial, Pierre had gone to Vondra's. We had also made several démarches to the communist government, under the Vienna document, seeking his release. Saša was in his twenties and rather quiet, and we got along well. I think it was because of the fact that we had known each other during the dark days. He had a habit, after the revolution, of saying in front of others that the Canadian Embassy had been "number one" in terms of its commitment to the dissidents. I have to admit this never failed to bring a smile to my face. I felt both modest and proud about this recognition, and gratified that Barry, Pierre and I had acted on our convictions.

I told Saša that Barry and I wanted to come and see him about the visit to North America. He invited us to the Castle the next day. On our arrival, we were surprised to find ourselves ushered into Havel's personal office. The furniture was modernist in style, in contrast with the baroque architecture. There was a huge expressionist painting on the wall by a Czech dissident artist. It exuded hot reds and pinks and oranges. It was an expressionist rendering of Adam and Eve in their innocent and naked state. I liked it very much. I remembered another painting by the same artist over Havel's couch in his apartment. This painting was also full of hot colours and there were two round balls on pedestals. The balls turned out to be talking heads. I liked this painting too, but I am not sure I would have wanted to live with it. Suddenly Havel walked in and Barry and I instinctively stood up. He was wearing his usual white shirt without a tie, his sleeves rolled up. Saša Vondra followed, wearing jeans as always. I felt a little overdressed in my blue suit. With friendly greetings and without any ceremony at all Havel invited us over to a couch and arm chairs around a coffee table. He took out his agenda and opened it on the table.

This was the way we planned the Czechoslovak President's official visit to Canada. It was no doubt unlike any other President's visit before or since. Michael Žantovský, Havel's spokesperson, joined us. We had known Michael when he was in the opposition, doubling as a journalist for Reuters. He had a soft spot for Canada, having attended McGill University in Montreal in the late 1960s.

Ambassador Barry Mawhinney, the author, and President Havel

Havel said that he wanted to stop in Iceland on the way to the U.S. A theatre in Reykjavik was putting on one of his plays and he was invited. Saša wondered if there was time to visit Canada and suggested that perhaps a few hours in Ottawa en route to Washington might be possible. Fortunately Michael intervened at this point. He argued that Canada was important. Havel would have to spend at least one night.

Among other things, Michael must have been thinking about the sizeable Czech and Slovak communities in Canada and the need to establish a new relationship with them. I knew that there were others in Havel's office who hoped their former countrymen might play a decisive role in assisting Czechoslovakia with its reintegration into the West. Following Michael's point that one night was the minimum for Havel's visit to Canada, there was a lot of discussion. We supported the idea that one or two nights simply had to be scheduled somehow. Eventually it was agreed that tentative plans for a visit to Ireland on the way might have to be changed, and that the dates for Iceland could be moved forward. Havel would arrive on a Sunday morning in Ottawa, stay the night, travel to Toronto for the day on Monday, and then leave for Washington late in the afternoon. It was still only one night, but there would be two full days of program.

The Sunday in Ottawa would be made up of official meetings, some contact with the local Czech and Slovak communities, and an official dinner. In Toronto we hoped to include the Premier of Ontario. We knew that Mr. Bata and other businessmen would want to be involved. Havel's own team organized a meeting at the University of Toronto with the large Czech and Slovak communities in that city. But the high point for Havel was to be a visit to the little publishing house of Josef and Zdena Škvorecký, 68 Publishers. This was the small renovated house in downtown Toronto that I had visited in 1989. It had kept Czechoslovak culture and history alive since 1968. Zdena and Josef published the books in Czech and in Slovak. These were novels and plays and poetry and political essays and histories and biographies and just about anything literary. But they all had one thing in common, which was that they were banned in communist Czechoslovakia.

Havel's plays and essays figured prominently in this list, not to mention Josef Škvorecký's own novels. Zdena was in a real sense the publisher. When I saw her during my visit the year previous, she came to the door apologizing, since she was covered up to the elbows with ink and grease from the printing machine. By publishing these works in their original language, the Škvoreckýs were very much keeping Czechoslovak culture alive. The whole literature of a nation would have remained unknown otherwise, its collective memory wiped out by the regime. The books produced by 68 Publishers circulated among the exiled communities in Canada, the United States, Australia, and Europe and so on. More crucially, they found their way to the readers held hostage in Czechoslovakia. I will never forget the surprise I felt in having managed to get a few of these books into Prague, by mail, during the fall of 1989. I brought them to our Pen International lunch that October, and they caused quite a stir with Havel, Klíma, and Urbánek. Our guests asked politely if the books might not be borrowed. They disappeared like hot cakes. What few books in any language ever managed to get into the country in those days were highly valued. The books published by Josef and Zdena in Czech and Slovak even more so. When he became President, Havel's pilgrimage to 68 Publishers in Toronto was to turn into a homecoming.

The irony of the struggle over Havel's agenda was that it was to be perfectly matched by a struggle over similar agendas in Ottawa. Wrapped up as we were in events in Prague, it was easy for us to forget that politicians everywhere had their own priorities, and that these affected their schedules. Czechoslovakia was a fascinating place to be in at that moment. But to many in the West it was still a far away country about which little was known. As with every official visit, we had a hard time getting the program in place, and the Sunday arrival did not help. There was the additional pressure, felt most keenly at the Canadian Embassy in Prague, that was created by the need to ensure that Canada was reacting quickly to the sweeping changes affecting Central and Eastern Europe. I was sensitive to the fact that high-level visitors, theatre troops, orchestras, and political advisors had started arriving in Prague from all points of the compass in the first days of Havel's presidency. At long last, the plans for Havel's visit to Canada were confirmed by both sides, and we began working hard at hammering out the details.

The objective of the visit to Canada was simple: to affirm the special bond between our two countries. But the visit would also reveal a troubling sign for the future, in the form of calls within the Slovak community in Canada for more autonomy, if not outright independence, for Slovakia itself. At the Embassy, of course, we wanted the visit to dwell on the common experiences and shared values linking out two countries. Canadians of Czech and Slovak origin, many of whom had left their homeland at different times throughout this century to start a new life in Canada, constituted an important human bridge. There were other ties, too, which gave the relationship a flavour all its own. One was the exodus of people to Canada after the Warsaw Pact invasion of Czechoslovakia in 1968. These people had sought asylum from political persecution. They had left family and friends behind to begin from scratch in a faraway country about which they knew little.

What made these immigrants different from most was the fact that they were practically barred from any contact with their homeland. Virtually all had assumed that this break was final. These people were among the most surprised at the suddenness of the change. Nothing could return the lost twenty years, however. Parents had passed away, friendships had faded. Even spouses who remarried were persecuted in their turn for being related to those now in Canada. Indeed the relatives who remained behind had the worst of both worlds: many lost their jobs or had careers blocked from further advancement because a brother or daughter had defected. Did they take solace in the personal freedom won by their kin? I wonder.

Against this background, Havel's visit brought friends and relatives together again, both symbolically and in reality. They were finding each other again, and one could say that together they were finding history, too. Czechoslovakia had been thrown back into time now that it had broken free from the glacis of communism, and from the national conflicts of World War II. The revolution signified that Czechoslovakia was moving back to its rightful place at the heart of Europe. It had long been a political and spiritual crossroads, and Czechoslovak history had frequently been traversed by events that affected other nations in Europe and beyond.

The irony was that Czechoslovakia had been the only democratic country in central Europe between the wars. Now, belatedly, it was to become so again, seeking to catch up with its central European neighbours, Germany and Austria. History had not been kind to Czechoslovakia the last time around. Its betrayal by the West in 1938, its absorption into Stalin's empire in 1948, and its conquest and humiliation in 1968, all of this had been history in the guise of a nightmare, and a nightmare from which its people were only now beginning to awake. Under the communist regime, history, and the beating heart of Europe, had come to a stop. Hope for the future had simply vanished and many had lost heart, in Czechoslovakia and in Canada. Many, but not all.

A few brave individuals inside Czechoslovakia kept up the fight at great personal sacrifice. There was a Canadian connection here, too. A number of Canadians, such as Zdena and Josef Škvorecký and others, did not forget their friends and acquaintances far away, or their ideals. Somehow, across an ocean, both sides shared the memory and dream of a free Czechoslovakia, and the desire for a whole and living culture. Gordon Skilling, at the University of Toronto, was another who devoted himself to the importance of the democratic opposition in Czechoslovakia. How right all of these people turned out to be.

The Canadian government, on behalf of all Canadians, played its role as well. We took a tough stand on human rights. We held the communist regime to the commitments it had made under international law. We supported the opposition in every way. I remember debates in Prague's diplomatic community about whether it was worth it. How could support for a band of utopian intellectuals change anything? For these diplomats, realpolitik and strategic gains were the only factors; or so the argument went. But we did support the opposition, and at the end of the day one could say about the little band of heroes that made up the opposition: "Never has so much been owed by so many to so few."

These few were not only brave, but modest. It is said now that all Czechs and Slovaks, together, accomplished the great task. That is true, and many did come forward to be counted at the crucial moment. But it was also true that the persistent expansion of the horizons of freedom was the personal affair of a relatively few individuals, who suffered persecution and jail over years on end. Theirs is the lesson of the value and strength of human dignity. And it is something about which we should not be mistaken. It is a lesson not only for the people of Central Europe. It is as much a lesson for the sometimes blasé and disenchanted people of the West. For us, political struggle and personal sacrifice is a fading memory and "historic" in the negative sense of that word. It is, for us, no longer alive.

Some Canadians understood this lesson perfectly. The common struggle that linked Canadians and Czechoslovaks on both sides of the ocean can be best characterized as, "words, words, words." It was no coincidence that many involved in the fight against repression in Czechoslovakia, and in the revolution, were intimately associated with words, with the positively liberating nature of literature, and with the power of language. It was symbolic, and perfectly appropriate, that the revolutionary President was a playwright and essayist, and that Canadian assistance was led by writers.

In an essay written a month before the revolution, Havel noted prophetically that in some situations, "words can prove mightier than ten military divisions." And they did. The revolution was in no small part prepared by his words and those of others. Perhaps this explains the rapidity of the change that occurred, and its peaceful character. Later, in the same essay, Havel said, "all important events in the real world are always spearheaded in the realm of words." This belief was shared on both sides of the Atlantic, and it was the key to unlocking the prison of repression.

This story of words, and their power, was not over with the revolution. Words again made history in the first months of 1990. Election issues were debated, political and economic laws were drafted that affected every citizen intimately, and the government took dramatically new stands on international issues. The approach to age-old problems was fresh, a freshness which seemed to draw its strength from firmly held moral values and from a lively and rejuvenated spiritual life.

Havel said that responsibility for and towards words is a task which is intrinsically ethical. He carried this admonition into politics with great effect. In so doing, he resurrected Czechoslovakia's traditional role as the spiritual crossroads of Europe. But one was also led to conclude that the national conflict between Czechs and Slovaks after the revolution was in its way, too, a sign of the times for Europe and for us. The only question was whether such national politics were the last gasp of the nation-state or its renaissance.

I had always felt that Canada, with its people coming from all the corners of Europe, and all the corners of the globe, was linked to the crossroads of Central Europe. The liberation of that geographical and spiritual centre from East-West confrontation, itself global, was also our liberation. I think this is what Havel meant in his first speech as President, when he talked about the rebirth of this spiritual crossroads as Czechoslovakia's special contribution. It was also a contribution to history, which has so often been made on Czechoslovak soil.

Canada was a part of that struggle for freedom, and many Canadians wanted to be a part of the history which had come back to Czechoslovakia. These were the ties, perhaps only fleeting, between a young country and an old country made young again. There was much to learn from each other, materially and spiritually. And the rush of Canadians to Czechoslovakia in 1990, whether as volunteer teachers, relatives, or businessmen, contributed to a crescendo of mutual rediscovery. We found that we shared much, for better and for worse.

It was this opening up on to a new world that we hoped would characterize Havel's visit to Canada that February. As chargé d'affaires during the Ambassador's absence in Canada, my role was to see Havel off at the airport. Knowing that the new President, the ministers, and the staff accompanying him would not object, I decided to bring Lynn, Kevan and Laura. Kevan was six and Laura was three and they tore around the VIP lounge as children do at that age. For a brief moment, I got them on to a chesterfield for a family photo with Havel. He was pleased to accommodate. Then they were off again, giving the high five to several ministers as they ran by. Havel was sipping a glass of orange juice while we talked. I blanched at one point when Laura waltzed up and nonchalantly drank from his glass. She was thirsty, she said.

I burdened Havel with a book or two. One was the traditional book of Canadian landscape photographs and the other the no less traditional novel by Margaret Atwood. We talked about the program and about Canadian politics. I mentioned that Lynn was Québécoise (a Massicotte), from Quebec City. The constitutional debate in Canada was sensitive at the time, although this was hardly news. He avowed he would not touch the subject even if his life depended on it. I nodded and said that this was probably a wise decision. As always, he seemed caught up in his own thoughts. He looked uncomfortable in his suit and tie, obviously new and rather stiff. His French cuffs extended well beyond the sleeves of his suit. It appeared as if the clothes had been bought over the telephone. Seeing him this way, you could be sure he was longing for the moment when he would change back into his sweater and jeans.

The government ministers accompanying Havel were no less unorthodox. They were mostly self-educated intellectuals, or theorists who had survived in the bowels of the Academy of Sciences. A few were former communist functionaries and were part of the government of national understanding, as it was called. I liked most of the ministers on a personal basis. But I was staggered by what lay ahead of them. The political culture of the country might be marginally improved by passing a few laws, but changing the economy from top to bottom and revolutionizing the material interests of the population was something else.

For all that, Havel and his team climbed on to the waiting plane buoyed by hope and a broadly shared unity of purpose. Their trip to North America was in some ways a homecoming too: they would meet for the first time in twenty years those who had worked with them, and supported them, to keep the flame alive. They would revel in the friendships found again, and stumble a little over the differences that had opened up over the years. But as the plane took off, I was enthused by the human potential that this visit would unleash.

33

HUMAN BRIDGES

IN ADDITION to the increasing number of official visits in both directions, I soon felt that the most tangible Canadian involvement in post-revolutionary Czechoslovakia was occurring at the grass roots. This reflected not only a strong interest by many Canadians in what was going on in the world. There was also a degree of personal commitment that was refreshing. Two endeavours stood out in this regard. The first was a truly visionary scheme that worked. The second became recognized as nothing less than a Czechoslovak institution.

The visionary scheme was hatched by John Hasek, a retired major from the Canadian Armed Forces and of Czech origin. John came back to Czechoslovakia for a visit within days of the revolution. He quickly got involved with Civic Forum and worked as one of their spokespersons. But he wanted to organize some kind of specifically Canadian contribution to the cause. He asked his Czech friends what they needed most at that moment. They replied unequivocally that what they needed most urgently, and what was key to whatever other assistance they might receive, was English-language training. John was off and running. Within days, he came to see me at the Embassy. His idea was to create something like a peace corps of Canadian volunteers to teach English in Czechoslovakia. They would not be, nor could they be in the circumstances, people with teaching certificates or specialists in teaching English. They would be Canadians from every walk of life who would offer conversational English. Many Czechs had the basics, but what they needed was to learn from native speakers. The volunteers would pay their own airfare, but once they arrived they would be housed and provided with a small salary in Czech crowns by the Czechoslovak government.

I asked John how many people he had in mind. I thought that 20 or 30 spread around the country would have a real impact, if we could find them. John said that he was aiming for 300, maybe 500 volunteers. I said he must be joking. This would be far and away the biggest single Canadian initiative ever launched in Czechoslovakia. The logistics of finding the Canadians in the first place, and then organizing their arrival, meeting them, finding places for them to teach, to live, etc., etc., were formidable in a country such as Czechoslovakia was at that time. Communist systems were still in place, though being dismantled, while Western ways of doing things had not yet been created. During these revolutionary days one occasionally had the impression that nothing worked at all and that just about everything was being done ad hoc. More immediately, I was concerned that all of these well-intentioned but innocent Canadians were going to have a massive case of culture shock and land on the doorstep of the Canadian Embassy looking for help. But John was a man possessed by an idea. He was not going to be put off by the recalcitrance of a bureaucrat. He caught the next plane to Canada in order to launch "Education for Democracy."

John's strategy was brilliant. He managed to get on the CBC radio show, Morningside. John was the kind of person who could sell Niagara Falls, and I had no trouble imagining the success he would have over the airwaves. The offer, in a sense, was irresistible. For the price of the airfare one could, for once, make a real contribution to what one knew was the right thing. And then there were the romantic beauties of Prague, in a country governed by a playwright. One did not have to join the army or the foreign service to find adventure overseas and gain a little experience. John had found the perfect match between the needs of Czechoslovaks at a crucial moment in their history and that international civic duty that seemed to be a genetic endowment in all Canadians. Within weeks of his broadcast, there were hundreds of Canadians teaching English from Plzeň to Košice.

Most of the volunteers were either young and just out of university, or elderly and retired. I suppose both sorts of people were, at this time in their lives, relatively free from the usual constraints that governed others. Maybe both the young and the old had a better appreciation of what was really important in the larger scheme of things and they knew they wanted to be a part of it. I met a lot of these volunteers, and they came in all shapes and sizes. Some were wild. But at bottom they shared one characteristic, and it was a reflection of what Havel stood for. They all wanted to help people they did not know, and they all wanted to make a new life. It was a remarkable display of civic duty. For their part, the Czechs and Slovaks could not have been happier with this display of Canadian friendship and the media gave it great coverage. And of course the Canadian Embassy basked in the reflected glory.

The fact that the volunteers were for the most part not professionals proved to be immaterial in those early days. It is difficult now to appreciate the extent to which Czechoslovakia had been isolated from the West under communism. These Canadians going off to the far reaches of the country provided many Czechs and Slovaks with their first close encounters with people from the other side of the former iron curtain. And because they were typically good-natured Canadians, this was the best way to promote Canada. I remember one young chap, about twenty, who was wearing a baseball cap and chewing gum. I could not decide who was having the culture shock, the Canadian, or the Czechs to whom he was explaining the finer points of North American life. He told me his students in Plzeň really liked learning English. There was only one thing they liked more: drinking beer. So he moved his class into a pub. Now they were in heaven, he said.

There was another, very distinguished gentleman who came to see me at the Embassy. A Canadian, he had spent his career in the foreign service and was retired. Now aged seventy, he was relishing this opportunity to be overseas again. We talked for a while and he said his students in Prague were wonderful. There was only one problem. The Czech government had assigned him his accommodation and it was very comfortable indeed. It turned out that he had to share a very small apartment with a rather attractive twenty-four year-old Czech woman. This had been going on, happily, for some months now. It seemed that he had never got around to telling his wife, who was back in Canada, about his attractive room-mate. His wife had just phoned to announce that she was making a surprise visit to Prague to see him. He threw up his hands in mock horror and said she was to arrive tomorrow. I laughed and could tell from his world-weary sense of humour, seasoned by thirty years in foreign affairs, that he would work it out somehow.

The other example of the Canadian contribution to revolutionary Czechoslovakia was also characterized by authentic civic commitment. This was a travelling exhibition devoted to Zdena and Josef Škvorecký's publishing house, 68 Publishers. The idea for the exhibit had been Pierre's, and it perfectly captured the unique relationship between the two countries. In Prague the exhibit was set up in the Museum of National Literature. This was located in the Strahov Monastery on Petřín Hill. Somehow the modest, highly personal endeavour which was 68 Publishers fitted in perfectly with the Romanesque arches and stone walls of the monastery. The monastery was once again to house books that kept the thread of humanist thought alive during a time of darkness. But the idea behind the exhibit belonged entirely to the twentieth century. For those who could not visit this bit of Czech history in Toronto, history would come to them.

There were documents and newspaper clippings describing the founding of the publishing house after the Soviet invasion in 1968. Glass cases were full of the many books published over twenty years. These included books of Havel's plays and political essays. Most of the material for the exhibit came from the Škvoreckýs themselves, or from Luba Hussel at the University of Toronto Library's Rare Book Room. The opening of the exhibit coincided with the return of Zdena and Josef Škvorecký to Czechoslovakia, and it was a triumph. Virtually the who's who of dissident life and the revolution turned out, including Havel himself. I remember him standing and looking at his books in the glass cases. It was as if his literary life was laid out before him, the peaks of mountainous effort. Indeed, the exhibit was a reminder of the drama of writing books under communism. The first challenge was to avoid having one's manuscript confiscated by the StB. This involved elaborate precautions such as multiple hand-written or typed copies and several secret hiding places. There were few copying machines allowed into Czechoslovakia, and access to them was tightly controlled. And then there was the problem of smuggling the manuscripts out of the country.

At any step, the regime might discover the network of couriers, and confiscation of the material could lead to charges of anti-socialist subversion and a stint in jail. Being a writer in Czechoslovakia in those days was truly a vocation. Just knowing that a manuscript was safely beyond the border was about all one could hope for. That the Škvoreckýs would turn it into a real book, and that this book might just make it back into the country and into the author's own hands, was nothing short of miraculous. Zdena and Josef understood the

Václav Havel, Zdena and Josef Škvorecký, and Islay and Barry Mawhinney, at the opening of the 68 Publishers exhibit in Prague

miracle, better than anyone in the West. But to their fellow publishers in the West, they seemed not only to be losing money, but also were apparently obsessed with publishing obscure authors writing in an incomprehensible language from a small Central European country locked in the grip of the Soviet Union. In so doing they single-handedly saved a national culture from extinction and preserved the collective memory of a people.

In the early days after the revolution, there was another kind of contribution that was less welcome and less than altruistic. From all over the West groups of wealthy entrepreneurs arrived to look over investment opportunities. Many were rather well known international names and had little difficulty obtaining meetings with ministers, even with Havel himself. But these visits were for the most part unsuccessful. I remember one group, typical of the others, that met with Saša Vondra and with Havel's principal economic advisor. They wanted to build a huge shopping centre in Prague. It would be linked with the airport by a new eight-lane highway. There would be conference halls and hotel towers and highway overpasses and so on. I could see the eyes of the Czechs glaze over.

Finally, Saša interrupted to say that, in the past, they had associated the building of glass and steel abominations in historic Prague with the communists. The communists had actually succeeded in putting a highway through the middle of the city. With some Western "help," they also threw up some towering and exceedingly ugly hotels. Saša hoped this experience would not be repeated. The businessmen reacted by agreeing totally. Yes, there would never be such eyesores again in Prague. But what about environmentally friendly hotels? Alas, the game was up, and the businessmen set out for Berlin to promote their schemes there.

This did not mean that the government, encouraged by Klaus, did not support a fast transition to the market. It did. But those who had been associated with Charter and the opposition were particularly sensitive to what development might mean for the city and for its citizens. This was in line with Civic Forum's position on political issues: the grass roots mattered regardless of the prerogatives of the market. Pressure from citizens in various districts of the city would ensure that no office towers or modern hotels would replace the historic character of the neighbourhoods. This policy would hold despite the obvious need to accommodate the flood of tourists rediscovering Prague.

For the most part, the communists had done little either to restore or to demolish historic buildings. The whole city was a museum of European architecture. War had left it virtually untouched. On any block you could see a medieval house beside a renaissance arcade between baroque palaces facing art nouveau apartments across the street. But it was all in desperate need of restoration after forty years of neglect. The old town was a maze of scaffolding. Yet, under the communists, I never once saw any workmen on them and never once in my time in Prague did I see any of the scaffolding come down. My theory about this was that the scaffolding was symbolic of the good intentions of late socialism. The regime no doubt assumed that, like the state, the scaffolding would one day whither away. The buildings would no doubt be restored by each according to his ability for each according to his need.

The fact that the communists had left the city almost untouched was definitely the lesser of possible evils. What they did do was bad enough. If they had been less Stalinist, and less suspicious of capitalism, they might have transformed the entire city with their legendary bad taste. The apparatchik browns and sputnik aesthetics were enough to make one want to run screaming into the street. The revolution, from this standpoint, came just in time to begin the real restoration of this wondrous city before it was too late. But the goal in the first months of Havel's presidency was to keep development to a human scale, to make development fit into the city rather than to let development destroy it. The slower and more meticulous approach to restoration carried the day.

I think there was also an underlying political reason for this. People felt that their cultural patrimony had been returned to them at long last. They were not about to turn around and sell it to carpet-baggers from the West. Neighbourhoods would be consulted before any hotels or highways were planned. The overwhelming desire was to humanize as much as possible the change that was upon them, to make the market serve civic life rather than the reverse. I think this approach deterred some foreign businessmen from investing during those first months. But others were willing to adapt to a reawakened citizenry. Many of the most successful were German businessmen willing to stay the course, over years if necessary, in order to gain a foothold.

In those early months of the revolution, John Hasek, the Škvoreckýs, and the first forays of investors were typical of the human bridge that had sprung up linking Czechoslovakia and Canada. Hasek's "English for Democracy" drew on the best in Canadian voluntarism, the perfect trampoline to help launch Czechoslovakia's entry into the Western world. The Škvoreckýs returned a cultural patrimony to a nation, and so helped make a people whole again, in mind and spirit. More Canadian investors would come in the future, and those would succeed who had a feel for the human ties that connected our countries.

And ties there were. The ties of family were the most obvious. But there was another tie, that was evident even in the dark days. This was the startling similarity in political traditions between the two countries, traditions based in both cases more on humane principles than on interests. Both Canadians, and those Czechoslovaks in the tradition of Masaryk and Havel, practiced moral politics. Canada's obsession with human rights was one dimension of this. But so was Havel's total commitment to their defense. It was this common conviction that political action should be rooted in moral principle that defeated distance and bridged the Atlantic. For a variety of reasons, Czechoslovaks and Canadians had come to share the same political culture, a culture based not on the realpolitik of big powers, but on principle-centred political leadership.

34

A NEW/OLD POLITICAL SYSTEM

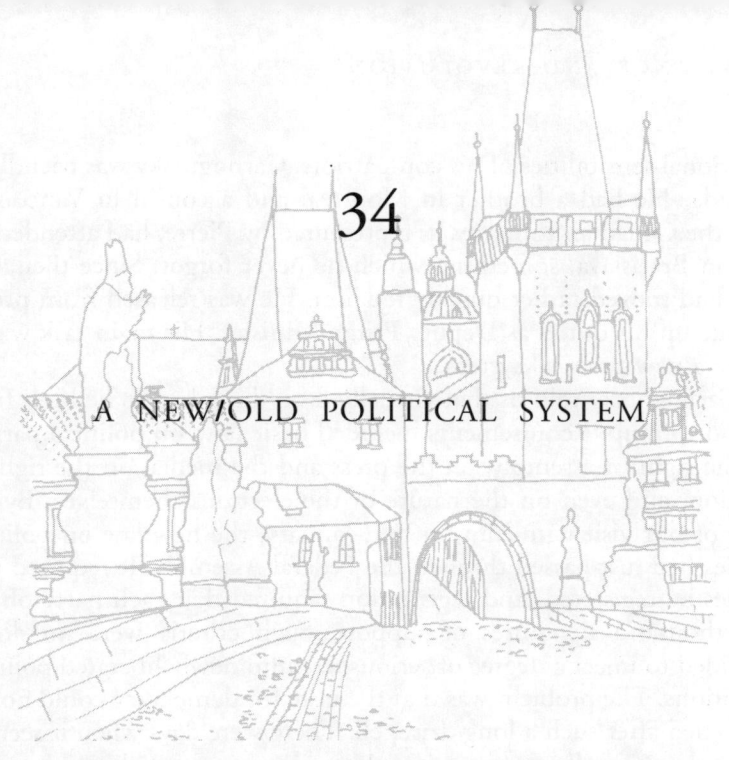

ALL NEW VENTURES, whether cooperative, cultural, or commercial, faced one thing in common. Newly liberated Czechoslovakia was a very politicized country. Everyone had rediscovered politics and no local decision, however insignificant, could escape scrutiny. In reaction to what had been an irresponsible and illegitimate regime people now wanted a say in everything. There could be no interest other than civic interest in any decision, large or small. That was the only criterion, and at this point it displaced the left-right spectrum we took for granted in the West. It was still too early for people to adopt views about the proper roles of governments and markets with respect to specific issues. The first priority was to ensure that decisions were transparent and that citizens had a say.

This sine qua non applied no less to preparations for the elections in June. Deputy Prime Minister Ján Čarnogursky, a Slovak, was in charge. Barry and I went to see him in January to get a sense of what lay ahead. Carnogursky was ideal for the job due to his legal background. But he was also one of the few Slovak dissidents under the communist regime, as well as being a nationalist and an ardent Catholic. He seemed to possess all of the qualities that would enable him to act as a powerful voice for the Slovak cause. His principal difficulty was that he was a quiet, temperate man, one might even say ascetic. In the end this personal style failed to resonate with the emotional sensibilities of his compatriots. Carnogursky was friendly to Canada. He had a brother in Montreal and a cousin in Vancouver. And the Canadian Embassy, as represented by Pierre, had attended his trial in Bratislava, something which he never forgot. Since then, history had moved rather quickly for him. He was released from prison to take up his duties as Deputy Prime Minister. His main task was to create a new political system.

Carnogursky told us that virtually everything had to be built from the bottom up. Requirements included basic laws on political parties, on the right of assembly, on the press and the media, on the right of petition, and even on the nature of the elections themselves. By the time of our visit with him, in mid-January, the new law on political parties had just passed through the Federal Assembly. It required that parties be registered, and registration required that each party obtain one thousand signatures of support. Such criteria were no doubt intended to inject a degree of seriousness into newly liberated political ambitions. The problem was that the taste for democracy could not be quenched after such a long dry spell. There were days when it seemed to me that virtually everyone was determined to found his or her own party. In fact, this was consistent with Havel's vision of a new age of independent candidates immune from the baser political calculations of traditional parties. Many of the new parties reflected the sheer exhilaration of standing for anything. I wondered about the membership of the Friends of Beer Party and the Erotic Party. But who could deny them the exuberance of the historical moment?

The experts drafting the electoral law turned naturally to the proportional system that had been in place between the wars. It had worked well for the country when it was an island of political stability in Central Europe. But the internal and external pressures on the nation were now very different. I was not convinced that current problems could be solved by a proportional electoral system. I think Havel was of the same view. It was here, as on other issues, that Masaryk's influence came into play in those early days.

Masaryk's so-called Golden Age was connected in most people's minds with the system of proportional representation then in place. Who could doubt the wisdom of his political vision? He was born of a Czech father and a Slovak mother and he was literally the founding father of the nation. In this role, he was unassailable as an authority within the Czechoslovak political tradition. But by the time of the revolution Masaryk had been dead for fifty years. During the intervening period, characterized mostly by enforced political paralysis, there had been subterranean political change, like the imperceptible shift of tectonic plates. Havel and the nation would discover a whole new set of fault-lines that were totally unexpected. Moreover, a proportional system was not necessarily the best after forty years of political inexperience.

Carnogursky said that the splintering of parties was the greatest threat. In principle, a proportional system would simply encourage small parties to carry on, even if they won just a few seats. Everyone wanted to experiment with politics. It seemed there was no one willing to abide by party rules that were not of his or her own making. Already, there were upwards of seventy political parties registered five months before the elections. This meant, he said, that any government capable of obtaining a majority in the Assembly would almost certainly be the product of a coalition. And all coalitions were inevitably unstable. The other problem facing the drafters of the new electoral law was the need to allow for the election of independent candidates, no easy thing in a proportional system where people voted for parties. Havel placed great store on the role of independent deputies in the new Assembly. He hoped that independents, free of the influence of party machines and party lines, would see the issues for what they were and vote both wisely and ethically.

This difficulty of trying to make room for such candidates within a proportional system perfectly symbolized the uneasy relationship of the revolution to the historical past. Havel valued independence of conscience and criticized party discipline because the Communist Party had been the epitome of machination and personal interest masquerading as civic duty. This anti-party bias was reflected later in Civic Forum's campaign slogan: "Parties are for Party Members. Civic Forum is for Everyone." In a conversation with Saša Vondra at this time I was struck by the seriousness with which this issue was being treated in the Castle. Not only were independents to be an important part of the new system; Saša was wondering out loud whether the electoral law should permit party politics at all.

Here was an instance in which the individualism of dissidence came close to revolutionizing the entire political system. It would have involved throwing the tried and true system inherited from the past out of the window. Would such a defenestration have saved the country from its future internal conflicts? Probably. But it was too radically new at a time when people were turning toward Masaryk's golden age for guidance, continuity, and tradition. I suppose the revolution was as conservative in some respects as it was creative in others. Still, the way the past was resurrected after forty years of institutional amnesia was no less revolutionary.

Listening to Saša speak, I finally grasped what Havel had in mind for the country. This was to be one of those historical watersheds in the life of a nation, a time of liberation and great political change. Enormous decisions lay ahead that could set the course for literally a hundred years. Hence it was vital that deputies vote on the basis of far-sighted judgment informed by conscience. It was as if Havel had in mind the period of the American Revolution and the framing of the American constitution, when great individuals emerged during the tumult of the times to fashion a truly unique form of government and seal the destiny of a people.

I think that, for Havel, party politics were just too mundane when compared with the unique opportunity that confronted the nation. He hoped that great-souled individuals, independent spirits, would rise above day-to-day business to craft a simple and profound expression of the common aspirations of Czechs and Slovaks. It was a worthy vision. But I think that Havel was one of the few political figures, if not the only one, who at that time would have been able to realize it. The less inspiring conflict and interplay of interests—regional, sectoral, ideological, and personal—would win the day.

Many such interests coalesced in Slovakia behind the demand for greater autonomy. Already, in January 1990, Carnogursky was taking the political temperature there. He had just founded the Christian Democratic Movement. He said that his approach was to build up from the grass roots. If there was sufficient commitment, the movement would become a party. Too many parties, he said, were being formed and all of them from the top down. During our conversation with him, we asked whether or not broad political movements, such as Civic Forum or the Christian Democratic Movement, might not themselves lead to monopolies of power.

Carnogursky thought not. There were already parties forming outside of the movements. He thought that the greater danger was the unknown strength of the Communist Party. Whatever support it retained, especially in the countryside, was still untested. This support could be magnified by the apathy of voters turned off by the sterility of politics over the past forty years. Carnogursky said that Civic Forum would have to counter the danger of indifference by fostering political pluralism within its ranks. The trick was to back away from direct political action, such as demonstrations, while keeping Forum from splitting up before the June elections. Only through civic participation, especially in the countryside, could disenchantment be overcome.

As to Havel's future, Carnogursky thought that he was basically a literary man thrown into politics by chance. He believed Havel would return to literary life when the political situation was stable. In this respect he shared Václav Malý's view. But Carnogursky went on to say that if Havel stayed on it would be a sign that the political life of the nation was not yet healthy. For the moment, the prognosis was good. No tensions had yet arisen between the Czechs and Slovaks. During the revolution there had been a common goal and both sides had worked together enthusiastically. Carnogursky concluded from this that when political movements were responsive to the grass roots, tensions could be avoided. Listening to the argument, I thought to myself that the corollary was also true. Party leaders, divorced from grass roots control, would likely, even inevitably, stir up trouble. And this was exactly what happened.

At the end of our conversation, Carnogursky made a point to thank the Embassy and Canada for their support over the difficult years. Pierre had been virtually the only Western diplomat to attend Carnogursky's trial in Bratislava. Such actions had been hugely important in those days, both for the individuals in question and for the human values they were trying to uphold. Carnogursky's compliment, like the many others we received those days, was mixed with a strong affection for all things Canadian.

This affection was fostered by a plethora of family ties that linked both countries, as well as a similarity of national traits. Both Czechs and Slovaks tended to be deferential, and uncertain about their identity. They tended to focus on their weaknesses rather than their strengths. The shared sense of uncertainty, the distinct lack of national self-confidence, led Canadians, Slovaks and Czechs to let down their barriers with each other, something that would have been unthinkable with the British, French, Germans, or Americans. Being a Canadian in Czechoslovakia had its own special privileges. It was a connection that was to take on a new meaning, and seriousness, as the national question came to the fore in both countries.

35

THE ECONOMIC CHALLENGE

THE ECONOMIC SITUATION of Czechoslovakia at this time could be summarized as an unworkable centrally planned economy, shoddy goods, antiquated factories and high levels of energy consumption and pollution. Could the new government put in place a market economy within two to three years as promised? I wondered. And where to begin? Probably everywhere. There was already talk of devaluing the currency so as to make it nearly convertible with Western currencies. There were also plans to introduce a restrictive budget so as to force state enterprises to rationalize operations before breaking them up and selling them off. But none of this could be done without financial assistance from the International Monetary Fund (IMF), and from Western countries.

Even if the state enterprises survived this shake-up they would only last as long as their ability to trade. And this was far from assured. The USSR, easily the largest customer, could no longer afford to buy Czech goods, now offered for hard currency. Meanwhile, the Czechs had to begin paying for their Soviet oil in dollars. Aside from the question of the balance of trade, where was the hard currency to come from? Trade with the former East Germany also fell. This was due to the enforced constriction of that economy and the new option adopted there of "importing" goods from West Germany. The technical assistance and training offered to Czechoslovakia by Canada and other Western countries was all fine and good but what the Czechs needed more was good old-fashioned trade. Without trade all of the cooperative assistance in the world could not keep an economy going.

The difficulty facing Havel and his government in early 1990 was that the economy, indeed the whole society, was organized to function as an integral part of the Soviet empire. Now there was a great rush to throw off this unnatural subjugation to the East and return to the more traditional embrace of the West. Psychologically, too, people felt that everything Soviet or East European (hence almost everything) was bad, and everything Western was therefore good. The latter was an assumption that did not necessarily follow from the first. But it was easier to fulfil the desire to return to Western political traditions than to adopt Western economic organization, or to accept the social dislocation that often accompanied it. The political laws were well drafted, were based on consensus, and passed through parliament like clockwork. The newspapers, too, seemed to adopt the habits of their Western counterparts overnight, for better and for worse. In the early days those habits were decidedly yellow. Newspapers in particular took their independence seriously and pushed the limits. In fact, when it came to libel, there were no limits. And everyone, with the sometime exception of Havel, was fair game.

The creaking Soviet-style economy of Czechoslovakia could not be easily transformed into a modern Western economy. Certainly all Czechs seemed to want a market economy, tomorrow if they could have it. But their starting point was a confusing set of administrative and ad hoc arrangements blessed by the heirs of Stalin and Brezhnev. These uneconomic arrangements had a rather peculiar effect on the family. Before the revolution people were afraid to express their opinions outside the close-knit circle of the family for fear of financial reprisals or worse. The duplicity required to safeguard even a modest standard of living put tremendous strain on relations between parents and children; it was difficult for the younger generation to understand their elders having to pay such a high personal price. There was no room for material or spiritual aspirations. Even travel outside the communist bloc was banned for almost all except communist officials. The result was often alcoholism and divorce.

After the revolution, it seemed that, paradoxically, the opening up of society brought families together by unblocking the normal channels of initiative and by simply making "success" possible. Any kind of success. This renaissance of the family, though subject to the strain of new demands for independence and freedom from spouses and children, became itself a kind of microcosm of the revolution. An artificial complicity was being exchanged for new responsibilities at work and at home. But this sense of responsibility was not something that could be inculcated overnight, especially in the first days of new-found liberty.

36

THE REBIRTH OF PARTY POLITICS

ALTHOUGH THE GOVERNMENT'S AGENDA of political legislation was well under control party, politics in the spring of 1990 were wild and furious. It was impossible to predict who would be the big winners and losers in the June elections. Certainly Civic Forum and its Slovak counterpart, Public Against Violence, remained popular. But who could say what might strike the fancy of a new and untested electorate in the months to come? The proliferation of political parties, which numbered over one hundred in May, expressed the sheer sense of unlimited possibility. At first sight, this multiplication of parties in a proportional system seemed to portend the fragmentation of democratic forces. It also appeared to provide a recipe for unstable government coalitions. But there were a number of reasons why neither of these things would result, at least initially.

The proliferation of parties was due to a Czechoslovak tradition of political clubs, reaction against one-party rule, and the requirement of only one thousand signatures for the registration of a party. The new electoral law, however, would go a long way towards separating the wheat from the chaff. Havel noted at the time that even two hundred parties would be understandable at this stage in Czechoslovakia's political awakening. Green sprouts were needed at the grass roots to ensure a healthy democracy. The electoral law required ten thousand signatures in one of the country's twelve constituencies for a party to be registered on the ballot in all twelve. This eliminated a lot of splinter parties even before the elections.

But the real crunch came in the form of a five percent cutoff when the votes were counted. Any party receiving less than this in either the Czech or the Slovak Republic would not obtain seats in the Federal Assembly. The Federal Assembly would be bicameral, with 49 Slovak and 101 Czech seats in the lower House of the People; and 75 Slovak and 75 Czech seats in the upper House of the Nations. The President would be elected by the Assembly, and to be successful a candidate would have to obtain a majority in the lower house, and in each of the two halves of the upper house.

The very prospect of the five percent cutoff forced many of the smaller parties into amalgamation with one another and with some of the larger parties. But those small parties that wanted to remain independent could go under the Civic Forum umbrella. Forum itself was not a political party and did not want to become one, at least for these elections. It was a movement and the electoral law permitted the listing of both parties and movements on the ballot. This provision was both innovative and necessary for the time.

Civic Forum was made up of people with a wide range of views, but who all supported the reestablishment of democracy. There would have been no point in trying to get them to agree to one political platform, beyond basic democratic principles. This would only have broken up what was then a stabilizing force in the country. Furthermore, Havel was a strong supporter of independent candidates and suspicious of party politics during the delicate transition to a new statehood. The Civic Forum umbrella, listed on the ballot, was the only way in which the small parties or the independents could be elected in a proportional system. But the small parties, and the independents, would have to be accepted into Civic Forum first. And this meant that they had to support unequivocally and responsibly Forum's basic democratic goals.

Despite all the adjustments, the electoral law was in my mind far from ideal. I understood why it was adopted. It was a throwback to the proportional system that had worked relatively well between the wars. But I was not the only critic of the new version. Slovaks were now saying that the system in effect between the wars, and the governments it produced, had not been sensitive to Slovak aspirations. I think the problem in that period had been to a large extent attributable to the fact that the founding of the country in 1918 brought together two somewhat unequal partners. The Czechs were urbane and well-educated while the Slovaks were rural and relatively inexperienced in political life. Though I believe Czech intentions were mostly honourable, the governments of the First Republic did not always understand how a given political decision might be received in Slovakia.

Slovak sensitivities after the revolution were if anything sharper, and the possibility for misunderstanding was correspondingly greater. Despite its weaknesses, it was true that the proportional system was traditional in Czechoslovakia and hence a source of stability. There would be no fractious debate and no experiments with new systems. Almost all agreed that it was simply a question of modifying a proven vehicle. Even some in Civic Forum argued that it would prevent an electoral outcome where Forum might conceivably win every seat in the Federal Assembly. This was held out as a distinct possibility if a majority system was adopted.

On the other hand, almost all agreed the proportional system was devilishly complicated. A day or so before the election, the voter would be given a pile of papers with the name of a party or movement at the top of each. On this piece of paper, below the name of the party or movement, would be a list of names. These were the candidates of the party or movement for the given constituency. The party or movement would determine the priority of names on its list. The voter would go to the voting booth on the day of the election, put the list of the party or movement of his choice in the ballot box, and return the unused lists. Depending on the percentage of votes cast for the party within the constituency, a percentage of the candidates on the party list would obtain seats.

There would be two innovations this time that differentiated the system from that in practice between the wars. The voter would be able to rearrange the list of candidates on the party ticket according to his own order of preference. If a given candidate was "promoted" by enough people, the party would agree to place the candidate higher on its list. The candidate would thus be more likely to obtain a seat. Secondly, it was customary between the wars for each party to demand a blank letter of resignation from every party candidate. Once elected, the party would use these letters to enforce discipline. Since the deputies had already signed the letters, only the date had to be filled in if a deputy broke party ranks.

The parties could thereby dispose of candidates on its lists who proved to be unworthy. The deputy would be replaced by the candidate next highest on the party's list from the most recent election.

Constituents did not particularly mind because there were only twelve constituencies in the entire country, and each had more than ten deputies. Hence there was no special relationship between the deputy and his constituents that the party might be accused of attempting to breach. After the revolution it was agreed that there would be no such party control of deputies. The result was that the government coalition of the day could not count on an automatic majority to get its bills through parliament.

The other main result of these innovations was that independent candidates were able to get elected without party affiliation, aside from a very general allegiance to Forum. This only reinforced the tendency whereby deputies affiliated with parties were basically immune to party control. But neither were deputies directly responsible to constituents, as in a majority system. It was true, as many argued at the time, that the proportional system best reflected the relative popularity of the whole array of parties and movements. But once elected, the deputies were unusually free to vote on the basis of their personal judgment. This was exactly what Havel wanted from his parliament as it tackled the difficult job of drafting a new constitution.

The dangers implicit in this political system were soon apparent. Parties that managed to exert control over their deputies, and many did, showed that they were more concerned with promoting their own agendas than with pursuing the interests of their constituents. The relationship between a deputy and his constituency was tenuous at best and any kind of direct accountability was lacking. This allowed parties to pursue political goals, even the division of the country, over the heads of the electorate. Havel sought to counteract "party politics" by calling for a referendum on important constitutional questions. This call was largely ignored by the parties themselves. The other main difficulty with the new system was that, if the two big winners in Slovakia and the Czech Lands could not agree to form a government, they could ensure that no one else would either. And there was no provision in the existing constitution to permit Havel to call a new election in order to resolve any deadlock.

Havel's vision for the future of the country in the spring of 1990 was totally different from what eventually transpired. He wanted the Federal Assembly, and the Presidency, to be restricted to a special two-year term after the June elections. His rationale was that the first elections would be largely a referendum on the future of communism in Czechoslovakia. Not that there was any doubt how that referendum would come out. But the real political and economic issues that would determine what kind of society would emerge in the future had not yet been properly debated. The debate would come only in the following elections. Furthermore, Havel wanted the Assembly to use this two-year term to prepare and adopt a new constitution.

The two-year limit was a kind of pressure tactic, I think, intended to get the country to lay the basis quickly for its entry into the new Europe. It would also provide a useful deadline for the task of putting all the principal political laws and economic reforms in place. The Assembly for the special two-year term would become a crucible in which the leading personalities of the day would create a political system that ideally expressed the unique traditions of the country. It was an imaginative throwback to early Americana, and bold for all of that. But party politics reasserted itself despite Havel's leadership. The prospect of a simple, visionary constitution slipped further and further beyond his grasp.

Havel sensed where some of the dangers lay ahead, even if their true import was not obvious at the time. To provide an additional check to party discord and the potential for political deadlock he proposed at an early stage the creation of a truly executive presidency. Under the communist regime, the role of the presidency had been emasculated because the Communist Party's General Secretary made all of the important decisions. Havel moved quickly to increase the staff and powers of the presidency to the extent he could under existing legislation. But it was virtually impossible to return the office overnight to the prestige and power it wielded in Masaryk's time.

However, like Masaryk, Havel possessed great moral authority and exerted a calming influence on political life. He used this moral authority to create a new role for Czechoslovakia on the international scene. He did so largely through the personal charisma attributed to him by Western publics. Even at home, his influence on the decisions of government, including issues for which he had no direct responsibility, was really a function of his personal authority. It was often sufficient for the decision making process if "the Castle" was for or against this or that decision or this or that appointment.

In fact Havel and his staff may have dabbled too much in the day-to-day workings of government. More of an effort might have been made to direct the Castle's influence, and Havel's involvement, to the big issues, and in so doing enhance his impact. His single most important power was the authority, after a federal election, to select the individual who, as prime minister, would be asked to form the next government. This was no easy task in a proportional system. The choice was critical for political stability, since any government would, of necessity, be a coalition.

37

CONSTITUTIONAL CRISIS

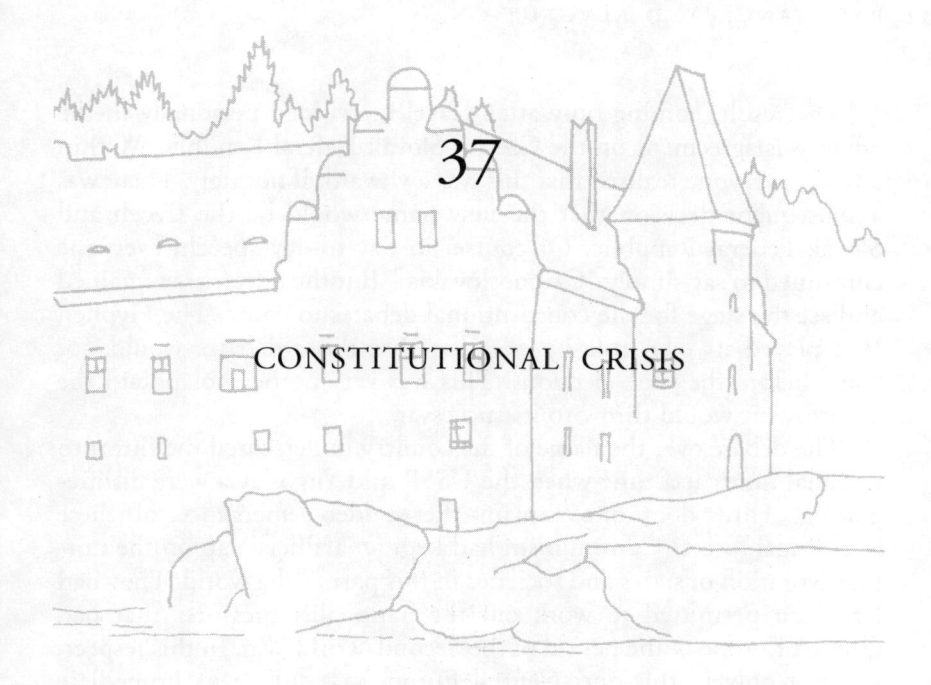

IT WAS WIDELY ACCEPTED that many of the ministers in the government, the "Government of National Understanding," would run in the June 1990 elections. This fact lay at the root of the cabinet dispute over economic reform and the attempt of those around Komarek to delay tough economic decisions until after the elections. But it also influenced the way in which the government dealt with relations between Czechs and Slovaks. Cabinet seemed reluctant to come out and say where it stood, or to convey its vision of the country's future as a federation. Consequently national unity did not come across as a priority.

Some Slovak deputies and many Slovaks were already pushing for greater political autonomy. There was even a party advocating outright Slovak independence. But the depth of these feelings was revealed almost inadvertently. Havel wanted to change the name of the country from the Czechoslovak Socialist Republic (the name of the country under the communist regime) to the Czechoslovak Republic, or Czechoslovak Federal Republic. Slovak nationalists insisted there be greater emphasis on the Slovak part of the name. They were tired of being grammatically second-class citizens. After days and days of protracted negotiation, and increasingly aggressive debate, the papers began calling it the "Hyphen War." I think that the Czechs were totally unprepared for the degree of resentment felt by their Slovak colleagues, resentment that had accumulated over long years.

The result, coming only after Havel intervened personally in the affair, was agreement on the Czecho-Slovak Federal Republic. Within a week, everyone realised that this was awkward, if not ugly. There was a subsequent decision that the new name would be the Czech and Slovak Federal Republic. Of course, in day-to-day speech, everyone continued to say simply "Czechoslovakia." But the bitterness remained and set the stage for the constitutional debates to come. The Hyphen War played its own role by ensuring that those debates would not come before the June elections. This was yet another hot potato the government would throw to its successor.

The debate over the name of the country underscored the threat to national unity at a time when the USSR and Yugoslavia were disintegrating. How does one explain the sudden emergence of these centrifugal forces? Communism had kept an artificial cap on the normal evolution of states and societies in this part of the world. They had not been permitted to work out the nationalist pressures that had gripped Europe in the period of the Second World War. In this respect, and not only in this one, Central Europe was still in its immediate postwar phase.

The communists had kept the lid on Slovak nationalism by equating it with fascism. And, indeed, the Slovaks had obtained independence only once in their history, as a Nazi puppet state. There was nonetheless progress under Dubček's brief leadership towards federalizing the country by creating real local governments in the Czech Lands and in Slovakia. This was formalized in a new constitution. After Dubček's ouster, and the reassertion of neo-Stalinism under Husák, this limited decentralization was reversed. Husák did this by ensuring that all important decisions were taken by the Party leadership, the politburo, in Prague. The Slovak local government, and the Czech local government, would slavishly follow the Party line laid down by the Party's leaders. And so the new "Republic" of Slovakia once again became a puppet.

Compensation for the loss of local autonomy came in the form of economic benefit. In the 1970s and 1980s, a massive regional development program was undertaken in Slovakia in order to make it an economic partner with the Czech Lands. For instance, a huge heavy arms industry designed to supply the Warsaw Pact with such things as T-72 tanks was built there. Although it had only one third of the population of the country Slovakia received one half of all government subsidies for economic development. Under a regime with virtually 100 percent state ownership of business, factories, shops, and even restaurants, this financial support was massive. It transformed rural Slovakia into a network of single industry towns. But what could not have been predicted at the time, least of all by the communists, was that the cold war would end sooner rather than later. The demand for heavy weapons of Soviet design would drop dramatically. Slovakia would be thrown into a recession that coincided with the shift to a market economy. And in the age of the market economy, the economic power of Prague as the city of business would soar.

Nor did it take long after the revolution for this communist regional development scheme to come under fire. There was a perception in the Czech Lands that most modern factories were located in Slovakia, while the Czechs laboured in factories that dated back to the industrial revolution. By March 1990, the Premier of the Czech Lands was calling for an end to transfer payments to Slovakia. This was partly based on the perception that the Slovak economy had been unduly favoured in recent years. More importantly, it was also based on the conviction, frequently mentioned by many Czechs at the time, that the Slovaks were not particularly grateful for the financial support. These Czech sentiments grew in direct proportion to the rise of Slovak nationalism during 1990. The skirmishes over transfer payments and over the name of the Republic only seemed to confirm the concern of some cabinet ministers that Havel's constitutional agenda might do more damage than good. They believed Havel was in too much of a hurry.

The President wanted to have a new constitution in place by the end of 1991. If he could achieve this, the campaign for the next elections in June, 1992, would benefit from the new constitutional consensus. The "national question" would be settled and the parties in this election campaign would be able to tackle the urgent issues of economic policy and the social safety net. However some cabinet ministers feared that, in the interim period, acrimonious constitutional debates would cripple the government. They believed that the decisions required to implement economic reforms could not be delayed for two years while the nation lost itself in endless discussion over the symbols of sovereignty. In their view, the Czechs and Slovaks should give themselves twenty years to reflect on the kind of country they wanted before rushing into a deal that would only unravel a few years later. There was also the growing concern among the Czechs—and this became significant—that the kind of decentralization the Slovaks were seeking would leave the people of Czechoslovakia without a country at all.

This is not to say that all Slovak politicians were by definition political chauvinists. Ján Čarnogursky was a Slovak leader who had great intellectual and moral standing in both parts of the country. He had created the Christian Democratic Movement in Slovakia after his release from a communist prison. His following tended to be conservative and Roman Catholic. But even Carnogursky's long-term political goal was formulated early and his party never wavered from it: when the time came for entry into the European Union, Carnogursky wanted Slovakia to enter as an independent state. It was this kind of politics that drove the Czechs crazy. How could you say this, they argued, and be sincere when it came to negotiating political and economic reforms now?

It was natural for Carnogursky, as one of the leading Slovak political figures of the day, to want to be nominated as a Deputy Prime Minister in the new Government of National Understanding. The gains of the revolution still had to be consolidated. It may also have been that he believed the best place to protect Slovak interests in those days was in Prague. But he must have been thinking, even then, of his eventual return to Slovakia. When Barry and I went to see him again in March 1990, he expressed a moderate view of Slovak aspirations. He said most Slovaks wanted to remain a part of the federation. He emphasized that a policy of compromise between Czechs and Slovaks, and between Slovaks and the Hungarian minority in southern Slovakia, was the only way forward.

Carnogursky said that Canadians and Americans of Slovak origin were more radical in their political views than Slovaks in Slovakia. For over forty years there had been little contact between the émigrés and their homeland. During the period of communist rule, Slovaks in North America described themselves as the true representatives of the whole Slovak nation. This was no longer possible. Carnogursky had recently told Slovak émigrés that Slovaks in Slovakia wanted to remain a part of Czechoslovakia, and that the Slovak question had to be decided in this country, not somewhere else. He said he hoped that, with more contact, the Slovak émigré communities would change their views. He then praised Havel for adopting the principle of not excluding any interest group from taking part in discussions about the future of the country. Only an open, inclusive debate would help solve the problems that lay ahead.

It was at this time, when the Czechs and Slovaks were beginning to explore the constitutional issue, that Pierre Trudeau turned up in Prague. Barry received a phone call one morning in April from the former Prime Minister who said, nonchalantly, that he was in town as a guest of the Czechoslovak government. Barry and I were to meet Trudeau for breakfast at his hotel the next day. Probably like most Canadians, I had feelings about Trudeau that were a little ambivalent. On the one hand, he was something of a hero. I had seen him going all out at Laval University in Quebec City in 1980, fighting the referendum battle. The crowd of students was hostile, to say the least, but he was both fiery and forthright, and the students came around. It was not that they agreed with him; they came to appreciate him as a thoughtful opponent, and as a personality. He had them laughing at the end. On the other hand, many in the audience said that his rigid views probably did more to encourage both independence in Quebec and alienation in the West than just about anything else. The students I talked with afterwards argued that the country seemed to keep chasing its tail, constantly turning to the man who was as much a part of the problem as the solution.

So there we were, in the brown velveteen Hotel Panorama, standing by the elevator waiting for Pierre Trudeau to appear. Out came the former Prime Minister, instantly recognizable. He had a relaxed, friendly approach. There was none of the hardness that characterized his TV presence. As we made our way to the hotel restaurant I noticed he was wearing running shoes with his suit. I liked that. If anyone could wear running shoes with a suit and tie, I guess he could. He was exceedingly gracious over breakfast, and very interested in Czechoslovakia. He talked to us about the group of international experts he was with, which was consulting with the Czechoslovak government about constitutional issues. Trudeau said the Czechoslovaks were rushing things. If they kept decentralizing power as they said they would, there would be no federal government left worthy of the name. The breakfast ended with Barry offering to host a dinner in Trudeau's honour, while I expressed a willingness to organize some transportation for him to get around the country. As we walked out to the car I was genuinely won over by Trudeau's personal warmth. I looked forward to hearing some of his views about both Czechoslovakia and Canada.

The dinner party was an interesting group, led on the Czech side by the rather youthful Vladimír Dlouhý, the Federal Minister of the Economy. Dlouhy was clearly pleased to meet Trudeau. He told a touching story about how he had first heard the former Prime Minister's name. As a young boy Dlouhy was travelling from Czechoslovakia to Cuba with his father. His father was an engineer and their family had been posted to Cuba for a few years as part of

Pierre Guimond, Minister of the Economy Vladimir Dlouhy, Ambassador Barry Mawhinney, and the author at Hadovka

Czechoslovakia's "fraternal" assistance to another socialist state. The plane touched down in Gander, Newfoundland, for refuelling. The boy and his father decided to stretch their legs, got off the plane and walked to the transit lounge. Young Dlouhy was taken aback by the wealth of consumer goods on sale in this small facility, all beyond the reach of the citizens of Czechoslovakia. He thought, in his young mind, that this country must surely be paradise. And so he asked who was its far-seeing leader? His father told him it was Pierre Trudeau. Since that time Dlouhy had never forgotten this name.

A respectful silence descended on our dinner guests at the end of this story. I think everyone was moved by the way Dlouhy had recounted his experience, with such obvious affection for the former Prime Minister. Trudeau, for his part, was quiet and appreciative. He looked down, smiling shyly as the rest of us glanced at him. And then Islay, Barry's wife, made one of her mischievous interventions, as was her wont. She was at one end of the long table, facing Barry at the other end. Dlouhy and Trudeau were sitting on her left and right, according to the demands of protocol. During this pregnant pause, replete with the recollection of boyhood dreams, Islay turned to Trudeau and said ever so respectfully, "You probably never imagined that your legacy would be symbolized by the transit lounge of Gander airport." Everyone laughed of course, Trudeau with difficulty.

The discussion that evening ranged over many issues, not least the constitutional debates in both Canada and Czechoslovakia. Trudeau was forever the proponent of strong federal power. He wondered what kind of country the Czechs were seeking to create. When it came to Canada, he was even-tempered and analytical about the dangers facing the country. I could not resist asking the obvious question. If the federal government insisted that there be no delegation of powers to Quebec, or to the provinces generally, and if a "distinct society" clause for Quebec in the constitution was unacceptable, was there the risk that Quebec might separate after all? Did he think the threat was real? Trudeau's reply was that there would be no Canada if there was not a strong federal government. His message to both the Czechs and the Canadians was the same. There had to be a critical mass of federal power in order to provide the "glue" necessary to a federal system. Without it, special interests would come to dominate, and the shared ideal of a single state would be lost.

There was another memorable moment when we got talking about Cuba. This topic flowed from the first, occasioned by Dlouhy's mention of his boyhood there. He had been back to visit on a number of occasions. It was also a subject of interest to Trudeau because of his friendship with Fidel Castro. I suppose one could have predicted the outcome of this discussion from the start. Dlouhy had a feel for Cuba at the grass roots. As a member of Civic Forum, an opposition movement that had just overthrown a repressive communist regime, Dlouhy was predictably hostile to the Castro regime. Trudeau was not.

He admired what the Cuban government had achieved for its people. He compared the communist regime favourably to other governments in the region. Dlouhy tried to disagree politely, but Trudeau pursued the issue by pointing out how successful the medical system and the schooling were in a country that had once been largely illiterate. Dlouhy insisted on the price that had been paid in terms of human rights and political and economic freedoms. He emphasized the human potential that had been wasted. Finally, when Trudeau tried to lecture him a little about the social situation in Cuba, Dlouhy smiled back and said, "I know, I grew up there."

What I found most remarkable about this particular conversation, was that Trudeau's admiration for Cuba had a lot, if not everything, to do with his admiration for Castro as a man. It was a feeling inspired not by Castro the politician, or even by Castro the revolutionary. It was an appreciation of Castro the whole man: the athlete, the deep-sea diver, the prodigious eater, drinker, and smoker, the intellectual, and the leader. One could see in Trudeau's description of Castro his own ideal of the multifaceted human being. But it was at odds with the kind of moral sensibility that motivated people like Dlouhy, not to mention Havel. Once Trudeau got on to the issue of Castro as an individual, the Czechs quietly dropped the subject.

I took Trudeau to the airport and we spent some time talking in the departure lounge. I enjoyed his company. He took a real interest in what I was doing and what I thought about the current situation in Czechoslovakia. There was this look he had when you first met him. It was very direct and very present, and yet somehow shy. You could not help liking him on a personal basis, and there was never any hint of condescension. He was friendly and polite to everyone he met during his visit. I think he was surprised by the Czechs and Slovaks, who were even then moving to a very decentralized system. It seemed to be his view that they were not very serious about wanting to have a country that they all shared. I gave him a book of Havel's political essays and he much appreciated it. He clearly admired Havel, though, curiously, not in the same way that he seemed to admire someone like Castro.

We talked a little about Canada. Trudeau joked that, when my assignment in Czechoslovakia was over, I would be leaving one country in transition and returning to another. Like Canada, the Czechs and Slovaks, who were just now emerging from communism, were about to be engulfed by a debate over national unity. They, too, would be forced to examine their attachment to Czechoslovakia as a political ideal. This was hardly something to be left to inertia. I said that the work of Havel and the others in the opposition showed how important it was for citizens to get involved in politics. Neither country would make its way through the difficulties that lay ahead unless more people shouldered some of the political responsibility.

38

DUBČEK REMEMBERS

NOT LONG after Trudeau's trip to Czechoslovakia, Alexander Dubček announced his intention to visit Canada. Dubček was the President of the Federal Assembly and was ranked third in protocol terms after the President of the Republic and the Prime Minister. As a Slovak, his principal purpose in visiting Canada and the United States at this time was to speak to the Slovak communities. There was growing concern in the federal government that some elements in the émigré communities were sowing discord between the Czechs and Slovaks in their country of origin. More specifically, it was believed that the Slovak communities might be funnelling substantial financial resources to the pro-independence groups in Slovakia. Though this issue was raised as a sensitive development in Canada-Czechoslovak relations, there was never any charge that Canada was trying to interfere in domestic politics.

People like Carnogursky and Dubček saw the issue as something to be dealt with by the Slovak community that linked both countries. Dubček intended to speak to the émigré Slovaks in order to explain better where the country was going and how Slovak concerns were being handled. He also wanted to redirect their activities into channels that the Czechoslovak government considered to be more useful. In the spring and summer of 1990 Dubček and Carnogursky made real progress in bringing the émigrés on board. But in a way, it was already too late. The debate inside the country began to heat up, and the foreign connection to the Slovak émigrés was largely forgotten.

I saw Dubček off at the airport. I had already met Dubček many times since the revolution and liked him very much. He had an engaging manner and a ready handshake, and he never forgot people he had met before. He did not look much different from the photos taken of him in 1968, except that his hair was now white. There was the same light build and the sloping shoulders, and that famous smile. He had a way of putting everyone around him at ease. He talked a lot in a rambling sort of way, but it was always interesting, reflecting a long and fascinating experience of political life. At the time we spoke, Lithuania was much in the news for trying to stand up to the USSR by declaring its independence. I asked Dubček if there was a parallel between Czechoslovakia in 1968 and Lithuania now. He thought there was, except that Gorbachov was giving Lithuania some room to manoeuvre. The Balts had a right to independence and Dubček thought they would get it sooner or later. The question was into whose hands the independence movements were playing.

With amazing prescience Dubček said there was a group waiting to replace Gorbachov. The independence movements were hurting Gorbachov and strengthening the hands of the conservatives. This was a real dilemma. The only solution, said Dubček, was for the Balts to stretch the process out at this stage. The economic problems that were putting pressure on Gorbachov were not especially new to the Russians. The average Russian seemed capable of tightening his belt almost indefinitely. But the nationalist tensions were a threat to the very existence of the USSR and would affect Gorbachov's survival.

I asked Dubček to compare Czechoslovakia in 1968 with Czechoslovakia in 1990. He said that, of course, "we have already gone much further now." Smiling, he recalled that in 1968, when he proposed a return to political pluralism, even the puppet parties thought he was crazy. He said that getting reform bills through the Federal Assembly in 1968 was no easy task. They had, at least, succeeded in completely removing censorship. The current situation in Czechoslovakia was much more favourable.

As President of the new Assembly Dubček emphasized that it was working hard to pass an enormous amount of new legislation. Deputies were sitting far into the night and on weekends, too, in order to deal with the volume of economic and political bills that required attention. This was a huge task not only because of the work involved. The deputies were, as one might expect, largely inexperienced parliamentarians with a rudimentary knowledge of parliamentary procedure. Later that year one of Forum's new deputies, Stanislav Chylek, contacted me at the embassy seeking Canadian assistance in the parliamentary field. I leapt at the opportunity, and arranged for Stan and a group of Czech and Slovak parliamentarians to spend a couple of weeks studying Canadian legislative procedure in Ottawa. (Stan's Canadian connection was about to begin: he became the Ambassador of the Czech Republic to Canada in 1993.)

The deputies of the Federal Assembly acted as if they were literally driven by their determination to complete their legislative task in as short a time as possible. There was such an incredible desire to change the country overnight. People wanted to live in a "normal" Western democracy. Of course, for Czechoslovakia, this was as much a return to the past, to the interwar period, as it was the creation of something totally new. Given the speed of the transformation under way, Dubček thought that the situation of Czechoslovakia in 1990 was now irreversible, no matter what happened in Moscow. If anyone was in a position to know, he was.

39

SLOVAK NATIONALISM

DURING MY CONVERSATION with Dubček I could not resist asking him, since he was a Slovak, about the issue of Slovak nationalism. He replied that political and economic reforms would be most effectively, and most quickly, implemented through the existing federal system. He thought that the majority of Slovaks understood this. He added that some Slovaks of Canadian origin were out of touch with developments. They would come to understand that the democratic process was working well and that Slovaks could speak for themselves.

My own feeling, based on trips to Slovakia at the time, was that the Czech and Slovak economies were so intertwined as to make Slovak independence at this stage untenable. Interestingly, when Civic Forum's counterpart in Slovakia, Public Against Violence, eventually split up after the June elections, both economic and nationalist considerations were foremost. One half supported rapid economic reforms and close cooperation with Civic Forum. But the other half, led by Vladimir Mečiar, wanted to slow down economic reforms, retain a greater degree of state ownership, and adopted a distinctly nationalist platform. Dubček came out in support of Mečiar at that juncture.

Barry and I made a trip to Slovakia in early 1990 in order to get a feel for the views of the new Slovak leaders. Slovak Premier Čič was a former communist who had become a member of Public Against Violence. When we called on him in the ornate palace that was the

Premier's office, we found him to be a friendly, welcoming man whose principal desire was to return to the practice of law. He regarded his tenure as Premier to be something of a fluke and probably not long-term. In this he reminded one of Prime Minister Čalfa: a capable and urbane politician who had come up through communist ranks and, though active in support of the revolution, knew his background would prevent him from remaining in high office in the future. When we asked him about the nature of Slovak political aspirations, Čič said that the Czech Republic and the Slovak Republic had agreed that a looser arrangement between them was desirable. The idea, as he explained it, was that the two Republics would retain all residual powers. Only very specific powers would be transferred to the federal government.

I suppose what Čič was really saying was that the Republics would be sovereign, but would delegate certain powers to the federal level, to be exercised in the mutual interest of the two Republics. In retrospect, I find incredible the extent to which Čič's two successors as Premier, Carnogursky and Mečiar, basically adopted the same position. What changed was the formula used to give it expression. Two years later, this position ran smack into Václav Klaus's unswerving federalism. His approach to the promotion of federalism was the "take it or leave it" variety. The Slovak politicians of the day, principally Mečiar, opted to leave it.

There was a tendency during the early days after the revolution, and increasingly so thereafter, for the Czechs to view Slovak nationalism as simply a power grab. It was the equivalent in many minds of an attempt to get something for nothing. What could the Slovaks possibly lack in the current arrangements? From exactly what, or whom, were they suffering? Neither Czech politicians, nor Czech journalists, could come up with an answer that sounded plausible in Czech ears. Ján Buday was at the time the leader of Public Against Violence in Slovakia. Like Civic Forum in the Czech Lands, it had been the main vehicle in Slovakia for the public protests that toppled the communist regime. And like Forum it was a mass movement which bridged many contradictory political streams.

Buday was young, dark, and charismatic. At the time we met him in early 1990, he was the most powerful political figure in Slovakia. What we did not know was that, a day after the June elections, he would resign and withdraw his candidacy. It would emerge that he had foolishly signed a piece of paper for the StB in the 1970s in order to obtain an exit permit for a trip abroad. Though he refused to cooperate with the StB after that trip, and suffered the consequences for a decade or more, the fact that he had briefly wavered was enough to end his political career. There were rumours at the time that the information about Buday had been leaked by Mečiar. Mečiar was the Minister of the Interior at the time, and a fellow member of Public Against Violence. With Buday's resignation, Mečiar became Premier of Slovakia after the June elections. As they say, the rest is history. An inquiry held in the following year into Mečiar's conduct as Minister of the Interior failed to turn up any proof of his involvement in the Buday scandal.

When we asked about the new Slovak nationalism Buday put a philosophical spin on the issue. He argued that patriotism was an entirely normal sentiment for the citizen of any country. But this had to be distinguished from nationalism. Nationalism was always directed against someone else. Buday said that if civic interests, a social safety net, and rapid economic change remained priorities for the federal government, the federation would continue to be supported in Slovakia. Uncertainty, even fear about the continuation of a social safety-net under Klaus's economic policies, was one of the important factors that led to the erosion of support for the federal government. But the biggest challenge, according to Buday, was not so much the question of Slovak autonomy as the task of extending the revolution into the countryside, where the communists were still entrenched.

Buday was convinced that the communists would play on people's anxieties about change. I could see his point, but I was more concerned about the potential for mischief through creating anti-Czech, or anti-Slovak, feelings. In conversations that Barry and I had with other political figures in Slovakia, an identifiable theme emerged. This was the belief in the emergence of a new Czech "mafia" that was, of course, detrimental to Slovak interests. The only reasonable reaction, according to this argument, was the struggle for maximum decentralization as soon as possible. This would be followed, step by step, by real independence. Both the Christian Democratic Movement under Ján Čarnogursky, and the Movement for a Democratic Slovakia established by Vladimir Mečiar soon after the June elections, sought to combine these elements by linking Slovak nationalism to doubts about rapid economic change. It was a potent mixture and attracted support from the former communist party and the Slovak separatist party. It also had the political advantage of giving shape to the belief in a Czech conspiracy.

40

AN INDEPENDENT FOREIGN POLICY

AS EXPECTED, the new Czechoslovak foreign policy made a revolutionary break with the past. Less expected was its rapid evolution from Charter 77 positions, and its surprising early successes. In June 1989, during the communist regime, I received a letter from Charter 77 addressed to the NATO Foreign Ministers who were about to hold one of their biannual meetings. The Charter letter was signed by Havel, Dienstbier, and Malý. It called for the dissolution of both NATO and the Warsaw Pact.

The argument supporting this proposal was that the bipolar world created by the two alliances would forever condemn Czechoslovakia and many other countries to political no man's land. In the early months of Havel's presidency, this theme was picked up again. There was a new element this time. It was suggested that the Conference on Security and Cooperation in Europe (CSCE), which had been created by the Helsinki Accords in the 1970s and was in large part a human rights mechanism, might be adapted to political security matters. Once the two alliances were abolished the CSCE would take over a political security function for all of Europe.

This would be possible, so the argument went, because the CSCE (today the Organization for Security and Cooperation in Europe or OSCE) already incorporated the USSR and European countries, as well as Canada and the United States. It was the logical institution to build on.

Implicit in the proposal, however, was the need for a CSCE security force to back up what Havel proposed would be binding non-aggression treaties. My first reaction was that this required too much of the NATO countries, and was too forward-looking for its time. NATO had proved to be a success, after all. It had deterred a military threat from a totalitarian empire for forty years. The USSR appeared at the time to be on a reform track under Gorbachov, but either a putsch or political chaos was a possibility in the medium term. There simply was no political predictability where the USSR was concerned. This security environment, including the overwhelming power of the weapons systems still very much in existence, seemed to require NATO more than ever.

Of course both Charter and the new government were decidedly pro-Western in foreign policy orientation. The only Soviet issue that preoccupied Havel's government was the removal of Soviet troops from Czechoslovakia. These numbered about 75,000. They had been stationed in this relatively small country since the 1968 Warsaw Pact invasion. Whole sections of the countryside where Soviet troops were stationed were fenced off and guarded. Negotiations proceeded rather quickly here, and an agreement was reached to have all foreign troops out of the country by June, 1991. The principal point of contention, in fact, was who would pay for cleaning up the land that was contaminated at the bases, and who would pay for the buildings erected there over the past forty years. Both sides finally agreed that neither country owed the other one anything. This single-minded preoccupation with one issue in bilateral relations with the USSR contrasted with the avalanche of new relations Czechoslovakia established with Western countries during the same period.

In the first six months of 1990 alone, Havel made back to back visits to Canada, the U.S., Germany, France, and Britain, as well as other countries. The TV clips of Havel with Mrs. Thatcher, Havel with Mitterrand, or Havel with Bush, left many Czech heads swimming after the forty-year spectacle of sterile communist hobnobbing. A lot of effort was also put into the resurrection of Central Europe as a political and economic region in its own right. There were visits to Hungary and Poland and a schedule of ministerial meetings established to promote common foreign policy approaches and the coordination of economic decisions and trade flows. Relations with Austria and Germany were intensified and returned to a level of activity that had been traditional between the wars, at least on the commercial front.

But the most radical foreign policy innovation was the emphasis Havel and Dienstbier placed on moral considerations. They argued that it was not enough to seek what was in Czechoslovakia's interest as a country. Every foreign policy decision had to be considered from a higher, moral standpoint, as to its benefits to the international community as a whole. Moral politics had been the heart of Charter 77's appeal. Its translation into foreign policy was to a large extent consonant with traditional Canadian foreign policy themes.

One of the first things that Havel did, and it was the first example of this new approach, was to make a statement on the expulsion of the Sudeten Germans from Czechoslovakia after the war. The Sudeten Germans had enthusiastically supported Hitler in the 1930s and 1940s. It was their plea to Hitler for liberation from the Czechs that led to the Munich Agreement, the Nazi invasion, and the breakup of the country at the start of World War II. Hence there was strong pressure from the Czech population after the war to expel the Sudeten Germans from the country. This decision was approved by the Allied powers and carried out with dispatch.

It was doubtful whether any government of the day could have done anything different, given the very emotional context. But what Havel said he objected to was the use by the government of the day of collective guilt to condemn all individuals. He argued that each Sudeten German should have been given the benefit of a hearing before any action was taken. This was a morally perceptive analysis of a dramatic event in recent Czech history. It was in direct contrast to what the communists did to the "bourgeoisie" after 1948, and to what many people intended to do to the communists in 1990.

Havel's position outraged many, if not most people, in Czechoslovakia. They saw it as an indirect apology to the Sudeten Germans. Any kind of apology was simply unacceptable to those who had suffered at German hands. There were numerous letters to the editor that described what the Nazis had done during the war and made the obvious comparison with the milder fate suffered by the Sudeten Germans afterwards. At the time, I felt that the root of the controversy was that Havel, unlike just about everybody else, did not have a vengeful bone in his body. This was true whether it was a question of German or communist interest. Such a disposition, since it was more than a position, was remarkable in a person who had spent over five years in a communist prison.

After the outrage had swept the nation, Havel's refined moral stand began to sink in here and there. One could see, after only a few days into his presidency, that he was not about to pander to anybody, even to the electorate. He was going to be a difficult leader. The more important question for the coming year was the attitude the average person, and the government, would take towards former communists. Havel knew that the same arguments he was applying to the Sudeten Germans applied no less to those who had been active inside the regime. But the range of collaboration was enormous, stretching from those who had been members of the Communist Party to former StB agents. There would be a tendency on the part of many to blacken all with a broad brush.

Havel's moral imperatives provoked criticism with respect to other foreign policy issues too, in addition to the question of the Sudeten Germans. There were some who said that he simply did not understand that foreign policy should be nothing more nor less than the pursuit of national interests. Not long after the Sudeten German controversy he invited the Dalai Lama to visit. This was the first time any head of state in any country had done so and it angered the Chinese government. Of course in light of Havel's own role in the opposition under communism, this initiative made perfect sense. The Dalai Lama had been the Nobel Peace Prize recipient in 1989, the year in which Havel had been widely expected to win. But there was a significant amount of grumbling in Czech political circles to the refrain of "there he goes again." The argument was that he was putting one of Czechoslovakia's biggest markets at risk. Havel replied that there were some issues that were of greater import to the international community as a whole. The benefits of doing the right thing, though less direct, were no less real. Later, he noted that no markets had been lost despite the uproar.

Finally, there was the question of the manufacture and sale of armaments to third world countries. If ever there was a foreign policy issue which imposed on the state a clear moral responsibility, this was it. But the issue also had significant domestic repercussions: the heavy arms industry was concentrated in Slovakia. It was in fact one of the few modern industries in that part of the country. Economic reform and the restriction of arms sales would deal a double blow to the Slovak economy. Nonetheless, Havel stated early on that all international arms sales would be phased out once existing contracts were fulfilled. Months later, as it became clear what the results of this policy would mean to Slovakia, the decision was, as one might say, modified. The arms industry would be privatized, just as it was in the U.S. or Britain. Proposed sales by the private companies would have to be approved by the government. As in the West, restrictions on sales would apply to any countries that supported terrorism, were engaged in war, and so on.

The debate over this issue took six months or more. It was a classic confrontation between principles and the urgent interests of domestic politics. Barry and I talked to Dienstbier about it, and it was clear that he was not pleased by the about-turn in policy. But he acquiesced largely because the moral considerations were overtaken by "national policy" considerations. This meant relations between the Czechs and Slovaks. Dienstbier also noted that there was no point trying to be holier-than-thou when most other countries tolerated, even promoted, arms sales. And he particularly resented pressure from some Western countries to restrict sales when those same countries would never dream of doing so themselves.

I had the impression that Havel's initial inclination to phase out arms sales, regardless of the economic consequences, was linked to an assumption about the amount of assistance Czechoslovakia would receive from overseas. After the country returned to the Western fold, many Czechs assumed that there would be a huge influx of capital and investment both from Western governments and from the Czech and Slovak émigré communities. These communities were concentrated in Canada, the U.S., and Australia. During the years of repression, and especially just after the 1968 Warsaw Pact invasion, hundreds of thousands of Czechoslovaks had emigrated to those countries. There was a deep conviction among the members of the opposition, shared by the population at large, that the thousands of émigrés constituted a massive and vocal opposition to the regime. Everyone remembered how, under Nazi occupation, many Czechs and Slovaks had made it to the West and formed Czechoslovak Legions within the Allied armies. Most of these soldiers had returned home after the war to help rebuild the nation.

Even before the revolution many Czechs assumed that the "foreign legions" of Czech and Slovak émigrés would return home again, too. They believed that one day, when freedom finally came to Czechoslovakia, there would be a vast homecoming. That was the unspoken expectation. Unfortunately, what the people who remained in Czechoslovakia did not understand was that, after a year or so of active interest in their country of origin, the émigrés began building new lives in their adopted countries. So it was that after the revolution the vast majority did not think twice about moving back. This was not to say that they did not want to visit, and a significant minority even got involved politically. But after twenty years the average émigré felt more Canadian, American, or Australian, than Czech or Slovak. I think that this came as something of a shock to those who had stayed behind.

A second assumption about the émigré communities proved equally false. Everyone had an uncle or cousin "in America." And naturally everyone's uncle or cousin was rich. I suppose that in some respects, though not all, they were rich when compared with their kin back home. But it was widely believed after the revolution that the rich uncles would return with lots of money to help get their homeland back on its feet, even if they did not move back themselves.

In fact, while a few of the émigrés were wealthy, most of them were solid middle-class citizens with mortgages to pay. This was partly due to the fact that the émigrés tended to be well-educated professionals with, naturally, little entrepreneurial experience. There was money to visit, and perhaps to pay for a relative's trip to America, but little to invest in risky business opportunities. In the early days of the revolution, there was an assumption in the government that an avalanche of financial assistance would flow from the émigrés to help modernize the economy. Within months, it was clear this was not going to happen. Nor would Western governments provide more than technical assistance to help get things going. There would simply have to be some tough sledding by the Czechs and Slovaks themselves to get through the period of adjustment. It was this growing realization that lay behind the waffling over arms sales.

By springtime, 1990 Czechoslovak thinking about the future shape of Europe had taken another step forward. Military blocs had never been kind to Czechoslovakia, and understandably the government wanted to put security in Europe on a new basis. There had been some further reflection about how the CSCE might be able to fill the security vacuum. At first glance, this body seemed hardly prepared to do the job, having been a forum for East-West debate over human rights issues, economic cooperation issues, and disarmament. A whole new set of treaties would be required to enforce cooperative security arrangements. There would have to be some sort of multinational military force to back them up.

That was not all. The security structures would be meaningless unless East-West political, economic, environmental, and cultural relations were "thickened." Security was based on trust and this would come only with the genuine reunification of "Europe" in the broadest sense (from Vladivostok to Vancouver). In this scenario, the unification of Germany was key, both to the future abolition of blocs and to the creation of a new Europe. In the spring of 1990, Havel said he did not believe German unification would be successful without some kind of pan-European reconciliation. The ideal instrument for this, in Czech eyes, was still the CSCE. I was not convinced, feeling that there were many problems with this strategy. It underestimated both the political and strategic decline of the USSR and the perception in the West that the USSR remained a significant threat. But the strategy also failed to anticipate the speed and "logic" of German unification, and the exclusive nature of European Community integration. German unification indeed took place, but without the broad European reconciliation for which Havel hoped.

This was not to deny the appeal of Czechoslovak thinking. Barry and I went to talk to Zdeněk Matejka, the Deputy Minister of Foreign Affairs, to get a better sense of where Czechoslovak security policy was going. Matejka insisted that the CSCE could provide the necessary security structures. Permanent institutions would be required, even a CSCE secretariat located, perhaps, in Brussels. But the way towards this goal was not simply the unilateral dissolution of the Warsaw Pact. What was required was the rapid dissolution of both the Warsaw Pact and NATO together. At the time we were speaking, Gorbachov and Shevardnadze were firmly encamped on the liberal wing of the Soviet political spectrum. Matejka said, "thank God for Gorbachov." He was hopeful that Gorbachov would lead the USSR to a market economy and political pluralism. But he admitted, even then, that there was worrying resistance to Gorbachov in the Party apparatus and in the security structures. He thought the Baltic Republics might obtain more independence, but that any steps towards genuine autonomy in the Central Asian republics might meet with repression from the centre.

The complicating factor for Gorbachov, according to Matejka, was that the Party structures in the USSR were basically unreformable. The Soviet people might suddenly lose patience with both Gorbachov and the Party, which could lead to a cataclysm. This was very worrying indeed, because the Czechs and Slovaks could hardly ignore what was going on in a country that bordered theirs. There were also significant economic links that had been built up in the communist period, including the importation from the USSR of virtually all of Czechoslovakia's oil and gas. Moreover, Matejka admitted Czechoslovakia was not necessarily immune from the tide of nationalism sweeping the USSR and the other countries of Central and Eastern Europe.

By June of 1990, Havel and Dienstbier began to back away from their demand that both NATO and the Warsaw Pact be abolished. They now argued that NATO was clearly a useful, and necessary, institution. But their change of heart was based on the belief that NATO could provide the basis on which to build their proposed CSCE security organization. They expressed continuing concern about the tension produced by superpower rivalry in the Third World. They were more than a little sensitive to the potential for conflict in what appeared, at the time, to be the ineluctable tendency in the USSR towards dissolution.

Yet their call for a new body, something they called a "Commission on European Security," fell on deaf ears. The NATO states argued that any CSCE security structure would have to complement, not replace, NATO. Warsaw Pact states, for their part, tended to support Havel's call for a new CSCE security system. The Czechs were mainly interested in the kind of guarantees that would prevent a repeat of the Munich debacle of 1938 or the Warsaw Pact invasion of 1968. It was against this background that Dienstbier referred disapprovingly to NATO states as a privileged club of sixteen countries. He wondered if it seemed to NATO that Czechoslovakia was still a faraway country when it came to hard security guarantees.

But what the Czechs had not considered fully was how to provide the USSR sufficient security assurances. That country would not react well to a NATO that expanded its membership to the East, indeed, to its very borders. Such a move would only play into the hands of the conservatives in the Russian leadership. The strategy NATO had adopted in negotiations with the USSR had been to maintain the existing balance of power in Europe but at greatly reduced levels of armament. It was in fact this strategy that had led, in part, to the revolutions in Central Europe. Gorbachov had given priority to political over military means, cooperation over confrontation, in dealing with East-West issues. But the balance of power was still the key to stability.

The Czechoslovaks proposed abolishing the balance of power. They argued that the unification of Germany made balance of power politics a matter of form rather than substance. The question, for them, was how to get from a balance of power to consensus. This question was important because any kind of CSCE security organization that bridged both East and West would have to work on the basis of consensus. But the development of such a consensus on European security issues implied a degree of political transparency in the USSR that neither existed, nor was likely to exist for some time. Political transparency implied a stable and democratic political system as well as predictability of intentions. These characteristics were hardly typical of Soviet political culture.

Still, the Czechoslovaks knew that the central front had disappeared. They had been that front. Now they were in a kind of no man's land, or security vacuum, as they liked to call it. The only organization that could fill that vacuum was a revitalized CSCE with the muscle to intervene, or NATO. Czechoslovak membership in NATO was, at the time, anathema to most NATO states because it would anger the USSR. Nonetheless, NATO was convinced of the importance of reaching out to the Central European countries, short of offering membership in the Alliance.

An important step in this direction was the visit of NATO's Political Committee to Prague in the spring of 1991. I played a key role in the visit because a Canadian was the current dean of the NATO committee. I emphasized the importance of the visit to Saša Vondra, Havel's foreign policy advisor. The Czechoslovaks knew they had to seize every opportunity at a time when new security structures in Europe were at least on everyone's mind. I suggested that a meeting between NATO's Political Committee and Havel might help get across to NATO the seriousness with which the Czechoslovaks regarded the security vacuum, and the implications of this vacuum for NATO. Saša agreed, and we arranged the surprise meeting with Havel.

During the discussions between the NATO committee and some of Havel's advisors, one or two of the NATO representatives explained the obvious facts about Russian sensitivity to any kind of Czechoslovak membership in the Alliance. They suggested that Czechoslovakia might be a little more accommodating to Russian sensibilities. The Czechoslovaks replied that they had tried to be accommodating in the past. In 1948, and again in 1968, they had been very accommodating, and look where that got them! They admitted, however, that in the first days after the revolution there had been little regard for Soviet feelings. Their attitudes had bordered on the reckless, but surely the way to avoid a power vacuum was not to turn once again to the Russians. In fact the approach that Czechoslovakia had adopted since the revolution was to build up a web of bilateral treaties, contacts, and indirect security guarantees, while working hard to get the CSCE to provide the superstructure. Neutrality, they argued, was out of the question. This would simply end in creating a new bloc between East and West. It would turn the people of Czechoslovakia into second-class citizens when it came to security.

It would also complicate future membership in the European Community. The Community might itself one day have a security function. The Czechoslovaks suggested that the way to build up the CSCE in the meantime was to create a permanent secretariat. This would be a first step towards "institutionalizing" the CSCE, which until then had been simply a series of diplomatic conferences on East-West issues. And of course the Czechoslovaks proposed to their CSCE colleagues that the secretariat be based in Prague. I do not think any of us, including the Czechoslovak representatives, realized that their proposal would be accepted at the November 1990 summit of the CSCE states in Paris. The secretariat would become a reality only a stone's throw from the Prague Castle by the following spring. The CSCE would itself become a fully fledged international organization (the OSCE) shortly after. It would play a key role in preparing the elections in Bosnia in 1996.

These important and early foreign policy successes for Czechoslovakia were based on a visceral understanding that the East-West security matrix had collapsed. The Czechoslovaks knew this better than most because they were at the heart of it, they were the crossroads of Europe. Like a man possessed, Dienstbier pursued new paths to escape the security limbo in which Czechoslovakia found itself. His actions were partly inspired by a meeting not long after the revolution with Dick Cheney, the U.S. Secretary of Defense, in Cairo. Dienstbier asked Cheney if the U.S. had abrogated the Yalta Accords. In other words, he wanted to know if the Americans no longer recognized Czechoslovakia as falling within the Soviet "sphere of influence."

To Dienstbier's horror Cheney did not know what to reply. He failed to confirm that the Yalta deal was dead. Dienstbier did not fully appreciate the fact that, as long as the USSR represented a potential threat, negative security guarantees were the most Czechoslovakia could hope for from NATO. A negative security guarantee would exist if Czechoslovakia obtained international recognition of its undertaking not to allow another country to use its territory to launch an attack. This was hardly tantamount to the NATO nuclear umbrella.

This sense of insecurity in Central Europe was reinforced by the feeling that the state was under pressure from all sides. Central European economies were opening themselves to the world economy and were suffering market shock. At the same time, there was an increase in nationalist tensions within these states. Whether in terms of the security vacuum, the economic changes or the rise of nationalism, there was an absence of arrangements or agreed rules for resolving conflicts and for reinforcing the sovereignty of the state. Hence governments and their parliaments in transitional countries became even more important as sources of order and as the generators of new schemes. This was happening at a time when these same governments and parliaments were already overburdened with the political work of creating electoral systems, extending human rights, and so on.

The Czechoslovaks felt particularly vulnerable while witnessing, at close range, the unification of Germany and turmoil in the USSR. It was the sudden unpredictability of events along their borders and the impact of these events on everything, from trade to exchange rates, from international security to the rights of minorities, that created a sense of vertigo. The changes also strengthened fears about a security vacuum. Havel and Dienstbier responded to the vulnerability of their country by seeking new international agreements, even temporary arrangements, to bring stability and a degree of predictability to their relations with other countries.

All such schemes presupposed that states were in control, that internal instability was being managed. The Czechoslovaks were increasingly aware that this was a large assumption indeed, not least in their own case. Internal stability was becoming more a function of economic change and trade than of international security systems. The CSCE secretariat in Prague was important, but the onus remained on the West to open the door to favourable terms of trade.

41

THE CAMPAIGN

THE CAMPAIGN leading up to the elections on June 8-9 was surprisingly quiet. I saw the posters go up. I listened to the endless debates on TV. But aside from what was clearly some libellous character assassination on one or two occasions, the campaign lacked life. The main reason, in my mind, was that there were no real issues to debate. The issue on which everyone agreed was that the communist regime had been an unmitigated disaster for the country and its people from just about every standpoint.

In terms of economic issues, the government was still at the stage of drawing up a plan for privatization. Who could disagree with that? Indeed, all of the issues were so fundamental that there was not a lot of room for developing options that could be put to the electorate. Even foreign policy was devoid of debate. Everyone wanted to get the 70,000 or so Russian soldiers out of the country as fast as possible. And generally, people wanted to distance themselves from everything Soviet and get closer to everything Western. The government agreed. Nor was there any doubt about domestic economic policy. People were looking for the kind of affluence they hoped a market economy would provide. The government was hoping for the same thing. Finally, people wanted free elections, and the government was delivering them.

The only real decision for voters was whether to vote against the communists and against the past forty years. And if you were voting against the communists, you were probably supporting Civic Forum and Václav Havel. A few people had some kind of historical or family tie to the pre-1948 political parties, but Civic Forum was clearly the emotional favourite. Support for Civic Forum amounted to a catharsis for many people: a very personal rejection of forty years of compromise and deceit.

Hence the campaign had an almost kafkaesque quality. Politicians and the public were going through the motions of democracy, but the outcome seemed to be preordained. Then a bomb exploded on a sunny day in early June, right in the middle of the Old Town Square. I can still remember it. One of our Czech employees at the Embassy came rushing up shouting that a bomb had just gone off downtown. We were stunned. I do not think that either the foreign diplomats and journalists, or the Czechoslovaks, believed it could happen here. A lot of people in the square had been hurt, including one German tourist who had a severe head injury. A few children too had been injured and taken to hospital. The bomb itself had been placed purposefully at head height on the statue of Jan Hus. It was obviously intended to kill. Only by some miracle had it failed to do so.

Strangely, the bombing only made the campaign more unreal. Some mysterious group seemed to have taken responsibility, but there was no indication of what their political goals might be. The event was all the more disturbing because it came against the background of what was then an extremely peaceful and law-abiding society. Under the police state of the communist regime violent crime was virtually unknown.

The bomb was a pipe-bomb, and a fairly sophisticated one at that. The quiet of the election campaign continued as if nothing had happened, but there was a new tension in the air that was difficult to describe. The Minister of the Interior went on TV and asked people to telephone a special police number with any information. He said that the bomb was quite clearly the work of terrorists. He then held up a drawing of a house in the countryside and asked viewers if they could identify the location. I could not quite figure that one out. How did the Minister obtain this drawing? The only thing I could come up with was that it must have been sketched or described by a psychic. Havel simply announced that an emergency team had been created to investigate the incident. He noted the obvious, which was that someone evidently wanted to disrupt the elections. Everyone assumed the perpetrators were former agents of the StB. It so happened that hundreds of them were getting their pink slips at this very time. Not a few of them had walked out of StB headquarters making parting threats to the new management.

Going into the elections, Civic Forum had come up with a great campaign slogan. It was aimed at people who were fed up with the Communist Party, and with all political parties. It was: "Parties are for Party Members. Civic Forum is for Everyone." There were two messages here. One was populist and participatory, telling the average Czech that Civic Forum welcomed him/her and his/her concerns. The other, more subtle message, was a plea for consensus politics that looked beyond the more narrow interests of traditional political parties. Both of these messages were vintage Havel. The slogan must have pleased him, if he did not come up with it himself. Consensus politics was what Havel had practised since November 1989. It was the basis for the creation of the Government of National Understanding. He was concerned that either fanatical anti-communism or extreme Slovak nationalism would rip the country apart. He wanted to maintain a firm grip on the centre, nudging society into an entirely new political system, without chaos and within the law. The revolution was fine in its day, but Havel did not want anyone to resort to extra-parliamentary means during this time of real change.

Civic Forum was the ideal instrument for consensus politics. Who could be against it, except the few die-hard communists? "Civic Forum is for Everyone." It was created by Havel and others on November 19, and had led the mass protests and the negotiations that toppled the communist regime. Since then, it had been the leading political and social force in society, with its members holding the key cabinet positions, including the posts of prime minister at both the federal and the republic levels, as well as the presidency. But Civic Forum was also instrumental throughout this period in turning over positions in the factories, hospitals, universities, and so on. It refused to become a party, saying that, as a popular movement, it was open to everyone. Its platform was vaguely centrist and decidedly democratic. As a registered political movement under the new electoral law, Civic Forum was running in the election with a slate of candidates.

This combination of roles was more than a little complicated. The Civic Forum slate contained both independents and many small parties which were under the Forum umbrella. Moreover, Civic Forum and its Slovak counterpart, Public Against Violence, represented virtually all of the well-known political personalities of the day. These included Prime Minister Čalfa, Alexander Dubček, Finance Minister

Klaus, Economy Minister Dlouhy, Foreign Minister Dienstbier, Labour Minister Miller, Czech Premier Pithart, and so on. Its broad decentralized structure led to more than a few conflicts between competing factions at the local level. These conflicts, over personalities and over policies, were both noisy and libellous. This was rather unhelpful during the election campaign and for a while, in March and April, Civic Forum slumped in the polls.

I somehow could not really take this drop in popularity seriously. Who else was there? For a while, it appeared that Civic Forum was coming apart at the seams, and Havel was reluctant to intervene too directly. The conflicts resulted from the fact that the movement lacked both discipline and cohesion. Yet Havel was himself hesitant to impose the kind of order typical of a party. As president he was expected to remain above party politics generally. Any partisan involvement with Forum would have led other parties to cry foul. Finally, Civic Forum headquarters took matters into its hands. Forum rebounded in June, peaking in popularity at the time of the elections as if it had all been carefully planned.

The main electoral contenders running against Forum were the Christian Democratic Union (CDU), the Greens, and the Communist Party. The last poll before the June 8 elections gave Forum and its Slovak partner, Public Against Violence, about 42 percent, the CDU 15 percent, the Communists 7 percent, and the Greens 4 percent. The parties that had been expected to do well on the basis of their interwar popularity, but did not, were the Social Democratic Party (4 percent), and the Socialist Party, which changed its name back to the National Social Party (2 percent). What these figures did not reveal was that the CDU was more popular in Slovakia, a Catholic stronghold, while Forum was polling about 50 percent in the Czech Lands.

One of the things that was the most difficult to ascertain during the election campaign was the real strength of the Communist Party. Although the polls seemed to suggest there was nothing to worry about, the pollsters tended to be youthful supporters of Civic Forum. Despite everything that had happened, there remained a lingering doubt that the wicked witch of the East was really dead. Barry Mawhinney, the Ambassador, and I decided to go and see for ourselves how the campaign looked from Communist Party headquarters. The offices were still located on the banks of the Vltava River in a huge stone building dating from the early years of the century. The building had housed the Ministry of Transport between the wars, and it had a massive, muscular feel to it.

We had been there only twice under the old regime. Those were the days when the parking lot in front of the building had been jammed with brooding black Tatras and Zils, the vehicles of choice for party apparatchiks. Our silver Embassy Chev lacked seriousness, not to say menace, in comparison. On one occasion, a year before, in the spring of 1989, we had gone to see Rudolf Hegenbart, then head of the Communist Party department responsible for security. The call had been at his request. As we made our way through the cavernous marble lobby, past the obligatory bronze statue of noble workers earning an honest day's wage, and up the sweeping staircase to the wood-panelled suites of the party elite, we were a little mystified as to why Hegenbart wanted to see the bad boys of the diplomatic corps. I do not think we ever got a straight answer.

Hegenbart seemed to want to tell us that he had been put in this thankless job against his will. His real interest was in economic policy. He then said that he, and others he knew within the system, were closet reformers and supported Gorbachov's perestroika. They were only waiting for the right moment to come out. This was all a little disingenuous, coming from someone who was running probably the most repressive state security apparatus in the bloc. What did it mean? Later we wondered whether Hegenbart was behind the regime's overreaction on November 17, hoping that public pressure would lead to the replacement of the regime's Stalinists by Gorbachov-like reformers? If so, he badly miscalculated.

I think Hegenbart must have concluded, as we had months earlier, that the end was near. We wondered what kind of credit he thought he was building up with us while the clouds gathered on the horizon. Perhaps he felt we might convey his "true" colours to the opposition as a kind of insurance policy against future need. Even during the height of the mass demonstrations he sought an urgent meeting with Barry, the Ambassador, in what looked like an StB transit flat. An ashen-faced Hegenbart claimed that he had refused to return calls from Jakeš, the Party's General Secretary. The implication was that Jakeš had wanted Hegenbart to take action against the demonstrators. Who knows. His real stroke of luck was that the revolution turned out to be relatively forgiving. No one would be hanged from lampposts.

Now, as we pulled up in front of Communist Party headquarters in democratic Czechoslovakia, the scene could not have been more different. There were a lot of empty parking spaces. In fact there was not a single Tatra limousine in sight. As we strode into the building it seemed to be virtually abandoned. We found the modest office of the new General Secretary, Vasil Mohorita, tucked away in a corner on the first floor. The corridors were mostly dark. The government was reappropriating the building for use, once again, by the Ministry of Transport. Indeed, Mohorita's main preoccupation was fighting to hold on to some of the massive holdings of the Party all over the country. It was a losing battle. He would be thankful in the end that the Party was not banned all together, as some in Forum wished. As for the election campaign, this seemed to be the least of Mohorita's concerns. He knew the party was, as one might say, unpopular. His strategy was to keep its collective head down and not provide Forum with more of a target than was already the case. He would be the epitome of cooperation and democratic probity. It was a wise decision, and the party survived, if in a reduced state. But our suspicions were confirmed. The communists were in disarray. There was no evidence of any support from a so far untapped silent majority. As we left the building we could not help remarking that most of the Party campaign workers seemed to be well over sixty.

Civic Forum's campaign strategy was fairly straightforward. It simply emphasized the importance of voting against the communists. Havel called the elections a dress rehearsal for the elections of 1992. Since the government's economic policy was still coming to grips with the most basic questions, the parties seemed to have a hard time differentiating themselves. The only real debate was whether the new Ministry of the Interior was doing what it was supposed to be doing in this sensitive post-totalitarian phase. The current Minister, Rudolf Sacher, was a member of the CDU. Civic Forum representatives criticized him for going too slow when it came to cleaning up the StB. This was a forerunner of the debate about how to deal with the many Czechs and Slovaks who had been agents, informers, or collaborators for the StB. Initially, both debates were confused by what was or was not known of the StB, and the reliability of its records. Some people were not aware that they had been described in the files as informers or as "cooperative." Nor had it always been made known to them that the person with whom they had been dealing was an StB agent. The sometimes subjective retrospective assessment of whether someone had actually known they were collaborating with the StB became the benchmark for public condemnation.

The passion of the parties to the right of centre, which wanted to expose the informers, would eventually lead to an occasional disregard for archival accuracy, in favour of what was thought to be the cleansing of society from its corrupt past. Names upon names would be printed in the newspapers under the headings "agent," "informer," and so on. There was no doubt that many of these names deserved to be made public. The guilty fully merited punishment for the harm that they had caused their neighbours and their families. But there were some names that were obviously wrong, and their publication wreaked personal havoc. It was a version of collective guilt all over again. For those who were unjustly condemned there was the presumption of guilt without the means to prove their innocence. Havel had been right, if unsuccessful, in trying to prevent this peculiar form of catharsis. He knew full well the damage that would result to the moral fabric of society.

An equally important issue during the campaign, though far less debated, was the difference of opinion over the nature and the pace of political change. Havel supported and encouraged the election of strong, independent personalities. Only these could draft the new constitution according to the dictates of reason, morality, and a sensibility imbued with Czechoslovak traditions. Throughout the spring, Havel seemed particularly concerned about achieving consensus on important issues. He then criticized the election campaign as reflecting "an inability to go from political rivalry to human reconciliation." Havel wanted society to move forward together, and sought broad-based support on important decisions. Hence it was assumed that, after the elections, he would turn once again to Prime Minister Čalfa to continue basically the work of his Government of National Understanding.

It was also assumed that the cabinet would again be a coalition of political forces, with many of the same ministers. This was exactly what happened. The only real difference from the government that had ruled between December and June was that the new government would not contain a single communist. Under the constitution, the new cabinet, once it had been proposed by the Prime Minister, would table its program in the Federal Assembly. It would be this program, rather than the cabinet itself, that would be subject to approval by means of a vote. The Federal Assembly would also elect the President, this time for the same two-year term as the Assembly itself. It was widely assumed that Havel would be elected by acclamation.

The sticking point in this scenario was that the parties other than Civic Forum complained, with some justification, that there was just not enough competition between parties and their platforms. In the weeks before the elections they took issue with the omnipresence of Civic Forum and the President on TV and in the media generally. On the other hand, Civic Forum ran the most sophisticated campaign of all of the parties, largely because of its store of talent. It was that talent that won the day, despite the attempt of the CDU to portray Forum (falsely) as moving to the left. The CDU tried to present itself as the only genuinely right-wing, anti-communist alternative. Indeed, one of the most striking aspects of the campaign was the sudden decline in the CDU's popularity in the last few weeks, even in Slovakia. This was due, in my view, to its vague economic program and to some stumbling over the abortion issue. But it had correctly calculated the potential for support on the right of the political spectrum. Other parties would do better in tapping into this support during the next elections.

Barry and I went to see Prime Minister Čalfa in the last days of the campaign. Čalfa told us privately that his main concern after the elections would be the potential for conflict between the Czechs and Slovaks during the drafting of the new constitution. The leader of the CDU in Slovakia, Ján Čarnogursky, occasionally played up to Slovak nationalist sentiments by holding out the prospect of independence at the time when Slovakia would be ready to enter the European Community. That was likely to happen ten years hence, if not more. Carnogursky said that what he wanted now was a stronger Slovakia within the federation. "Czechoslovakism" would no longer wash. It was seen in Slovakia as a code word for the suppression of Slovak interests. Though a federal Deputy Prime Minister, Carnogursky would return to the local Slovak political scene after the elections. He judged, correctly, that this was where the action was going to be. When Barry and I asked Premier Pithart of the Czech Republic if he agreed, Pithart said that he too supported more powerful republics within the federation. Indeed he seemed to agree with the Slovak line that the republics should delegate only limited powers to the federal government. For his part, Havel had been relatively open-minded about the demand for more regional power, as long as it was supported through democratic means.

I felt that a shift to a decentralized federation would make it more difficult for Civic Forum and Public Against Violence to become political parties like the rest. The President and his movement were the glue necessary to ensure national consensus on the difficult economic and constitutional issues that lay ahead. But Pithart, perhaps reflecting at least one stream of thought within Forum, agreed with the other parties that sooner or later more partisan politics must take hold. Only with partisan debate would political and economic issues become more clearly defined. Only this kind of debate would clarify the options and offer some kind of counterweight to an invigorated presidency.

42

THE FIRST FREE ELECTIONS

THE OBJECT of the elections, the Federal Assembly, was divided into two chambers. This was to become a significant fact in terms of the ultimate fate of the country. The lower chamber, the House of People, contained 150 seats and these were distributed by population: 101 for the Czechs, and 49 for the Slovaks. But the upper chamber, the House of Nations, also contained 150 seats, except that these were evenly split: 75 for the Czechs and 75 for the Slovaks. Legislation had to pass all three parts of the Federal Assembly: the House of People and both halves of the House of Nations. Although this arrangement no doubt sought to ensure that both "nations" would be protected from legislation that might be considered detrimental to Czech or Slovak interests, in fact it created an arena where the two nations could do battle.

This situation was only reinforced by the fact that the federal elections were held simultaneously with elections in the two republics. The result was that the prospective voter had to choose three party lists to insert into the ballot box: a party list for the House of People, one for the House of Nations, and one for the Czech or Slovak Republic. The simultaneous vote obscured the distinction between federal parties and parties in the two republics. In fact, all of the federal parties were republic parties running at the federal level. These parties were expected to protect republic interests rather than to try to serve the country as a whole. This tendency was only amplified by the separation of the upper chamber of the Federal Assembly into two halves, ideally guaranteed to protect each republic's interests.

The result was a cacophony of regional parties, each seeking to defend both its party's agenda and the Czech or Slovak "national honour." The constitutional fault-line dividing Czechs and Slovaks had in the past been counterbalanced by the authoritarian and centralizing power of the communist regime. With the regime's disappearance there was no "glue" to hold the country together. There had been little in the way of Czechoslovak nationalism under the regime, and people had come to dislike the federal government because it merely provided the outer trappings for a communist oligarchy. It appeared sometimes as if Havel was the last Czechoslovak, in the same way Masaryk had been the first. The Czechoslovak idea, after suffering the blows of six years of Nazi terror and forty years of communism, had been killed at the root.

Prior to the June elections Havel was one of the main proponents of the decision to limit the parliamentary term to two years instead of the usual five. This would permit another set of elections in 1992 on the basis of a wholly new, and hopefully improved, constitution. The goal proved overly optimistic. The constitutional talks ran into roadblock after roadblock. The 1992 elections, tragically, had to be held using the existing electoral laws and the existing constitution. This, almost inevitably, led the Czechs and Slovaks on to a collision course from which they could not escape. In 1992, when Havel recognized the constitutional cul-de-sac for what it was, he resigned.

But in June 1990, both Civic Forum and Public Against Violence emerged from the first free elections in over forty years with a slim majority in the two houses of the Federal Assembly. In the 150-seat lower house, the House of People, Forum and Public Against Violence together polled 84 seats, a clear majority. The Communists polled 20 seats, the CDU 16, the Moravian and Silesian Party 9, the Hungarian Party 4, and the Slovak National Party 4 seats.

In the House of Nations, the 150-seat upper house, Forum and Public Against Violence polled 80 seats, another clear majority. The Communist Party carried 20 seats, the CDU 17, the Moravian and Silesian Party 7, the Slovak National Party 7, and the Hungarian Party 6 seats. The seats that were nominally won by other parties according to the percentage of votes cast, but which obtained less than 5 percent of the vote, were redistributed to the parties listed above on a proportional basis. The single most important outcome at the federal level was that the centrist parties, led for the most part by former dissidents, had a working majority in both houses. The inherent weaknesses of the proportional system had, for the moment, been overcome by the strong showing of the revolutionary movements.

Simultaneous with the federal elections were the elections in each of the two republics. Civic Forum did even better in the Czech National Assembly, with 126 seats out of 216. The Communist Party got 30 seats, the Moravian and Silesian Party 22, and the CDU 18 seats. In the Slovak Republic, Public Against Violence obtained 46 out of 138 seats, the CDU 30, the separatist Slovak National Party 21, the Communist Party 20, the Hungarian Party 12, the Democratic Party 6, and the Green Party 3 seats. Unlike Civic Forum, Public Against Violence, the federalist party, was in a minority position in the Slovak National Assembly. This would bode ill for the future. The turnout was high in all three elections, with 95 percent of all those eligible voting. What had appeared as public apathy towards politics in the spring had undergone a dramatic transformation by the time of this historic ballot.

The big surprise of the elections was the weakness of the conservative CDU. Only a month before the elections, it was riding high in the polls, when Public Against Violence had difficulty in exceeding 5 percent. Yet at the time of the elections, the more centrist Public Against Violence obtained twice the number of seats secured by the CDU in the Federal Assembly's lower house, the House of People. The second surprise was the relative strength of the Communist Party. It obtained about 13 percent of the vote across the country, whereas the polls had shown it to have been only half that level of support. Though small in comparison with Civic Forum, the Communist Party became the second largest party in the Federal Assembly.

The support extended to the communists was, in my view, a function of two factors. First, there were those people who had been part of the nomenclature and had benefited from various economic and career privileges. They saw absolutely no personal interest in changing horses now. These were people who had not participated in the revolution but were not necessarily hardline supporters of the regime either. In fact, those who voted for the Communist Party in the elections did not constitute a majority of former Communist Party members. Many communists had seen the writing on the wall in the first days of the revolution. They became ardent revolutionaries for the same self-serving reasons that had once made them ardent communists.

The second factor that explains the residual support for the Communist Party was demographic. A lot of older people who had grown up in the Party and seen their whole lives shaped by it, even in retirement, were simply not prepared to see their world turned upside down. It was not as if they had particularly benefited from the party in any material way. It was more that their lives, whether at work, at sports events, or even at home, had been wrapped up in Party cells, Party teams, Party clubs and Party associations of every conceivable kind.

Almost as striking as the failure of the CDU was the fact that the non-communist left was virtually wiped out in the elections. Though popular between the wars, the Social Democratic Party and the National Social Party failed to make the 5 percent cutoff at the polls and so did not receive any seats in the Federal Assembly. Former communists who deserted the Communist Party did not tend to defect to left-wing variants. Most of them appeared to have been picked up by Civic Forum. The Green Party met the same fate as the smaller socialist parties, despite the fact that it had done well in opinion polls in the run-up to the elections. It failed to capitalize on its earlier support because it remained highly decentralized and hence almost leaderless. There was also a rumour during the campaign, which was later substantiated at least in part, that it had been heavily infiltrated by former StB agents. It went without saying that this was the kiss of death for any party, however attractive or worthy its platform might be.

In contrast to these parties, the separatist Slovak National Party, the Moravian and Silesian Party, and the regional Hungarian Party did surprisingly well. The underlying message from the electorate was that ethnic or regional interests were as important, if not more so, than policy differences along the traditional left-right political spectrum. Given the nature of the Czechoslovak constitution and the political system it expressed, this should have been taken as a warning about the constitutional negotiations to come.

With an overall majority at the federal level Civic Forum and Public Against Violence could have formed a cabinet alone. But they chose instead to form a coalition government along the lines of the Government of National Understanding. Havel asked Čalfa once again to take on the task of Prime Minister and to put together a cabinet. Many of the same personalities who had emerged during the revolution found their way into this new government and, not surprisingly, there was a basic continuity of policy.

The principal exception was in the economic area. First, Komarek was bounced from the cabinet. Then, during the summer months after the elections, Havel publicly admitted that he knew little of economic theory, but that he saw no point in delaying the painful transition to a market economy. Finance Minister Václav Klaus set an increasingly right-of-centre course as he launched his program of economic reform. When I asked him if the dramatic steps envisioned amounted to shock therapy he vehemently denied it. He argued that his radical program consisted of a carefully designed series of measures, for which sequence and coordination were key. Still, he intended to range across every sphere of economic life, privatizing and liberalizing as he went. His reforms would have a tangible impact on the nature of society and on day-to-day life in Czechoslovakia in a fairly short time-span.

Čalfa's constitutional proposals would grip the public mind in a different but equally dramatic fashion. There the story would be full of tragic twists and turns, with its fair share of anguish and hubris. It would turn out that these elections, and the parliament it produced, would be a lot more than the "dress rehearsal" Havel anticipated. For the audience, the spectacle would veer between social realism and the theatre of the absurd, and build towards an unexpected final act.

Ironically, the success of Civic Forum at the polls sowed the seeds of its dissolution. By far the largest party in the Federal Assembly, it sheltered a broad range of views under its umbrella. Right-of-centre and left-of-centre groups were already taking shape within this somewhat amorphous movement. This process was accelerated by the vacuum that had opened up at both ends of the political spectrum. The conservative CDU had only limped across the finish line, while the non-communist left had faded from sight. And though one could imagine that the Communist Party would capitalize on the unemployment and inflation expected to result from economic reform, its supporters were literally passing from the scene into the materialist's version of the afterlife.

The CDU had been especially hard hit just before the elections by reaction to its anti-abortion platform. In a country that had grown accustomed, if thoughtlessly, to abortion on demand, the stringent platform of the CDU frightened off some of its support. More damaging in the Czech Lands was the charge, only days before the elections, that its leader had been an StB informant. The charge, carried live on TV, was made by a Civic Forum Deputy Minister of the Interior. The CDU cried foul, and certainly the timing was suspect. But the charge stuck. There was no way the allegation could be investigated publicly, let alone overturned, in the hours before the elections themselves. With the CDU mortally wounded, at least in the Czech Lands, Finance Minister Václav Klaus began burnishing his right-wing credentials through the summer. A conservative, market-oriented economic policy, rather than CDU's Christian principles, would prove to be the drawing card.

Civic Forum had said that the elections were about voting against communists. On this score, 87 percent of the voters agreed. That was a fairly significant defeat, considering the depth and breadth of the penetration of communist patronage into Czechoslovak society. It was a defeat that, by its nature, led to a change in the Communist Party platform, in its leadership, even its name. But the elections were also about Slovak nationalism, where a polarization occurred. Public Against Violence, proposing a decentralized model of a federal state, did surprisingly well. The separatist Slovak National party, with about 14 percent of the vote, did likewise. This polarization contributed to the weakness of the CDU in Slovakia, where it had argued for a confederation of two sovereign states, while holding out the prospect of independence in the medium term. Oddly enough, when Vladimir Mečiar and his Movement for a Democratic Slovakia eventually split off from Public Against Violence about a year later, he adopted much of what Carnogursky and the CDU had championed. But his particular style, his charisma, turned this into a vote-getter by the time of the 1992 elections.

The Slovak political scene would become complicated, interesting, and at times unstable during the next two years. Already, Public Against Violence and the CDU were forced into a coalition government in order to govern in the Slovak National Assembly. The Slovak National Party and the Communist Party cooperated to form an effective opposition. They probed the weaknesses of the government on national issues and on the plans for economic reform being hatched by Klaus in Prague. As often as not, these two parties found themselves voting together on the same motions. They posed a tangible threat, even if they could not defeat the government outright. In this respect the Slovak Communist Party revealed a worrying tendency evident elsewhere in Central Europe: the use of nationalism to recapture a disaffected electorate. Scepticism with regard to economic reform, together with anti-federalist policies, would prove to be a heady, not to say intoxicating, brew.

43

THE END OF "CZECHOSLOVAKISM"

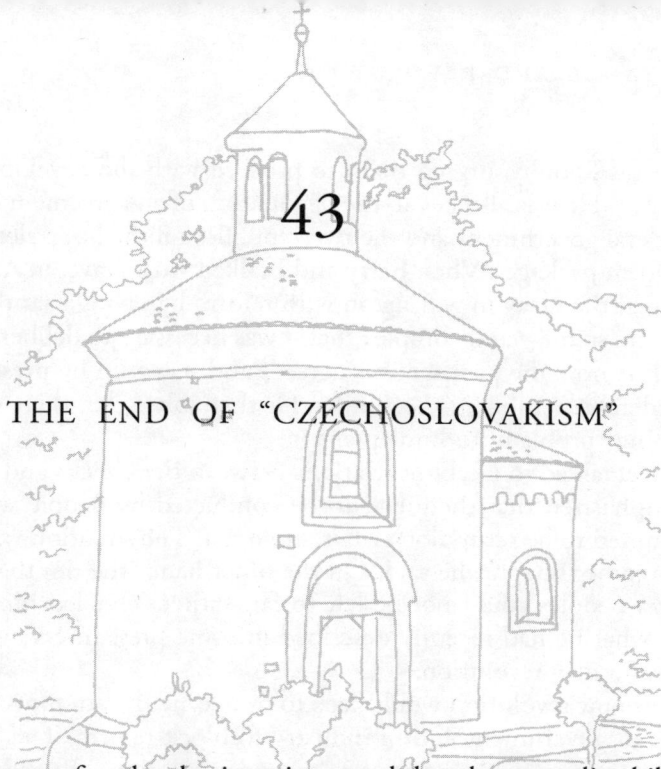

IMMEDIATELY after the elections, it seemed that the unpredictability of Slovak politics was counterbalanced by Havel's reelection as President. Havel had a way of pouring oil on troubled waters, exerting a calming influence across the political spectrum. He revealed in those days an uncanny knack of expressing people's thoughts and feelings, and their anxieties. He was able to say what people were thinking, even if they could not do so themselves. He placed these insights in the larger context of social and political change, describing with a poet's sensibility the truly existential nature of revolutionary life. Havel did this not from some moral height, not from the mountain top, but almost instinctively, by example and parable, so that both professor and bricklayer knew exactly what he meant. When he spoke, you hung on every word, even though he was not an innately talented public speaker. It was all in the words, in the path of words that led to the clearing of thought. It was to many nothing less than a revelation after the endless drone of communist mantras.

Havel's weak spot, and he knew it, was economic policy. He did not want people to suffer unduly from economic change. He understood the likely impact of that change on the livelihood of countless numbers of people, and on their families. This concern contributed to the prolonged stalemate in cabinet, before the elections, over the pace of economic reform. By the summer of 1990, Havel sensed his own limitations in this regard. He swung around and gave his support to

Klaus and Dlouhy, urging them to proceed with the development of their plan. He was also key to the negotiation of an agreement between the federal government and the two republics on the basic elements of the reform package. When Barry and I talked with Havel in August he explained the delay in getting on with reform by saying that the problems were so huge and complex that it was necessary to deliberate carefully. But now the package was agreed, and it would be presented to the Federal Assembly in short order. He then joked that there was only one minor problem: to implement it.

Havel talked to us about relations between the Czechs and Slovaks. He emphasized that these had to be conducted by people who were determined to be scrupulously fair and open. The situation was not as bad as some thought, he said. On the other hand, the ties that bound the two peoples could not be left to fate either. This led him to talk about what he had recently described in some press interviews as the need for a new revolution.

This new revolution would seek to overcome the attempts by some people in government and in industry to block reform. The idea had been referred to in the press as a "second revolution." But Havel told us it was not really a second revolution that he had in mind. Rather, what was required was a second phase of the current revolution. Changes had been made only at the top, at the level of elected representatives. Below that, in the bureaucracy and in the nomenclature, nothing had changed. What he wanted was a process of change, not a purge. More important was a change in attitude, since this had to precede any change in the system itself. The mind-set of the old regime had to be broken.

I was struck by what he had said about Czechs and Slovaks. It was becoming increasingly apparent that the term "Czechoslovak," as a common denominator for the national identity, and a name for the citizen of this country, was no longer palatable in Slovakia. This was due, in part, to what was for many an exciting rediscovery of cultural and political traditions in Slovakia (and in the Czech Lands) that had taken place in the months since the revolution. The most significant by-product of this development was the impression that no one seemed to know what it meant to be Czechoslovak any more. Even the parliamentary agreement on the new name of the country had substituted "Czech and Slovak" for Czechoslovak.

The erosion of the Czechoslovak identity parallelled the growth of the new nationalism, of course. Slovaks felt that "Czechoslovakism," as expressed by the leaders of the First Republic between the wars and the communists afterward, had sanctioned the dominant role of the Czechs. Now, even the Moravians, Silesians, Hungarians, and Gypsies were pushing for more local autonomy, for more self-determination. This in turn was leading to increased Czech self-awareness and sensitivity to specifically Czech interests inside the new federation. But what had catalyzed this rediscovery of ethnic roots was the opportunity to given them shape in a new constitution. Later, some would argue that the revolution had seemingly released long-suppressed passions that even the most evenly balanced constitution could not contain.

In the first year of the revolution the new regionalism led to a significant devolution of power. The constitutional debate, even in its earliest days, focused on the extent of this devolution rather than its desirability per se. Public Against Violence, Forum's Slovak counterpart, entered this debate soon after the 1990 elections with a new-found nationalism. Vladimir Mečiar garnered enough support within Public Against Violence to become the new Slovak Premier. He had previously been the Slovak Minister of the Interior, a responsibility that was to come back to haunt him a year later.

As Premier, Mečiar took the initiative in the constitutional talks. He did this by quickly imposing himself as the unchallenged spokesman for Slovak interests. First off, he made it clear to the federal authorities that he wanted his hands on all of the policy levers that affected Slovakia's economy. This led to demands for Czechoslovakia's central bank to be relocated to Bratislava, and so on. When Barry and I met with Mečiar at the end of August he was in no doubt about the future of Slovakia. He would seek greater Slovak autonomy. To our surprise, he then told us that he had learnt much from what Quebec had obtained, and was seeking, within the Canadian federation. He later expressed interest in the Meech Lake Accord.

Mečiar's main preoccupation in his meeting with us was what he described as the emergence of a new Czech mafia in Prague. He implied that things had not really changed much after the revolution, since the new circle around Havel were no less detrimental to Slovak interests. His second preoccupation was the management of relations with Hungary, in light of the sizeable ethnic Hungarian minority in Slovakia. There was, at the time, a vigorous debate over the effect of a new bill that would entrench Slovak as the official language of Slovakia.

To a Canadian, it all sounded too familiar. How do you protect an ethnic minority within a larger ethnic minority? How do you balance collective rights against individual rights? Can you create an equilibrium between the rights and responsibilities of two nations within a single federal state? Listening to Mečiar, I had a sinking feeling that my friends in Prague were in for a roller coaster ride during the constitutional talks. I had no idea then that the roller coaster would come off the tracks.

To put Mečiar's demands in perspective, it has to be remembered that the government of the Czech Republic was seeking more powers, too. The difference was that the leadership in the Czech Republic, prior to the 1992 elections, genuinely sought to spell out a role for the federal government as a counterpart to more powerful national republics. It was assumed, for example, that the federal government would continue to take the lead in developing and implementing a broad strategy for economic reform. The Czechs also endorsed the federal role of the Central Bank. They assumed that both defence and foreign policy would continue to be directed from Prague.

During these early months after the first real elections in forty years the receptive attitude of the Czechs to the decentralization of authority failed to arrest the growth in Slovak demands for more power. The fact, in Czech eyes, that the Slovaks seemed to be constantly shifting the goal posts would become significant in the longer term. It helped predispose the Czechs to "go it alone" when those demands seemed to change and grow after yet another (and surely the last!) constitutional compromise had finally been brokered. One might have hoped that the time spent renegotiating the various constitutional deals would have permitted the Slovaks and the Czechs to weigh the cost of autonomy.

Yet Slovak demands simply increased the desire for a separate existence on the part of the Czechs. The only person not caught up in this dialectic of national sensitivities was Havel. In a speech to the Federal Assembly in September, 1990, he ventured that "Czechoslovak identity is not a mere fiction or a virtue construed out of necessity. It is something clearly definable, which is not at all an artificial prison for Czech or Slovak national existence. It is their common denominator, and a hopeful framework for the construction of a stable and humane state."

What Havel was fighting, unsuccessfully in my view, was the "Czechoslovakism" that was associated in people's minds with communist centralism, where a handful of party secretaries decided the fate of the nation. After forty years of this sham federalism, "Czechoslovak" had a hollow ring to it. The challenge was to build up the idea of being Czechoslovak in a way that made it attractive to those born long after Masaryk's golden age. It had to mean more than admiration for the current President. It had to mean that Moravians, Silesians, Gypsies, Hungarians, Slovaks, and Czechs would all find recognition of their worth and their aspirations in that single word. But it could function in that way only to the extent that it signified, as it had in 1918, a tradition of political tolerance and acceptance. I think that the periods of Nazi rule and of communism had weakened the Czechoslovak tradition fatally, so that it no longer spoke to people as a living tradition. That, as much as anything, constituted the real death of the Czechoslovak idea.

44

THE NATIONAL AWAKENING

IN THE MONTHS after the elections of 1990, it seemed as if the more the revolution unfolded the more complicated every issue became. Part of the problem was the lack of understanding of Czechoslovakia as a national project, aside from specifically Slovak or Czech ethnic traditions. There was relatively little knowledge of Masaryk and the traditions of the First Republic. Even the mention of Masaryk's name had been banned for over forty years. The former dissidents, too, had difficulty portraying the new Czechoslovak democracy as the resumption of an inter-war democracy that had been suppressed for two generations. Instead, they turned instinctively to the more recent tradition of dissent and the vision of a morally-committed community that it had inspired.

There were moments when some of the former dissidents were almost nostalgic for the old days of life under the regime. The visit to Prague of Gordon Skilling in October, 1990, brought out this sense of shared values among a generation of people who were in numbers no more than the conscience of a generation. This, rather than Masaryk, was their tradition. But it was a tradition only for the relatively few.

Professor Skilling had written much about Czechoslovakia since his first visit in the 1930s. I remember him showing me a window in the Prague Castle from which Hitler had looked out on to the main square of the Hradčany in 1939. There had been a crowd in front of the

Castle gates. The Sudeten Germans in this crowd cheered while the Czechs stood at the back, tears streaming down their cheeks. In the 1970s and 1980s Skilling was close to the opposition. He wrote extensively about the Warsaw Pact invasion of 1968 and the creation of Charter 77. Hence his return to receive an honorary doctorate from the new Rector of Charles University, Radim Palouš, was something of a personal triumph.

Skilling had seen it all: the Nazi takeover of Czechoslovakia after the Munich debacle; the sad transition from liberal democracy to communist totalitarianism in 1948; the hope and the despair of 1968; and the heroism of the 1970s and 1980s. He had been detained by the StB, and on occasion banned from the country. Then, in October, 1990 he stood in the ancient Carolinium of Charles University, clad in ceremonial robes, while the Rector and his Deans, wearing the historic academic costumes of the University, extended their highest recognition. The hall was packed with people from the ranks of the former opposition. Skilling spoke about his many experiences in Prague. Palouš spoke movingly of Skilling's faith in his friends. There were damp eyes all around. The Czechoslovak national anthem was played, followed by "Oh Canada." I had the privilege of being chargé d'affaires at the time. I have rarely felt so proud to represent the Canadian people.

I hosted a lunch after the ceremony at our home. Skilling, Foreign Minister Jiří Dienstbier and other close acquaintances such as Zdeněk Urbánek, Dana Němcová, Vilém Prečan and Jiřína Šiklová were present. There was a lot of talk about old times, even a certain yearning for those times, though none wished to return to them. They all had too much work to do and they were all tired out. Then Dienstbier commented that it was not often that history offered the chance to see your values and your commitments vindicated during your lifetime. Not that these people had not paid a price. The periodic stints in jail, the tension of living with uncertainty, with the instability of one's personal life, had taken their toll, physically and mentally.

As we sat at our dining table, looking out over Prague and the Castle, I was struck by the full extent to which the lives of my Czech friends had been altered. Ivan Havel had become head of the new Centre for Theoretical Study, affiliated with Charles University. He returned to the work that had earned him a PhD at Berkeley almost twenty years before. Martin Palouš would soon be appointed Deputy Minister of Foreign Affairs. Zdeněk Urbánek, Czechoslovakia's most distinguished Shakespeare and Joyce scholar, had become the Rector

Jiřina Šiklová, Foreign Minister Jiří Dienstbier, the author, and Professor Gordon Skilling at the author's home

of the Academy of Musical Arts and Drama. Saša Vondra was Václav Havel's principal foreign policy advisor. Václav Malý had finally received a parish of his own, St. Gabriel's. Ivan Chvatik went into academic life and publishing. Others became journalists, MPs, and professors. Professor Jiří Fiala, who had attended my "underground" philosophy seminar in the old days, invited me to give a philosophy seminar at Charles University, which I did. I even knew one former dissident who went on to head up an important section of the new security service that replaced the StB.

But many others in the opposition did not fare so well. They were unable to make the transition from the closely knit dissident way of life to the open society that the revolution had created. Many were depressed, unable to find a new meaning in their lives. The overriding commitment to oppose the regime had affected every aspect of their existence. Their work, their families, and their friends were all intimately linked to the fact of their dissent. Oppositional life was a kind of counterculture, and I was reminded on more than one occasion of the similarity to the counterculture of the 1960s. Even the relaxed, somewhat scruffy, and occasionally promiscuous style was the same. I suppose the most important difference was that the perceived persecution was more real in one case than the other. Communal support was correspondingly more essential to one's mental well-being.

The other main difference was that the dissident counterculture of Czechoslovakia actually achieved its objective, unlike the counterculture of the 1960s, which was more utopian in its political aspirations. But success in one sense may well have been failure in another to those who had relished the crusade as a way of life. I do not think all of them had become aware of the extent to which their personalities were informed by their commitment. I suppose one might describe their post-revolution depression as a rather acute form of "future shock." It was, in fact, to deepen after the 1992 ballot, when many former dissidents failed to win reelection. One of the reasons for their failure to retain support in 1992 was that they were unable to communicate the experience, the tradition, of oppositional culture to the broader population. Yet it was paradoxically this tradition of personal allegiances that was most alive to them, that had carried them through the revolution and through the first elections.

At least for a while, the public seemed to have been won over to this counterculture of revolution and revolt. People adopted the persona of opposition life during the revolution and in the months soon after. It was almost like a religious conversion. Everyone was suddenly wearing jeans and sweaters. Anyone who was not was either a foreigner or a communist. But with privatization and the influx of foreign capital and goods I think most Czechs returned to what they were and had always been: the good burghers of Central Europe. And this explained the appeal of Václav Klaus. The ties and suits of business were suddenly back in, and oppositional culture again became the preserve of artists and intellectuals. One might say that the Czechs continued to support Havel with their hearts, but understood Klaus with their brains. It was the old Czech dilemma.

Although it was not true in every case, there was a sense in which the former dissidents who had entered politics remained the captives of oppositional culture and its traditions. They tended to work the "old boy" network of Charter 77 signatories. But they could not translate the traditions of dissident life into a political program or a vision of the future of Czechoslovakia. Havel came closest to doing so, and I think his pursuit of non-political politics and the moral essence of all political issues attracted broad support, even if it was not always fully understood.

Havel raised political life to a standard unheard of in the West. It was perhaps for that very reason that it could not be sustained. Most people could not keep up with him, whether in terms of moral commitment or of intellectual grasp. Of course, that was why the life of opposition had been the affair of the relatively few. The dissidents were a different kind of people and, when the popular romance with revolution waned, I think that sense of difference remained. It was hard for the average Czechoslovak to identify with the former dissidents as politicians, politicians who were expected to understand their mundane, and not always selfless, concerns.

The traditions of oppositional culture might have provided the substance of a new Czechoslovakia, and for a while after the revolution they did. But the commitment these traditions inspired ultimately proved to be fleeting. The material allure of the West, and the psychosocial attractions of nationalism, were too strong. There was a moment, however, during the first six months of 1990, when it seemed as if Havel might succeed in linking the revolution with the half-forgotten glory of Czechoslovakia between the wars. He made it fashionable to talk of Czechoslovakia once again as the crossroads of Europe. It was not only talk, we could see it with our own eyes. The division of the European continent, as artificial as everyone had known it to be, had collapsed swiftly and completely. Amidst the heady changes of whole political systems and economies, people spoke of a return to normalcy as if the last forty years had been a bad dream.

It was decided that elections would be held in Czechoslovakia and the other former bloc countries, just as in the West. Economies were privatized and the enthusiasm for "business" penetrated every facet of life, just as in the West. But what was this normalcy to which Czechoslovakia and Europe was to be delivered? Certainly the Europe between the wars, or at war, could hardly be described as normal. Nor was the nineteenth century world of empire particularly kind to Czechs and Slovaks. Even the First Republic, as magnificently led as it was, had an artificial existence, only fully revealed in 1938. Some would say that made it all the more noble, and indeed it was. But normal, I think not.

The return of Europe to a kind of normal life following the revolutions of 1989 turned out to be no return at all, but a project for the future. It was a project which T.G. Masaryk had already seen as vital to the survival of his country, and he had a particular insight, perhaps unique, into its necessary components. Masaryk's concern was based on his conviction that the survival and revival of his country was necessarily tied to the dynamism of European politics. In talking about the national awakening, he noted that "the idea of humanity did not stop before customs barriers and political border posts; on both sides of the borders, people yearned for the same goals of freedom and humaneness." But Masaryk quickly saw that only a dynamism rooted in natural right would provide Czechoslovakia with the security it needed to grow and prosper.

Masaryk believed the problem in his own day was that the political culture of Europe was not founded on a common spirit of humanism, on what might be called moral health. His understanding of humanism was imbued with the writings of Kant and John Stuart Mill: recognition of the rights and dignity of one's fellow man, and the tolerance, even the promotion, of diversity this implies. Masaryk concluded that "the political task of the democratic reconstruction of Europe must be attained and actually made possible by a moral reeducation of the nations." What, we may well ask, was a moral approach to politics? In the first instance, it was a kind of realism, but not the realism of realpolitik. Realism for Masaryk meant understanding everything in its concrete existence, both moral and material. It was the attempt to understand things as they were, not exclusively as part of some historical process.

In the field of politics, this meant evaluating nations, including one's own, objectively and without idealization. Conclusions regarding national character were generally incorrect. Rather, when looking at a nation, it was crucial to be attentive to soul and spirit. Masaryk said, "In disputes among nations, I am primarily concerned with the spiritual aspect of the struggle; ideas, feelings, moral goals are decisive. No nation has a right to its own special set of ethics." The moral education of nations was not only a matter of teaching people to respect the rights of others. It was, at the same time, an understanding of the relations between people and nations as essentially ethical. All nations have interests, but Masaryk was asking us to judge these interests on the basis of principle and moral imperative. The pursuit of interest, including the seemingly worthy pursuit of national prosperity, was not an end in itself. It was this ethical context, the higher ground of transcendent value, that gives meaning to Havel's phrase "unpolitical politics," which is perhaps the greatest specifically Czech contribution to political thought.

Unpolitical politics does not mean apathy. Shortly after we arrived in Prague in 1988 I was told by many Czechs, in order to explain the uncontested rule of the communists, that the political scene was rooted in the national character: Czechs tended to bend with the wind, to accommodate the latest wave of foreign domination. I disagreed with this assessment. In fact Masaryk put his finger on the matter when citing Palacký, the nineteenth-century Czech historian. Palacký noted, in 1864, "whenever we emerged victorious, it was primarily because of spiritual superiority rather than physical power, and whenever we were defeated the fault always lay in a lack of our spiritual strength, moral courage, and stamina." Masaryk's genius was to take this historic insight and apply it within the political arena. He declared;

> If humanism is the ultimate aim of all our thought, it must also be the ultimate goal of our political activity. We will achieve humanism only through humanistic means—enlightened heads and warm hearts.... Not with violence but with love, not with the sword but with the plough, not with blood but with work, not with death but with life—that is the answer of our Czech genius, the meaning of our history and the heritage of our great ancestors.

The key to Czech survival was, therefore, a high moral sensibility in matters political, combined with the courage to defend it. But it was the key to Czech survival in another sense too.

Only a Europe based upon a scrupulous regard for natural rights would be safe for a small country at its heart. During the period of totalitarian rule, when the rights of people were forsaken, that heart stopped beating. It was as if history itself, the history not only of Czechoslovakia but of Europe, had come to a stop. Just as Masaryk would have predicted, Czechoslovakia ceased to develop in a normal sense. It was civic life, rather than the state, that withered away (contradicting Marx). This fate befell Czechoslovakia because it was the crossroads of Europe. That geographic and spiritual location has not changed. When the forces that affect it are not directed to humane objectives, this crossroads and all of Europe suffer. This seems so obvious now, but it is no less true. Perhaps as important for the future is the logical counterpart of this conclusion, that when this crossroads is morally healthy, then the heart of Europe beats all the more strongly, is all the more alive.

This does not mean that Czechoslovakia, understood as an ideal, was simply the place where East met West. That Masaryk saw a clear distinction is evident from the following: "I should remark about a theory that is being promulgated in our land as if it were the infallible truth—namely, that we Czechs are destined to mediate between East and West. Actually, this theory has no substance." Masaryk went on to point out in the same passage that the border with the former USSR was rather small and, more importantly, that the Russians had always had direct ties with the Germans and the French and hardly required the Czechs to intervene. I think that what Masaryk really meant was that Czechoslovakia was a crossroads in the best sense when it was scrupulously sensitive to the broad diversity that is Europe. But Czechoslovakia could act as a crossroads only when its moral health permitted it to open out and affirm difference—indeed, when it promoted difference.

In this small country, it was Europe itself that was at the crossroads. The way of Czechoslovakia was and will be the way of Europe. The inequality, or intolerance, of Europeans at the crossroads is a sure indication of the moral ill health of the continent. Masaryk's idea of a Europe of the future was, rather, one of spiritual and material parity and respect. He did not have in mind the dead hand of uniformity, but a rich diversity rooted in acceptance and self-confidence.

At a time when Europe is at the crossroads in another sense, when the European Union is turning its attention to a possible confederation of the future, the moral imperative that Masaryk so well championed should not be forgotten. A Europe walled in on itself would diminish it. The Europe of the future that Masaryk hoped for is not so much an institutional structure as an idea. This is what he meant when he said that it was spiritual life that was key to political motives. It is the idea of Europe that is important. It is the idea of Europe as itself a crossroads of peoples and values that is the essence. And it is a crossroads that was once exemplified by the spiritual life of Czechoslovakia.

This, at least, is the way I interpret the reflections of Karel Čapek near the end of his life, in the spring of 1938. He said that being the heart of Europe, being its crossroads, implied the necessity

of seeking with other nations the path of understanding, peaceful cooperation and European solidarity. A thousand years of tradition suffice for a nation to learn once and for always these two things: to defend its existence, and with all its heart and all its strength to stand on the side of peace, liberty, European and world solidarity.

After all, in the Czechoslovak tradition it was the idea that counted, the moral idea of a nation rich in freedom and tolerance, rather than political power. It was the search for the principle in all things—what hides behind the interest. For this higher reckoning Masaryk had a peculiar talent.

I think that Havel had the same talent. The difference this time was that the Czechoslovak ideal, and the traditions of the First Republic, no longer found a resonance in public opinion. The remembrance of things past had been obliterated by half a century of enforced forgetfulness. Charter 77 had begun to create its own traditions of dissent and civic life, what was in effect an oppositional culture. But the public at large was oriented more towards the realities and the myths of 1968. Dubček's Prague Spring and the subsequent invasion was the closest thing most to what people recognized as a living tradition. It was the only period in living memory in which humane values were clearly opposed to the nihilism of communism. In the first days of the revolution, recollections and feelings associated with this time came rushing to the surface and Dubček's appearance alone was enough to bring the general population to tears. There was a great eagerness, a need, to talk about those years and to hear for the first time what had happened then from the people who had been directly, and heroically, involved.

Yet, for all that, this eagerness eventually faded. Some people began to question Dubček's role as President of the Federal Assembly. As clubs of right-wing Deputies sprang up in parliament there was more criticism of "socialism with a human face" as out of step with the new realities. There was also a reaction by many who had never been communists to those of the 1968 variety who had been communists in 1948 and overthrown Czechoslovak democracy in the first place. It was against this backdrop that opinion coalesced quite early in support of Havel's presidency. Not that Havel was right-wing, or left-wing. He was regarded as an ardent anti-communist. He reassured the non-communists in a way that Dubček and the others from 1968 did not.

There was a lingering belief that Dubček and his closest supporters had caved in to Soviet pressure, that the invasion and its follow-up should have been more actively resisted. The result was that, just as happened with dissident culture, the mythology surrounding 1968 did not, in the end, provide the kind of national tradition into which a new, liberated Czechoslovakia could sink its roots. For reasons different than those that applied to dissident culture, the Prague Spring did not prove to be a living tradition. It was not an ideal which could influence the political agenda of the Slovak and Czech leaderships after the 1992 elections.

Neither the moral ideal of opposition life, nor the mythology associated with the Prague Spring, had staying power in the public mind. Somehow, the moral and spiritual dimension of life described by Masaryk would take a back seat to the cut and thrust of partisan politics and entrepreneurial savvy. But these, too, were part of Czechoslovak tradition.

45

1968 AND 1989

THE CZECHOSLOVAKS were fond of saying that the number 8 had a special place in the history of Czechoslovakia. The country was founded in 1918. The Munich debacle occurred in 1938. The communist coup d'état took place in 1948. The Prague Spring riveted the world in 1968. One almost felt the 1989 revolution was freighted with destiny. But it was also true that each turning-point changed the way the previous events were viewed.

On August 21, 1990, the Ambassador and I went to see Oldřich Černík to obtain a sense of how the leading lights of the Prague Spring saw themselves fitting into the new politics. It happened to be the 22nd anniversary of the Warsaw Pact invasion. Černík had been Dubček's Prime Minister at the time. We met him in the lounge of the Alcron Hotel which, in those days, was a rather dreary example of what passed for a hotel under the communist regime. There were the usual dark brown velveteen curtains with nylon shears, lumpy chairs, and melmac tables boasting cigarette burns. You never knew what to order in these places. We had become accustomed over the years to thick coffee with lots of sugar, and so it was coffee all around. Černík was now heading up an association of towns and villages that were seeking to obtain some of the powers typical of municipalities in the West. Local elections would be held in November for the first time since 1948.

There were a lot of issues to settle before then, including the questions of how to develop the tax base of municipalities, and of how to proceed with privatization at the local level. But one decision had been taken, which was that the electoral system would be based on majority as opposed to proportional representation. Only this system would make sense in terms of ensuring that a representative was responsible to a specific geographic constituency. Individuals, rather than parties or movements, were what counted at the local level, according to Černík. The fact that the local elections were not being held at the same time as the federal and republic elections was also important. The local political scene would not be seen as a mere extension of the struggle between national parties. This seemed to be eminently sensible.

What we really wanted to hear, of course, was Černík's recollections of the Prague Spring and the invasion. He said that each minister, at the time of the invasion, had to face the key question of whether to pursue confrontation or compromise. Now, after twenty-two years, everyone had their own views. But Černík said that if he had to do it all over again, he would do the same thing. There were more than 800,000 heavily armed soldiers of the Warsaw Pact entering the country. President Johnson, after consulting Brezhnev, withdrew NATO forces from the Czechoslovak borders. It was tacitly accepted that Czechoslovakia fell within the Soviet sphere of influence. Nor did the mobilization plans for the Czechoslovak armed forces take into account an attack from the east. Those forces were concentrated in the western part of the country and, hence, of little use. On the other hand, there were millions of people in the streets facing the tanks and willing to do anything.

Obviously, said Černík, any popular resistance to the military invasion was out of the question. He said that the leadership had to finalize their talks in Moscow as soon as possible to avoid the danger of a conflict between the people and the army. Any resistance would have justified the Soviet claim that there was a counter-revolution that had to be put down. The Moscow Protocols negotiated by the Czechoslovak leaders were a compromise. The Czechoslovaks managed to get accepted their view that there was no counter-revolution and that the entry of the troops was unjustified. They also sought to demonstrate that the Soviet fears of an invasion from the West were unfounded, according to Černík. Dubček and his colleagues defended the policies of the Prague Spring. They fought for Russian recognition of the legitimacy of the 14th Party Congress, which had condemned the Warsaw Pact invasion. Husák intervened at this point in the negotiations with the Russians to say that the Congress had started without the Slovak representatives being present, and was therefore illegal. The Czechs had to concede on this point. It was in a way the beginning of the end.

Černík charged that during the tense days after the invasion, when the Czechoslovak leadership was held hostage in Moscow, Soviet pressure tactics were supported by the Slovak side. He said that one could already see the new hard line that would be adopted by the leadership afterwards. But the real question was whether 1968 could have been a success in any event. The designation of countries as falling into spheres of influence was broadly accepted in East and West. The heritage of Stalinism inside the USSR was still too strong, hindering social and political development in that country. The promise of the Prague Spring was based on political liberty and economic development. It would have led to pluralism if the international system would have permitted it. In any event, the Prague Spring was one of the most important postwar attempts to break out of the division of Europe. Černík added that he was honoured to have participated in this initiative, despite everything that happened afterward.

One of the most bizarre aspects of the whole affair was the role played by Gustav Husák. Černík said that, prior to 1968, Husák's position had been given to him by Dubček, largely because Husák had been a victim of Stalinism in the 1950s. Husák was Černík's First Deputy Prime Minister. In this role, Husák was present at the birth of the Prague Spring in January, 1968. He was one of the Slovaks most strongly opposed to Stalinism. After a visit to Moscow that spring, he returned saying that if Dubček fell he would fall too. There was no obvious tension between Husák and Dubček and the others who supported the reforms. All of that changed in Moscow, just after the invasion, when Husák realized that he, not Dubček, was backed by the Russians. Then Husák's approach reversed itself, according to Černík. He knew that the Russians were preparing to "normalize" Czechoslovakia. They would need a new man to support the Soviet presence inside the country. But the one thing he never understood, said Černík, was why Husák was in Moscow with the rest of the Czechoslovak party leadership. Unlike the others who had been kidnapped and spirited off to the USSR, Husák was not then a member of the Czechoslovak politburo. Had it all been planned long before?

The invasion had been the answer to a long-standing strategic dilemma for the Russians, said Černík. They had long wanted to have the Soviet army stationed in Czechoslovakia. It had never been stationed there before the 1968 invasion. Novotný, the General Secretary of the Communist Party before Dubček, had always resisted (this was a little odd, given Novotný's otherwise Stalinist tendencies). Hence the invasion solved a number of problems for the Russians. They were able to liquidate reform here and more actively suppress it in other bloc countries. Secondly, by occupation, they were able to deploy Soviet forces in a way that strengthened their geo-strategic position.

I could not resist asking Černík if he thought that a letter to Brezhnev had been written by conservatives in the Czechoslovak politburo inviting the invasion, as rumour had it. He said that it was his personal opinion that the letter existed. He was sure that its contents reflected the views of those in the leadership who were opposing reform at the time, people who were spouting the Soviet dogmas of the day. There was no doubt about their responsibility. They betrayed the principles of sovereignty and statehood and the right of nations to decide their own fate, said Černík. They violated their own constitution, which stated that such a request for assistance could only be extended by the duly constituted bodies. Černík added that he assumed the letter was still in the Soviet Union but that, in any case, everyone knew Slovak strongman Vasil Bilak had been the main culprit, and who the others were.

Turning to the present-day leadership, Černík said that he had met Havel only a few times before the revolution. He had much admired Havel's determination in opposing the regime. Moreover, the strategic thinking that led to the regrouping of all of the movements opposed to the regime had been brilliant. After November 17, Havel showed that he was not only a playwright and a dissident. His political touch, and his ability to direct Civic Forum, showed that a new political personality had been born. I detected in Černík's words the feeling that the torch had effectively been passed on to a younger generation. Černík was now occupying himself with the more immediate concerns of towns and villages. There was no nostalgia for the life of high politics. He wanted to reinvigorate decision making at the local level as soon as possible. This was the only way to begin rebuilding the countryside, which had suffered such economic and social neglect, not to mention environmental devastation, under the regime.

It was also clear that Černík considered the events of 1968 to have become largely a matter for the archivists. The revolution and its aftermath had created a new world. There were no traditions peculiar to the Prague Spring that were being passed on to the next generation.

In his mind, there was nothing in 1968 that might offer fertile ground for the development of a new Czechoslovak ideal. When our meeting was over, he stood up and smiled and shook hands. Then he walked off into the obscurity of the Alcron Hotel lobby, as if into history. I was struck by the degree to which Czech and Slovak rivalry was a constant minor theme in the history of this country. Even during the extraordinary times of the Prague Spring and its terrible aftermath, mutual suspicion ran like a fault line down the centre of the country.

46

HELLO GOOD-BYE

OCTOBER 28, 1990, was the first national day since the revolution. Czechoslovakia had been created seventy-two years before. It was still a young country. Perhaps, ultimately, it was too young to have suffered and survived the indignities of the past fifty years. These had turned out to be mortal wounds for a fledgling democracy. The injuries were internal and their severity was not yet fully appreciated in the first days and months of freedom. The so-called hyphen war had been an early indication that the patient was not well. Then the constitutional wrangling, and the searing debate over StB informers, the crime wave, ethnic tensions involving gypsies, the economic struggles, and the rise of nationalism and xenophobia confirmed the seriousness of the disease.

Havel fought hard and valiantly. Increasingly, though, he was overwhelmed by a mounting tide. The elections of 1992 would determine the fate of the country. The two parties led by Klaus and Mečiar would each dominate the parliaments of their two respective republics. Neither party would be able to dominate the Federal Assembly. The result was that the latter body came to be seen as an obstacle both to Klaus's economic reform program and to Mečiar's Slovak autonomy agenda. These two politicians would seek to remove the obstacle in their path, even at the expense of federal statehood.

But all of that lay ahead, on that first October 28 after the revolution. As chargé d'affaires, I was invited to the Castle to celebrate the country's independence. It was a glorious autumn evening in Prague. The air was moist and perfumed. The yellow and orange lights of the city flickered on the surface of the Vltava River as it wound its way below the Castle. I sat in the back of the official car, the Canadian flag fluttering on the standard, as we carefully navigated the narrow streets of the Hradčany. As almost everywhere in the city, the medieval and baroque houses on either side were a splendour of ochre, contrasting with the black ribbon of glistening cobblestones between.

The official cars were pulling up smartly in front of the Castle gates. The palace guards snapped to attention as yet another minister or ambassador emerged. When our car pulled up, there was a small crowd standing around, curious about the various dignitaries, and applauding occasionally. To a background chorus of clapping hands I jumped out of the car and walked quickly through the gates and across the courtyard toward the main entrance of the Castle. I always appreciated the ceremonial recognition and respect for Canada and its people. I was proud to be their representative on this symbolic day.

I suppose I looked a little young to be an ambassador. The guards at the main entrance gave both me and my invitation a careful look before ushering me through to the wide ceremonial staircase that led up to one of the baroque ballrooms inside. It was called the Spanish Hall, an exuberant expression of high baroque in white, gold, and cut glass. Scantily clad men, women, and cherubs in white plaster held up the decorated ceiling. I counted twelve chandeliers in all. Some of them were absolutely massive constructs of cut crystal that would have crushed twenty people if they had fallen.

A stage was set up at one end of the ballroom. The Czech Philharmonic was arrayed in preparation for a concert. There were rows of seats set up and the rather dignified crowd tended towards the glamorous in a few instances. There were lights and TV cameras. They would broadcast the concert live. I knew many of the Czech ministers from the days before the revolution and said hello to a few. When we were all seated, Olga and Václav Havel came in and everyone stood and clapped. It was a little incredible to think about it all, and to try to put it into perspective. A year ago Havel had been public enemy number one in a seemingly invincible totalitarian state. Now he was President of the Republic, presiding over national holiday celebrations in the Prague Castle. In that short time, the country had been liberated and put on the path towards prosperity and civic freedom. The applause that greeted the shy and modest President was loud and determined and so it should have been. I clapped loudly, too. Havel had changed history.

The Czech Philharmonic then played the Czechoslovak national anthem and we all rose from our seats. It is a beautiful anthem and I had heard it in many different circumstances since I had arrived in this country. Only a year previously, I had stood in the rain in Wenceslas Square watching as a demonstration against the regime had once again been brutally put down. I had narrowly escaped the bloody tactics that the police had devised to harm those foolish enough to sing the national anthem in Wenceslas Square. As they sang that anthem while the riot police beat them to the ground, I was moved by a love for this people, who stood there against hope and showed the world what Czechoslovakia was all about. Now I stood in this ornate baroque ballroom, moved by this same anthem and by all of the memories that collided in my brain, images of the individual struggles and the heroism of so many of the people I had come to know. I could only imagine what must have been going through the minds of my Czech friends.

Václav Havel carried the mantle of his office lightly and modestly, even with some embarrassment. The exercise of authority over others was not his style. He consistently sought to include people and to obtain consensus, if not agreement. He did this with the utmost seriousness and with respect. I think it was this above all that won him the affection of the people, even when some of them began shifting their support to political parties with a more self-serving agenda. Sometimes people asked me if he had changed. I kept seeing him on and off within the context of official visits, ceremonial events such as these, or simply in the hallways of the Castle. I could not say that he had changed at all. Although he had become a little more fearless about public speaking, he remained painfully shy with people he did not know.

I watched Havel now on this first national day after the revolution and remarked how this quietness, the awkwardness, exuded what could only be described as a kind of charisma. It was the charisma of the nonpolitical politician. Perhaps the revolution in his own life was not so surprising after all. He had been the real leader of his country all along, except that now more people understood it.

Havel's statement to the nation on this first national day after the revolution perfectly captured the feelings of accomplishment and foreboding that mixed uneasily in every breast. He said that for the first time in many decades people were free to profess the ideals with which October 28 was inseparably connected. These were freedom, pluralism, democracy, equality, social justice, humanity and independence. They were the ideals that the revolution had opposed to the totalitarian regime.

Now, almost a year later, it was important to ask if they were being implemented. He concluded: "I am afraid we do not have much reason to be content." It was a sign of Havel's honesty and his directness that he identified the relationship between Czechs and Slovaks as the main problem. The rest of his speech tried to offer an explanation of this and to point the way forward. He argued that the federation had to be given new meaning. "We are not one single Czechoslovak nation, but two nations, which have the right to the same measure of national specificity and sovereignty. We are at the same time a state with numerous national minorities, who also have their rights. One of these is the right to be equal citizens in our federal state."

He admonished the Czechs to rid themselves of feelings of superiority. He appealed to the Slovaks not to succumb to nationalist demagogy. He argued that sentimental explanations about the allegedly destitute, forgotten, and oppressed Slovak nation were insulting to the Slovak people. He asked that all Czechs, Slovaks, and the national minorities think of their federal state as a joint task and common inheritance. But Havel's final remarks were nothing short of prophetic: "The 28th of October 1918, and the 28th of October 1990, are interlinked by thousands of meaningful threads. On the 28th of October 1918, the Czechoslovak state was born. On the 28th of October 1990, the question arises in this state whether, due to our own fault, it is not dying, or whether its life has caught its second breath."

The concert that evening was a program of Czech and Slovak classical masterpieces: Smetana, Dvořák, Martinů, and so on. When the orchestra took a break half way through the performance the guests moved to an adjoining ballroom for refreshments. There was a great crush of people and everyone seemed desperate to be seen and to be heard. I thought I might shake Havel's hand and convey the best wishes of the government of Canada to his country on its national day. After all, Canada had played a key role in supporting the opposition in the old days, and in keeping up international pressure on the regime. Perhaps we had done our small part in helping to create the conditions for a peaceful and speedy transition. I said hello to a number of ambassadors and ministers. Ole Mikkelsen was there as chargé d'affaires of the Danish Embassy. We laughed about some of the adventures we had had before the revolution. It seemed like several lifetimes ago.

I then saw Havel across the room. I made my way towards him through the crowd. He was literally surrounded by a throng of ambassadors trying to get his ear, trying to be seen with him, trying to see in every word a meaning that somehow eluded them. I noticed that this particular group of ambassadors consisted of those who would not have been caught dead with him when he was a dissident. They had been too interested in currying favour with the regime. This moving throng came towards me, and as other ambassadors pushed in front in order to elbow their way closer, I saw that it was fruitless to try to extend my simple greeting. As Havel passed by, he looked up and saw me at the edge of this mob, smiled, and said hello. I waved back in return. Returning to the ballroom, it seemed to me that Havel's smile was the smile of a certain powerlessness, of one caught up in the current of history: a wistful smile of acceptance and reconciliation.

47

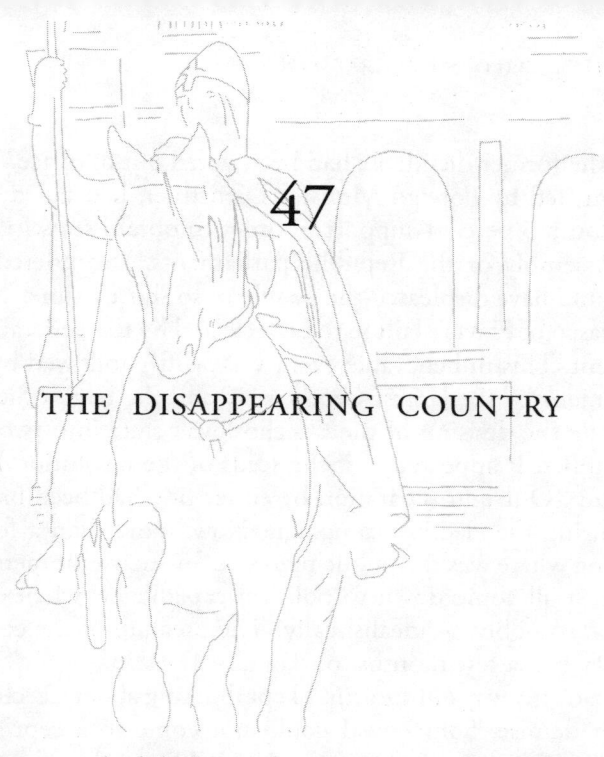

THE DISAPPEARING COUNTRY

AS THE PLANE touched down on the runway, I could barely suppress my excitement. I looked out of the window of the aircraft. The fields of grass beside the runway had turned brown from lack of rain. It had evidently been a hot summer. There was a low grey sky, so low that the airport seemed to crouch beneath it. Beyond the fields and the runways were the familiar houses with orange tile roofs and brown stucco walls. I took everything in. I knew it all so well and yet I wanted to impress every detail, every moment, on my memory. I was back, and in at least one sense I had the unmistakeable feeling that I was home. It was a warm and hazy September morning. And I was back in Prague.

We had left only a year before, in 1991. Lynn and I and our children had said a difficult farewell to our Czech friends. It seemed as if it might be a long time before we would see them again. Then, one day in the mail, like a bit of fate turning up on our doorstep, I received a letter from Ivan Havel. Could I attend a conference on political change in Central Europe? It would be held in September, 1992, at the Institute for East-West Studies in Štiřín, just outside of Prague. Ivan's own Centre for Theoretical Studies was a co-sponsor. My reply, of course, was unequivocal. So I returned to Prague, unexpectedly and full of excitement, only a year after our departure.

I confess I felt somewhat out of touch with developments in Czechoslovakia. There had been the elections of June 1992, during which many of the former dissidents had been voted out of office. The Civic Movement, led by Foreign Minister Dienstbier, had failed to receive the minimum 5 percent support in order to obtain seats in either the Federal Assembly or the Republic parliaments. I wondered how my friends could have displeased the people in so short a time. Then there was the fiasco of Havel's failure to be reelected by the Federal Assembly as President. This unbelievable event was swiftly followed by another, the agreement by the largest Czech party and the largest Slovak party to negotiate the division of the Czechoslovak state into two independent republics. It appeared as if the seeds of the revolution had borne poison fruit. Outright separation by either side had been barely mentioned during the election campaign. Now, more than a few Czechs were asking where was the public mandate for such a momentous decision? Did it all come down to political expediency, when everything had begun so nobly, so idealistically? The breakup of the country was to take place in a few months, on January 1, 1993.

As I made my way out to Štiřín I kept thinking about Czechoslovakia's imminent demise. Somehow I could not come to accept the disappearance of this country as either inevitable or desirable. Had the situation changed so dramatically, so fatefully in just one year? Certainly the first signs of tension, or misunderstanding, had become apparent only months after the revolution. Yet Czechs and Slovaks shared much, and had accomplished much together. Had Czechoslovak traditions so completely faded from the public mind? There was also the fact that the decision to separate was being taken by two parties that had as yet failed to obtain a mandate from the electorate on this specific issue. The argument deployed to defend the decision was that economic reform was the top priority, and that protracted constitutional debate would needlessly destabilize the country during a time of transition. I would hear a lot more about political expediency in the days to come.

The drastic decision to break up the country, and the seemingly passive response of people to this fate, appeared symptomatic of a more general problem. During the forty years of communist rule virtually everyone had built up a healthy scepticism with regard to political life. I think that the only exceptions were the dissident opposition and a few diehard communist ideologues. The vast majority had simply acquiesced in the charade of public life, as long as they were left alone to live their private lives. No one had actually believed the lies.

The revolution did not so much reveal the lies for what they were as (at least in one sense) confirm the scepticism that had been there all along. When the thrill of revolution, and the appeal of its ideals, began to fade, no strong social values or traditions were there to fill the vacuum. It seemed as if the scepticism engendered by the regime had left behind a kind of nihilism, and the paralysis of ethical vertigo. Havel remarked on this a number of times during his Presidency. He saw signs of it everywhere, in the rising crime rate, in the yellow journalism, in the ad hominem attacks that had become typical of political debate.

What struck most foreigners in the post-revolutionary period was the extent to which this spiritual vacuum was now being filled with the values of the market. Not only had numerous stores, restaurants, boutiques sprung up everywhere in Prague. Everyone seemed to have an angle. The smell of money was in the air. Was this any different from Western capitalism? Perhaps not. But the Czechs had not yet developed a comparably healthy scepticism with regard to unfettered entrepreneurship. It seemed to have gripped both the leading politicians and the people as if it was itself an ideology, a utopia, that would solve all of their problems. A sufficient dose of market scepticism might just reopen the door to a reappraisal of Czechoslovak traditions and values. Such a reappraisal would bring the kind of stability that the new government professed to champion. The completely unexpected decision to split the country was symptomatic of the fact that such a reappraisal of values and traditions had not yet occurred.

With my head buzzing with these thoughts, I arrived at the country manor where the conference was to take place. It was a gloriously sunny afternoon. The first person I saw was Ivan Havel. I was glad to see him again. It seemed only yesterday that we had said farewell. We had a lot to talk about, and I was brimming with questions about the future of the country. Then Martin Palouš arrived and the occasion began to feel like a homecoming. Although I had first met Ivan and Martin only four years before, it seemed a lifetime ago. Indeed the events of those years had changed all of our lives.

Martin promptly announced that he was quitting his job as First Deputy Minister of Foreign Affairs that very week. He could no longer support the government's policy of breaking up Czechoslovakia, at least not without a referendum. He could not defend a policy in which he did not believe. I suppose this was the dissident in Martin speaking, but he was speaking the truth on an issue of principle on which no compromise was possible. Others I would talk to did not necessarily disagree with him. They just did not think it helpful to face the issue squarely. They did not even want to think about it, because it was too painful and because, for some, it meant assuming personal responsibility.

I said that many of the same issues were at stake in Canada. The federal government had just called a referendum on a new constitutional proposal. The proposal was primarily designed to accommodate a desire in Quebec for special powers to protect its language and culture. But, regardless of the outcome, the point was that the Canadian electorate was being given the tools to understand the issues and to express its opinion. This included three important ingredients: the use of public forums to enable people to participate in the process; the availability of independent studies on the cost of separation in order to inform the electorate; and the use of a referendum to provide a mandate for the government to act. None of these mechanisms was being used in Czechoslovakia.

Next day, the conference was focused on Václav Havel's political thought. He had promised to attend for this discussion. It would be the first time I had seen him since the summer of 1991. He was now no longer president because he had not been supported by the Slovaks in parliament. I wondered how this might have affected him. The two and a half years of his presidency seemed, in retrospect, to have been a light that burned brightly and then was abruptly and unexpectedly extinguished. I waited downstairs in the hallway with Ivan. An Audi pulled up in front of the manor and came to a quick stop. A driver and a bodyguard jumped out. Havel emerged from the car, looking lithe and relaxed. He came striding up and laughed a little as he talked with Ivan. We shook hands. Havel looked very much like a president in a well-tailored olive-coloured suit. He did not have the preoccupied look that characterized his appearance in the last year of his presidency. He was in genuinely good spirits, and this started to lift my own.

There were about twenty of us in the baroque salon as Havel sat down and lit up a cigarette. The afternoon sun filtered through large open windows. There were pristine green lawns, a fountain, and a small lake in the distance. A few people asked some questions, and Havel talked for a while. He thought it amusing that he should be the subject of study. Then he talked about the importance of trying to pursue a different kind of politics. He said it had something to do with returning the transcendent human dimension to political culture. It was true that everything around us was finite. But this had to be seen against the backdrop of the infinite. Only such a perspective could provide a criterion, a standard, for action.

Havel then said that, all his life, he had been wondering why people behaved in a decent manner. Even when they did not, why did they try to portray their behaviour as decent after all? He had always taken an interest in the problem of the guilty conscience. It seemed to be related to the existence of a moral imperative. This was the only way to explain all of the problems that people had with morality. But even so, it was related to something else, something outside of human being.

Havel told the following story to illustrate his point. He asked us to imagine a situation under the old regime in which someone had been picked up for interrogation. The interrogators tell this person that either he informs on five friends, so he can go to the pub afterward, or he will be charged, and spend the next two years in jail. The person hesitates and decides to inform. But when he is in the pub and he is eating dinner he finds that he does not enjoy it at all. It would seem, said Havel, a human being's capacity for suffering is such that sometimes he finds prison food tastes better than dinner in a pub.

I asked him a rather long and complicated question. I was trying to get at the reason why the former dissidents had failed to communicate their vision of a new Czechoslovakia during the recent elections. I noted that in his essay, "The Power of the Powerless," written during the years of opposition, he had said that dissident movements turned away from abstract political visions of the future towards concrete human beings and the ways to defend them. These dissident movements, or parallel structures as they came to be called, were themselves expressions of living in truth. This was not to say that the opposition retreated into a ghetto, or that it was an exclusive group with exclusive interests. Rather, it was intended to serve as a point of departure for a new society.

This parallel polis opened a new vista and pointed beyond itself, though its primary purpose was to have an impact on society. As I understood Havel, such an impact was necessarily indirect. He said in his essay that these movements addressed "the hidden spheres of society." During the Prague Spring of 1968, these hidden spheres gradually opened out, though they never went further than reform. Havel predicted that, after 1968, either the parallel polis would gradually grow within society, or the regime would finally destroy it. These issues were of concern not only to totalitarian states; even in the West, Havel wondered whether a "parallel polis" might not offer an example for new post-democratic structures.

I said, as we now knew, neither of the alternatives described by Havel in the 1970s came to pass. There had not been the steady growth of the parallel polis, such as had occurred prior to 1968, and the regime had not succeeded in crushing all opposition. The parallel polis of the opposition had been swept up by revolution, after a long and difficult period of bare survival. I wondered about the capacity of that parallel polis, in the post-revolutionary period, to convey its values and its traditions to society at large, and whether it would have the kind of influence that Havel had once predicted for it.

He joked, in reply, that the overthrow of communism had surely been a success, after all. He went on to say that the question was complex. He could spend a lot of time on it. The situation in those European countries where totalitarianism had ceased to exist was similar in many ways to that of West Germany after the war. Those individuals who received the most recognition in the post-totalitarian period were those who had resisted the regime. They became the stars of the day, and were presented with both honours and political offices. But very soon, said Havel, a reaction sets in. Gradually these people are pushed out of power. There is a reason for this.

Those who had offered resistance to the regime were a minority. The result, said Havel, was that they held up a mirror to the majority that was not flattering. So the majority, some of whom were collaborators, began pretending after the revolution that they too had fought against the regime. Soon enough, they began to realize that they could not sustain this falsehood. They reacted by dumping those who symbolized their guilty conscience. Havel concluded his remarks by saying that these developments would require several years of reflection, during which a new generation would emerge. Perhaps this period would mark the comeback of the minority. He looked up and said to me that he realized he had not given a comprehensive reply to my question. But he hoped that he had touched on the reasons that led me to ask it.

In light of his own electoral defeat, and the defeat of the Civic Movement in the 1992 elections, Havel was asked with whom was he most angry? He smiled and said that he had tried to find a suitable object for his anger, but that he continually discovered that he could only be really angry with history.

More seriously, he emphasized the need to reinforce political stability in this time of change. He said that if democratic institutions were to function, if the state was to work, there must be something to hold things together. Ideology was the worst sort of instrument for this task. The glue that was required should be neither ideology nor utopia. Certainly these things were easy enough to invent and to have accepted. But the glue necessary to the complicated existence of democratic life had to be made up of values and ideals. But these required thinking, which was more difficult than belief in a doctrine.

Doctrines were always against people and against life. Instead, said Havel, we had to start with ourselves, we had to look at what we could do. The first thing to do was to try to express and explain the conditions of post-communist life. This was something that concerned the West, too, because it was a question of general human experience. The West had failed to prepare for a time when there would be no communism. Now there had to be an attempt to understand the general meaning of what had happened, since it affected the whole globe. I could not agree more.

Havel said it was true that in communist countries history had come to a standstill. When communism disappeared, history revealed itself with a new urgency. Countries seemed to be travelling backward. They suddenly became concerned with borders, nations, ethnic groups, and so on. Seeking to remember traditions leads to the remembrance of history. This in turn leads to a dynamic process which includes the differentiation of geographical contexts. The West, too, was frozen by communism and the communist threat. Now it was unfrozen. The West, too, had started to remember its own history in a new way.

As I listened to this talk of traditions and history in the post-communist world my thoughts kept turning again and again to the situation in present-day Czechoslovakia. Finally, I asked Havel about the fate of the Czechoslovak ideal in the light of recent political events. I mentioned an interview he had given that was published in *Le Monde* in early July, 1992. In that interview, he had said that he was no friend of the nation-state. Nor was he the partisan of any state that defined itself by ideology or by religion, because this put a single human dimension above the rest. Each of us was the member of a nation, and each had religious and political convictions. But when one of those dimensions was made the founding principle of a state, democracy was threatened.

I also referred to the remarks Havel had made to the Federal Assembly in September, 1990, when he had said that Czechoslovak identity was not at all an artificial prison for Czech or Slovak national existence. It was common denominator of the two nations and a hopeful framework for the construction of a stable and humane state. Against the background of these remarks, I asked Havel about the future of the Czechoslovak experiment in statehood. Masaryk, who had begun this experiment, had sought to build Czechoslovak statehood on transcendent human values. "Ideas, feelings, moral goals are decisive," said Masaryk. Havel's vision of Czechoslovakia seemed perfectly consonant with Masaryk's own. Now, it appeared, this vision had been forsaken irrevocably.

Havel replied simply. The force of his words came nonetheless as a blow. He said it appeared that the existence of Czechoslovakia was drawing to a close. What was at issue was the nature of the Czech state and of the Slovak state that would emerge from it, and the form of their cooperation. He added that much of what was to expire on January 1, 1993 would be taken up in a natural process by the Czech state. It was important to emphasize that this was a natural process. The identification of Czechoslovak statehood with Czech statehood was hardly automatic. It needed to be talked about, and nurtured. The media seemed to think the transition was only a technical matter. They were wrong.

The biggest problem, he said, was that the Czech state was not arising of its own will. In one sense, it was being founded by the Slovak state. This lack of will to have its own state was reflected in the lack of concern on the part of the Czechs about drafting a constitution. There were ongoing arguments between various political parties. Each party sought to add its own paragraph to the document in order to claim it was the father of the new constitution.

It was often said in Prague that the Czech state had a better starting position than Slovakia in terms of its economic development. Havel was not so sure the advantages were all on one side. The determination of the Slovaks to have their own state was also an advantage, and would reinforce both stability and international credibility. Meanwhile, the Czech state might fail to agree on a constitution. This would inspire a different kind of concern on the international scene. Havel joked that whatever Czech politicians had to say about the constitution they had already said a hundred times. What was needed now was to take three constitutional lawyers and lock them in the Castle until they produced a document.

Despite this comical aside it was clear that he took the issue very seriously. He said both republics were approaching the stage when they would be seeking international recognition. There were something like 2,000 international treaties in question. There was also the real importance of cooperating with the West in economic matters. In Slovakia, as a point of principle, when it was said that something would be done, it was done. In the Czech Republic it was often the case that foreign partners found they were dealing with one person one day and another the next. Havel seemed to be saying that there was, as yet, no shared allegiance to the soon-to-be-independent Republic as a collective project, as there was with regard to Slovakia. It was not just that there had been insufficient preparation for the drafting of the constitution. It was rather that there was not the kind of mental preparation for independence among the Czechs that was evident in Slovakia.

Havel ended his remarks by saying that this was something that he would like to talk to the Czech people about, sometime in the near future. I had the impression that it was a question of personal responsibility for him. He understood that many people looked to him for guidance in this confusing time, whether or not he was president. It was his sense of loyalty to these people, who had been with him since the revolution and before, that was guiding his own thinking about his future role, whatever that might be. As he got up to take his leave from our small group, there was a round of applause. It was a mark of appreciation for both the insights and the man.

Havel's thinking had a way of going to the heart of the matter which often surprised his listeners. He had done it again in his brief remarks. But I was particularly struck by the fact that he seemed to accept the dissolution of Czechoslovakia as inevitable. This conclusion was no doubt based on his assessment of the determination of the Czech and Slovak parties involved, and of the political and legal instruments at their disposal. I think there was also sensitivity on Havel's part to what he thought were the expressed wishes of the Slovak people. He had always emphasized public participation in politics, and was scrupulous in listening to people's concerns and sceptical with regard to party politics. In the circumstances that confronted him Havel felt he had to accept the fact that Slovaks were no longer interested in the Czechoslovak ideal or in Czechoslovakia.

The second issue was whether or not he should accept the presidency of the Czech Republic if it were offered. I had the impression at the time that he would. It was clearly a difficult question for Havel. I think that, as a writer, his personal inclination was to return to literary life. In the end, he was motivated once again by the moral imperative. He felt a strong sense of loyalty to the people who had followed him into the revolution. Everyone knew that his presence would be a stabilizing factor. He must have recognized this too. Ultimately, it was for him more important than defending the Czechoslovak ideal to the bitter end. Perhaps he could best defend that ideal by accepting the presidency of its "natural" successor, the Czech Republic.

Despite this reflection on the remaining practical steps to be taken in Czechoslovakia's end-game, the game itself continued to have for me an air of unreality. There was a sense in which the revolution was following the traditional pattern of all revolutions. It was devouring its children, except that, in this case, it was devouring a whole country. The former dissidents who had led the revolution were voted out of office, at least in part, because they were no longer regarded as being sufficiently revolutionary. What was "revolutionary" had come to be identified with those who promoted a far right-wing agenda, which included a combination of nationalism, virulent anti-communism (reflected in the publication of names of those thought to be former collaborators), and an almost exclusive reliance on the market to solve economic and social problems.

Havel and other former dissidents from the Civic Movement had already made clear their antipathy for states based on nations, their dislike for the presumption of collective guilt without due process, and the importance of a balance between market forces and a social safety net. In fact the dissidents, and the revolution, had sought to escape utopia, the communist utopia. Now it seemed that Czechoslovakia was rushing to embrace the new utopias represented not only by the market but by everything and anything from the West. Was it simply that one set of illusions was being exchanged for another?

Some on the right argued that dissident life, the "parallel structures," were themselves a kind of utopia. Were not the politics of the market, and national aspirations, the real world after all? These same critics went on to complain that the dissidents had always denigrated political power as inherently evil, and as innately manipulative. They claimed the dissidents had, in effect, no concept of authority. From this standpoint, the problems that had arisen in the post-revolutionary period were rooted in the difficulty of reconciling dissident notions of civic society with the political decisions that had to be taken.

What the dissidents did not understand, according to their critics, was that the revolution had reflected the desire of people to throw off all constraints. Most people wanted to open up society to a myriad of influences without the overburdening presence of the state. This view of the revolution had obvious implications for the priority given to the "free" market. But it also sanctioned the right of nationalities to be themselves free from constraint, including the constraints of human rights and democratic government. The common denominator in this view of the revolution was the assumption that people wanted the state to wither away, to get out of the way of the market and of national destiny.

If one accepted this reading of the revolution and its aftermath, the former dissidents had indeed failed. But it implied a view of their actions that was simply wrong-headed. It assumed that dissidence was all about the moral conversion of individuals. It led to the conclusion that, after the revolution, the only political action taken by the dissidents was to throw out moral imperatives for public consumption. When it was seen that this had no effect, and when the public had got tired of playing the dissident game, popular support for the dissidents collapsed. At the heart of this critique of dissident culture was the assumption that it was profoundly anti-political, or even apolitical. Dissident life, in this view, was inward-looking, and hence incapable of offering a practical vision of society after the revolution.

This attack on the dissidents simply did not correspond to my experience of them. Václav Havel (not to speak of Dienstbier, Carnogursky, and the others) was the epitome of the political man. These people had all been locked in political struggle with the regime. It involved them in negotiation, debate, declaration, and the development of positions that far surpassed what was accepted as political life inside the regime. They understood the Helsinki human rights agreements and positioned themselves to make the most of them. That was how they kept up international pressure on the regime. I was at one end of this political dynamic linking Canada to the East-West rivalry that centred on this small group of people. The fact that they succeeded in keeping the eyes of the world on this "faraway" place was no mean feat. It was hardly the work of romantic innocents.

Perhaps most importantly, these individuals kept the dream of democracy alive in their country. They passed on the political torch from the generation that had founded the democratic traditions of Czechoslovakia to the present generation that was experiencing democracy for the first time. On this point, their political instincts were right on. Most observers in the West, and in the East, had written off any future for democracy in this part of the world for a long time to come. The fact that many of the former dissidents faced a setback after the 1992 elections was not in itself, in my view, a major indictment of their approach to politics. Political culture is nurtured by defeat and debate. I was buoyed up by Havel's own optimism, and about the possibility that some of these extraordinary individuals might return to public life in the future.

After another full day of discussion in the baroque splendour of the manor Ivan and Martin suggested I come with them to a party for Michael Žantovský. Žantovský had been a member of the opposition under the old regime and Havel's official spokesperson during his Czechoslovak presidency. He had already begun to play that role during the press conference in the Havels' flat on November 20, 1989 when Václav Havel announced the creation of Civic Forum. Now he was going to Washington as Ambassador. He would be replacing Rita Klímová, who had also taken part in that first press conference.

The party for Michael was in a pub, not far from the Russian Embassy in Prague. It was crowded and noisy, with lots of familiar faces from Civic Forum. We made our way through the crush of people. I congratulated Michael on his appointment. He was surprised to see me again. That first morning of the revolution was fixed in both of our memories. With Václav Havel's resignation, and with Michael's departure for Washington, this strange and wonderful adventure had come full circle.

I was full of questions about the dramatic events of the day. A Canadian could not help drawing the parallels between Canada and Czechoslovakia. Both were facing constitutional decisions that involved the possible breakup of the country. Martin and Ivan had talked about this at length during the drive into Prague. What disturbed them was the fact that negotiations over the dissolution of Czechoslovakia were taking place without a public mandate, whether by means of an election or of a referendum. In Canada, at the time, we were having a referendum on a deal agreed to by the leaders of the federal government and the provinces. This had been preceded by government-organized public forums designed to permit people to participate in the process, and a series of independent studies that examined the economic and social impact of various outcomes. Martin said that none of these democratic instruments—the referendum, the forums, the studies—had been deployed in Czechoslovakia.

Others at Michael's party tended to agree that a decision about the future of Czechoslovakia was being taken "over the heads" of the people. This feeling was reinforced in a few instances by the belief that the federal state was being abandoned for partisan political reasons. They remarked that Slovak Prime Minister Mečiar's Movement for a Democratic Slovakia was pushing for an independent Slovakia when neither the recent elections nor the polls had demonstrated that a majority of Slovaks supported this option. On the Czech side, it turned out after the elections that the right-of-centre parties, including Václav Klaus' Civic Democratic Party, did not have a clear majority in the Federal Assembly. This meant that the federal government would have had a difficult time over the next four years pursuing the economic policies that had been championed by Klaus when he was Finance Minister.

It appeared that at least some of the Czech parties were predisposed to abandon the Federal Assembly in favour of the Czech Republic's National Assembly. In the Czech Republic, the Thatcherite proponents of rapid economic change would not have to contend with the Slovak nationalists. The general point made by several of the former dissidents during the evening was that the Federal Assembly had no defenders among the large parties because they saw it as an obstacle to their partisan goals.

The main issue for all my interlocutors was the lack of consultative mechanisms in the constitutional context. I talked first with Josef Zielenec, the Minister of Foreign Affairs in the Czech Republic. When I asked about the future of Czechoslovakia, he said simply "it's over." He said he was not happy about it, but there was nothing to be done. The federal government could not deal with two fundamental problems at the same time, economic transition and the constitution. The government had opted to give the market economy priority. To do this, they had to resolve the constitutional uncertainty as soon as possible. What had to be kept in mind was that the existing constitution dated from the time of the communists. This constitution had in part created the dilemma in which they found themselves.

If one part of the country held a referendum, and the result supported independence, the other part of the country would be regarded as the successor state to Czechoslovakia. It was the successor state that would continue to be recognized legally on the international scene. This was a great advantage. It also explained why neither side wanted to hold a referendum. In any event, said Zielenec, the Slovak parliament had voted for sovereignty. Though this was not tantamount to a vote for independence, it made cooperation at the federal level virtually impossible.

Saša Vondra held similar views. He had become Deputy Foreign Minister to Zielenec in the Czech Republic, after working as Havel's principal foreign policy advisor. When I said it appeared that at least some Czechs were concerned they were giving up too quickly on Czechoslovakia Saša laughed and said I must have been talking to Martin Palouš. He said Martin was the last Czech not to accept the fact that Czechoslovakia would soon disappear. As for a referendum, he said that it had been impossible for both sides to agree on a question to be used in both parts of the country. In any event, it was too dangerous now to have a referendum, given the heightened emotions. There might be a referendum later, when everything had already been settled. Saša added that even if there was a referendum in Slovakia it would pass there by 95 percent. When I noted that there was still no agreement on a Czech constitution he was not overly concerned. He thought the Czech Republic could continue for a while without one.

Vladimír Dlouhý came up to me at that point to say hello. He was now Minister of the Economy in the Czech Republic, after filling that role in the federal government. I remembered the bottle of champagne I had brought to Dlouhy's apartment two days after he and Klaus had been appointed Ministers in December, 1990. Now Dlouhy was very serious. He said that I knew he was a federalist, but he was telling me that it was over. I asked him if the government had done studies to determine the economic and social impact of separation. He shook his head and said that, in any case, it was a political question, not an economic one.

The point, he said, was to complete the constitutional negotiations over separation as quickly as possible. They had to put the uncertainty behind them. In fact this was the prevailing view in official circles. But not a few Czechs outside these circles were arguing that uncertainty was the essence of politics. It was by playing on political uncertainty that minorities typically sought to maximize their influence with majorities in a federal system. Of course it was maddening sometimes, but it was a tried and true strategy for managing the interests of unequal partners. One simply had to learn to live with it.

I saw Václav Havel come into the pub. Even among this group, which had known him when they were all members of the resistance, there continued to be much respect, even reverence. They all wanted to shake his hand and have a word with him. He looked relaxed in his white shirt sleeves, a cigarette in one hand. He came my way and said hello and I talked about his comments the day before, both in terms of his writings and of the future of Czechoslovakia. Somehow I could not bring myself to talk about referendums and so on. Havel needed no advice from me about the importance of being sensitive to the views of others, or about the principles of participatory democracy. I was sure he had gone over his options a thousand times. He had his own unique considerations.

The one person who was not at this gathering was Alexander Dubček. He had been critically injured in a car accident at the beginning of September. Tragically, he would survive only another month or so. Dubček's passing from the scene was for me, and I think for most Slovaks and Czechs, a sad and troubling event. He had a way of reaching out to people, of caring, that made his death a personal affair for everyone who had come in contact with him. Since the revolution, I had met Dubček many times. At official functions, we would greet each other, smiling, and take up our conversation where we had left off last time. He had come under increasing criticism from the right-wing parties in recent months, as had many from 1968, for having once been a communist at all. What I do not think the people in these parties fully appreciated was the imagination and bravery that was required to introduce democracy and economic reform in 1968, when the Soviet empire was at its zenith.

Dubček was a profoundly democratic man, who followed the will of the people in those tense months. He was also a scrupulously decent man who returned political life, briefly, to the moral standards of a Masaryk or a Havel. The last time I had spoken with him, in the summer of 1991 at a reception, he was telling me about the events immediately after the Warsaw Pact invasion. Jiří Hájek, his Foreign Minister at the time and a founder of Charter 77, came up to join us. Hájek listened and then broke in to tell Dubček what he (Hájek) was doing at the United Nations during the very days in which Dubček had been kidnapped and taken to Moscow.

Dubček interrupted and said in disbelief, "I didn't know that! Why didn't you tell me!" Hájek laughed and said he could not because Dubček was in Moscow. The two went on telling each other in excited voices what each was doing in those critical days. I had the unmistakable feeling I was witnessing a moment of history. Twenty years later, it was punctuated by a certain amount of backslapping and laughter. Dubček belongs in that spiritual pantheon of Czechoslovak heroes.

In the car, as we drove back to the manor, Ivan and Martin continued to voice their concerns about the current political situation. Discussion frequently came back to the point that uncertainty was an integral part of democratic political culture. The desire to "clarify" the situation bespoke anti-democratic inclinations. Martin argued that the clarity that was required was not the precision of an agreement between two parties to dissolve the state. It was the clarity that would be fostered by public debate. Ivan said that the recent political decisions to break up the country had practically passed without remark in the papers, or among people in the streets. This was partly because it was difficult to discuss the issues without knowing the facts regarding the negotiations between the parties or their likely political and economic impact.

Martin made the rather eloquent point that words were the place where democracy lived or died. You could not have democracy without open debate. It almost seemed as if there was a conspiracy of silence. The major political parties were determined to get the constitutional issue behind them. Yet the lack of public discussion was tantamount to disenfranchisement, particularly when the future of the state was at stake.

It was late by the time we got back. We trudged off to bed mentally and physically fatigued. Martin was convinced that a mistake of historic proportions was in the making. A noble ideal had been discarded. He continued to be troubled by its ghost.

I woke up early the next morning with the sun streaming through my window. I decided to go for a walk before breakfast on the rolling grounds of the manor. On a small lake there was a white gazebo, joined to the shore by a narrow walkway. The sun was shimmering over the tree tops. I sat on a wooden bench in the gazebo feeling the warm rays on my back. Everything was still and the trees surrounding the lake were reflected in the water. My mind was clearer now, and I was oddly reconciled to an apparent metaphysical absurdity. It seemed that I had become the patriot of a disappearing country. I suspected that my situation was more farce than tragedy, perfectly in keeping with one of Havel's darkly comic plays.

During our discussion that morning our small group had decided to form the Prague Circle of Political Philosophy. This had been one of Martin's goals for some time now. I was all for it, and wanted to take an active role. I thought that some, even most, would think this move the most irrelevant response to the Czechoslovak and European crisis of the day. Yet its aim was to understand the transcendent human dimension of what we all knew was a political watershed of vast extent, a watershed that effected Western culture as a whole.

The Circle would sanction a diversity of views. It would explore the issues of political responsibility, of the relationship of civic society to the state, of nationalism. It would grow from the very soil of Central Europe. I emphasized how important it was for the Circle to be conscious of its Central European roots. I was still convinced that Czechoslovakia really was the crossroads of Europe. Ivan made fun of my seriousness, and said not to worry. He pointed to the well-manicured grounds of the manor. The Circle would no doubt grow from this very lawn.

That evening, I met Ivan, Martin, Václav Malý, Ivan Chvatik, and Paul Wilson for dinner. Zdeněk Urbánek could not come. It was a wonderful occasion to see all these people together again. This group had encountered one another frequently in the bad old days. Now

Ivan Havel, Martin Palouš, Ivan Chvatik, Paul Wilson, Václav Maly, and the author

they barely had time to meet at all. Once the greetings were over, we immediately started talking about the political situation. Ivan pointed out how ironic it was that only the left-wing parties, including the former Communist Party, seemed to be supporting the continued existence of the federation. The result was that if you now questioned the decision to split the country, you were accused of being a supporter of 1948, the year of the communist coup. Someone said, in that event, should we not quote Lenin, in order to ask "what is to be done"? We all laughed.

Martin wondered what people were going to think in five or ten years. Would they not look back with disbelief at what was going on? Would they not ask why we did not do something about it? He said there must be a god of constitutions. He had no doubt that the people of Czechoslovakia had offended that god, and were going to pay a price. I could not help commenting that the only way to appease such gods was by making a sacrifice. Did he have anyone particular in mind? Martin smiled and said that he, like Havel, could only be really angry with history.

We all felt that there was more at stake than the continued existence of the Czechoslovak state, though that was important enough. There was the whole question of the survival of Czechoslovak traditions, as distinct from specifically Czech or Slovak traditions. I asked my friends what they understood by Czechoslovak traditions and got a variety of answers. But they all harked back to some of Masaryk's ideas about the importance of tolerance and the transcendent dimension of human life. It was a belief in this moral ground as the root of politics that seemed to distinguish the Czechoslovak tradition. In my mind, Havel and the dissidents were the direct inheritors of the ideas behind the birth of the state in 1918.

The fact that most of the former dissidents were out of office seemed to suggest that this tradition no longer had the same appeal, at least for now. Václav Malý agreed. He said that many of the former dissidents were shunned these days. "We are walking reminders." This would eventually change, but Malý said it was part of a larger spiritual crisis gripping the country. The nihilism left behind by the communists was being replaced by a new materialism, that of the consumer. Despite the fact that the church had regained much of its position, there had as yet been no moral reawakening among people.

Malý thought that the tradition of tolerance was already fading. The beginning of the end had been the mass expulsion of the Sudeten Germans after the war. He was, on this issue, in agreement with Havel, who had made a public apology for the expulsion soon after being elected President. The same question about the legitimacy of assigning collective guilt lay behind the controversy over the vetting of StB informers. Thousands of people had seen their names printed in newspapers because they had allegedly cooperated with the secret police, even though the evidence was sometimes uncertain. Such people were being condemned without being able to contest the evidence in a fair trial or being permitted in advance to check the evidence through an objective investigation. Those political parties, and individuals, who were pushing for the publication of the names did not as a rule include the former dissidents. They tended to be those who had, even passively, cooperated with the regime, and who now felt bitter about it. Unlike most, the dissidents had made their stand in opposition to the communist regime. As a result, they were largely unaffected by regrets and recriminations, even with regard to their former jailers.

If Malý was right, the return of the dissidents to public office presupposed the reinvigoration of moral sensibilities in society at large. Havel had stated that the moral fabric of society had been frayed by forty years of duplicity. It was this fact that had sharpened his suspicion of political parties, suspicions that seemed, in retrospect, to have been well-founded.

The evening ended appropriately enough with Paul Wilson telling the story of the rock band called Plastic People of the Universe. Paul and another Canadian, Don Sparling, had come to Czechoslovakia in the late sixties. They found minor jobs teaching English, got married, and settled down to the bizarre life of resident Westerners in what became "normalized" Czechoslovakia after the 1968 invasion. Don found a teaching position at the university in Brno, and stayed on in Czechoslovakia through thick and thin. Paul, on the other hand, joined a rock band, Plastic People of the Universe, as its lead singer. It turned out to be a risky, if historic, artistic debut.

The band became an underground hit with the young and disaffected. The music was raw and the lyrics poked fun at the regime. Paul described how the regime's prosecution of this band, and others, led to the founding of Charter 77 as a vehicle for protest. It was a good story, fully recounted by Gordon Skilling in his books. But Paul provided lots of colourful detail about his own experience. This included the events that led to his expulsion from Czechoslovakia. I found his account especially interesting, given my own close call early in 1989. Paul was a wonderful storyteller and we were all laughing at the absurd circumstances in which he and the StB frequently found themselves. It was enough to carry us out into the night, and to make us forget, for a moment, the seriousness of the crisis facing the country.

I finally caught up with Zdeněk Urbánek two days later. He would be turning seventy-five in a few days, and was his usual warm and cheerful self. We were having lunch with Martin. I had a profound affection for Zdeněk, which was shared by my wife, Lynn. It was not difficult to understand why Havel counted him his closest friend. I asked him whether, after all, there was any future for Czechoslovakia. He said that, unfortunately, it appeared to be a case of hope against hope. But he shared Martin's reluctance to accept the current political decisions as somehow inevitable. He worried about the lack of democracy when the government parties took the decision to break up the country.

When I joked that he risked being accused, as had Martin, of being the last Czechoslovak to accept the deal, Zdeněk said that he was indeed one of these "last Czechoslovaks." I wondered if he would be sharing his thoughts with Havel on this. Zdeněk spoke of the great admiration he felt for his friend. Havel had an extraordinary sense of personal responsibility. When he was released after spending four years in prison he refused the regime's offer of a passport and a one-way ticket to the West. He decided that he had to take responsibility for what he had started. He had to stand by the people he had seduced into following his lead, the people who had sacrificed everything to fight for human rights and human dignity, the people who were determined to live in truth. Zdeněk said that he would never think of suggesting anything to Havel on the constitutional issue, either way. He knew that Havel would think long about this, and then do the right thing.

Zdeněk had not been able to join our dinner a few days earlier because he had been at a meeting of Czechoslovak writers. Havel was there too, and there were many questions about the constitutional situation. Some writers suggested that Havel had made his commitment to the federation clear, and that he should not accept the presidency of the Czech Republic when it became independent. Zdeněk said that Havel seemed to want to keep Czechoslovak traditions alive in the remaining part of the country. He even wondered if the name of Czechoslovakia should not be retained. There were at least 500,000 Slovaks living on the territory of the Czech Republic.

For his part, Zdeněk said that he remained puzzled about the true nature of public support for the split. Many Slovak writers did not seem to support the leading Slovak political parties on this question. Perhaps Havel's strategy might be to keep Czechoslovak traditions alive until the present generation of political leaders passed from the scene. Czechoslovakia might then be reborn in more propitious circumstances, sometime in the future.

It had always been apparent to me that Václav Havel, Zdeněk Urbánek, Ivan Havel, Martin Palouš and Václav Malý had much in common. On the constitutional crisis, they shared both concern about the swift demise of Czechoslovakia and a guarded optimism that, just maybe, the country might be put back on its feet one day. It was hope against hope, as Zdeněk had said. But it was hope nonetheless. It was an example of the kind of impossible hope that had sustained the dissidents during the long night of the regime. I wondered if the constitutional debacle in Czechoslovakia was not part of a larger phenomenon. There was a crisis of confidence in constitutions generally, as if they no longer benefited from popular consent.

Havel and others had described the activities of the dissident opposition as the creation of a parallel polis, as a new civic society struggling to be free from a repressive communist state. But when civic society finally proclaimed itself after the revolution, the dissidents were shocked to see civic society redefined as ethnicity. These were not the independent civic structures they had in mind at all. Meanwhile, other political parties seemed content to abandon the individual to the individual's group. Though the dissidents sought to have transcendent human values recognized in a new constitution, their concern was overtaken by the national question and the relative powers of Czechs and Slovaks. It appeared as if someone had stood Masaryk on his head.

The original vision championed by Masaryk and Havel of a multi-ethnic state founded on humane values may yet survive. Perhaps it is a question of hope against hope after all. But the unspoken resentment against the dissidents, and against their unusual courage, will fade. Illusions about the market place, and the nation state, will dissipate in the cold light of reality. It is just possible that some half-forgotten Czechoslovak traditions will be rediscovered by a younger generation. The work, it would seem, of that extraordinary group of individuals who kept the dream of democracy alive in years past is not over. Another revolution is there for the making. It will take place in those hidden spheres of society where intolerance and the techniques of manipulation wage battle with conscience and care of the soul. This is the battleground of the next revolution. These are the people who are already leading it. As I took my farewell of Czechoslovakia for the last time, I knew it would pass into history before my return. Yet, with my memories of those heroic days and of those great-hearted friendships, I knew that I would always be carrying a part of it with me.

Postscript

THE NEXT REVOLUTION

AS I MADE MY WAY on a blustery winter evening to Gordon Skilling's flat in Toronto, my concern about Václav Havel continued to deepen. It was January 10, 1997 and Gordon had invited a few people over to celebrate the twentieth anniversary of the founding of Charter 77. Another anniversary was upon us, though there would be no demonstrations this time.

I was looking forward to see Gordon, and Paul Wilson, who would also be there. But the event was overshadowed in my mind by Havel's recent illness. This sudden, life-threatening event had come the same year that his wife Olga had passed away. I had heard that he would not be able to attend the Charter anniversary celebrations in Prague. The odd thing was that Havel himself did not seem to share my sense of foreboding. In his annual New Year's address the week before, he said the experience of coming face to face with death was a challenge to begin a new, more profound reflection on the world, on himself, on the mysterious order of Being, and on its hidden messages which we mostly ignore. "I also realized with a new urgency that the only source of the will to live lies in hope—an inner certainty that even things that may appear utterly meaningless can have a deep-rooted meaning, and that our task is to look for it."

Here was a meditation on death and on the apparent meaninglessness of human existence that put my more mundane concerns in a larger perspective. We had come to expect no less from Havel, even at a time of personal adversity. But his words also made clear what had motivated him during long years of opposition to the communist regime. From the meaninglessness of life under the regime, he found both meaning and hope.

Gordon Skilling had asked me to speak to the small group gathered in his flat on the significance of Charter 77. It was a daunting task to speak about Charter in the presence of Gordon and Paul. But I said that at the most basic level Charter was nothing more nor less than a set of individuals who had made an existential choice to risk all in order to say and do what they thought was right. I could not say where this particular strength of character came from, but it gave rise to a keenly felt moral imperative. And it was the importance of living according to virtue that linked Charter to Czechoslovak culture and traditions going back to Masaryk and Hus before him. In this way, Charter was the seed of an entire culture, a whole world in miniature, designed to weather the winter of the communist regime.

Charter was a whole world because it was a way of life. The dissidents were living in truth and living authentically not only individually but collectively through various cooperative endeavours. Their authenticity was the product not simply of "being towards death": it had a significant social dimension. Caring for the soul was interpreted as caring for others, others not only in the opposition but in society generally. Of course this refined moral sensibility had developed under what one might describe as the hothouse conditions of life under the regime. It was a sensibility that no longer existed in the West, having been eroded by the ease and induced somnolence of material comfort and personal freedom. As a voyager from the West to the strange land of Charter, I had quickly discovered that my own moral sensibility was no match for that of my dissident friends.

Surprisingly, the social dimension of Charter was balanced by a remarkable spirit of individualism. All Chartists tended to betray a dislike of rank and distrust of position, valuing instead the individual without titles. This individualism was part and parcel of an existential engagement with the world marked by wide-ranging interests in art, philosophy, science, psychology, ecology, and so on. Ivan Havel's weekly "salons" were a perfect reflection of this preoccupation with "higher things," and reflected an individualism informed by a renaissance humanism not unlike that of Erasmus. It had deep roots, but in the West we had almost forgotten what it meant for our day-to-day lives.

In other words, Charter was a civil society that successfully resisted the homogenization, repression, and conformity of the state apparatus. It was indeed a parallel polis but, more than that, it was for me an advanced form of human organization which offered important lessons for the future. Charter was a microcosm of the ways in which civil society can resist the flattening effects of globalization. By taking democracy back to its roots, Charter revealed that the mainspring of the democratic spirit was self-transcendence. In this it shared a long tradition with resistance movements everywhere, including the Czechoslovak resistance to Nazism during World War II. But its public dimension, specifically the non-violent demonstrations, also showed that it had absorbed the lessons of the student protest movements of the 1960s, which themselves had roots in Gandhi's pacifism. For Charter, as for its more recent antecedents, there was a conviction that individual example could have a radicalizing impact on society.

Its radicalizing role had great effect during the early days of Civic Forum when the latter was taking on thousands of new members. Charter was both the birth mother and beating heart of Civic Forum. This was not so surprising when one understood that the members of Charter had constituted the real moral leadership of Czechoslovakia for a number of years, and exercised considerable moral authority in the time of transition. Charter was the essential catalyst which turned resistance into revolution. It had no army, but it possessed and used to considerable effect "soft power" assets, especially during the crucial week of November 20, 1989.

Finally, Charter was the living thread of civilization linking men and women in a fabric of shared values that crossed both borders and time. In a sense, it included those veritable Chartists everywhere, both real and virtual, who were fighting intolerance and injustice and enlarging the sphere of freedom. For me, *this* was the battleground of the next revolution, a revolution still being waged by Václav Havel, but now on a global level.

My reflections on Charter 77 and its twentieth anniversary were received with appreciation and kindness by Gordon and Paul and by the students and friends of Gordon who had come together with us on that January 10. We raised our glasses to Charter and its noble ideal, though I think we all regretted a little the fact that we were not in Prague celebrating the anniversary with our friends there. Still, it was another occasion when we were reminded of the ties that bound that small country far away with our new country—ties based in part on a shared belief in the transcendent value of human rights. Of course the other characteristic that both countries exhibited was the struggle to build a multicultural and pluralist society in the face of nationalism and the spurious claims of what can only be described as a misguided ethnic determinism.

Czechoslovakia had, tragically, failed despite the universalism of Charter's appeal. Yet Havel had not, in the end, left matters there. In the years since the breakup of Czechoslovakia he had been leading a one-man crusade to understand the significance and the dangers of the present age. It was clear to me that he was searching for meaning in the seemingly ineluctable trends of globalization on the basis of his experience in Charter and his reflections on the tumultuous history of Czechoslovakia.

His view was that the modern age had come to an end, perhaps as long ago as 1969 when man had first walked on the moon and, from that vantage point, seen the globe as a single living entity. We were part of a transitional age, a temporal crucible in which cultures and traditions were mixed together and value-systems turned upside down. It was a postmodern multicultural era, the first era in which a truly global civilization was emerging. But this globalization had touched only the surface of our lives and, just as rational knowledge provided few answers to the fundamental questions of human being, so too were individuals turning to the ancient certainties of their tribe. Havel argued that an abyss had opened between the rational and the spiritual, the outer and the inner man, the objective and the subjective, the technical and the moral, and the universal and the unique. The one-dimensional development of civilization brought with it new problems every day.

In a series of speeches over the last few years, Havel has argued that the creation of new organizational or political instruments will not be sufficient to confront the threats facing contemporary humanity. Such solutions have to grow out of deeply held values based on the realization that human being is rooted in the Earth and the cosmos: respect for human rights should flow from respect for the miracle of Being. Only this kind of self-transcendence holds out the prospect of accommodating cultural differences in new forms of creative cooperation. In other words, "transcendence is the only real alternative to extinction."

What has clearly struck Havel in his travels as President is the extent to which globalization is forcing us all closer together in the new global village. This has heightened the perception of cultural and ethnic differences at a time when people are reacting to the levelling tendency of globalization by seeking security in tradition and tribal allegiance. The mix, when combined with the apparently objective advance of science and technology, is potentially explosive. The answer, according to Havel, is to seek those things that underlie all cultures and which are fundamental to our shared humanity. One of these is the experience of transcendence.

The point, I think, is that the mere transference of Western values and democratic traditions to the developing world will not be enough: these cannot be exported like cars or television sets. Rather, democracy and human rights must be understood as based in the spiritual dimension common to all humanity. He says, "If democracy is not only to survive but to expand successfully and resolve those conflicts of cultures, then, in my opinion, it must rediscover and renew its own transcendental origins." This means renewing respect for the non-material order as the only possible source of man's respect for himself and others. Havel believes that democracy should become a place for quest and creation and for creative dialogue. As our global civilization develops, a truly planetary democracy may begin to emerge, but only if it is based on the commonality of the human race as inhabitants of Earth. "If a renaissance of spirituality does occur, it will far more likely be a multi-levelled and multi-cultural reflection, with a new political ethos, spirit or style, and ultimately will give rise to a new civic behaviour."

What is noteworthy in Havel's view is that the way one accommodates this multicultural world, and roots it in our shared humanity, is through tolerance and creative dialogue. In this way we will discover a mutual respect for what transcends us, such as the mystery of Being, the moral order, the belief that our deeds will live after us, and our shared responsibility. Havel sees the latter to be the main challenge, arguing that the principal task for the coming era is a radical renewal of our sense of responsibility. In short, our conscience must catch up with our reason. Not only are we a part of the cosmic order, we share in it such that nothing of what we do is lost, but rather becomes part of the eternal memory of Being, where it is judged. This "Memory of Being" Havel sees as another common element to all cultures, and as a core belief original to human existence.

I think it is difficult to exaggerate the significance of this "Memory of Being" for Havel. In a curious way, it links his life in the opposition to his new role as international statesman. In a speech last year in Dublin, he said:

Once done, nothing can ever be undone, since every human life and every deed is recorded forever in the history of Being and has forever changed that history in some way or other. In this way, every human existence can be considered eternal. This is a great source of hope and meaning, but it is also a tremendous commitment and an appeal to responsibility. Knowing this, we must act so as to be able to justify ourselves not only in the imperfect sight of our fellow mortals but also in the perfect sight of eternity.

These words encapsulate that sense of responsibility Havel sees as crucial to the survival of humanity in the post-modern era. He has gone on to say in his most recent speeches that the one thing that can avert the impending disasters is "a revolution in the realm of the mind." Political reconciliation will not be enough, since to be successful it must be based on this sense of responsibility for the Earth and for each other. Nor does the propagation of global economic integration and the liberalization of markets offer a comprehensive solution: Havel argues it would be foolish to think that all of the problems of the world can be resolved by the laws of the market alone. The next revolution must begin as a revolution of the mind.

Surely this insight was the secret of Charter's strength. The members of the opposition were distinguished primarily by a sense of shared responsibility that not only provided mutual support during times of adversity, but proved to be catching. The spread of this revolution of the spirit also explained why the revolution of 1989 overturned the regime with such speed and without violence. Havel and the other dissidents provided the public with examples of a truly revolutionary turn of mind, and the transformation of public opinion that they effected gave the revolution a sense of direction and common purpose.

The next revolution, this revolution of the mind, will therefore not only transform the way we see the world. It will transform the way we live in the world. In the meantime, there is no point waiting and hoping to be rescued by some force or event outside of ourselves. Havel believes that the next revolution will occur only if we act because it is the right thing to do, regardless of whether or when it pays off. Doing the right thing, assuming responsibility for others and for our world, is ultimately rooted in hope and good faith. It is, as he says, ultimately the kind of hope that springs from the love of fellow humans.

INDEX

Adamec, Ladislav 59, 117, 124, 132, 144-45, 149-50, 153-56, 158-59, 161, 166, 187
Atwood, Margaret 204

Bakewell, Peter 11-12
Bata, Sonja 172, 173
Bata, Thomas Jr 169-79, 200
Bata, Thomas Sr 169, 172, 175
Beneš, Edvard 20, 162, 177-78
Bilak, Vasil 144, 157, 292
Black, Shirley Temple 103
Bond, Cliff 23, 193
Brezhnev, Leonid 12, 44, 50, 222, 290
Buday, Ján 244-45
Bush, George 132, 248

Čalfa, Marian 161-65, 170, 172, 174, 184, 188-89, 244, 261, 265-66, 270-71
Čapek, Karel 286
Čarnogursky, Ján 133, 162, 165, 215-19, 234, 239, 244-45, 266, 272, 311
Castro, Fidel 237-38
Černík, Oldřich 289-92
Cheney, Dick 256
Chvatik, Ivan 16, 72, 281, 316-17
Chylek, Stanislav 240-41
Čič, Milan 243-44

Daácar, Otto 170
Dienstbier, Jiří 161-62, 164, 167-68, 172, 177-78, 247, 249, 251, 254, 256-57, 262, 280-81, 302, 311
Dlouhý, Vladimír 166, 172-74, 176-77, 235-38, 262, 274, 314
Dubček, Alexander 1, 5, 17, 21, 43-47, 49, 76, 80, 82, 84, 100, 103, 112, 115, 132, 133, 135, 143-46, 153, 158, 161, 163-64, 167, 170, 184, 187, 192, 232, 239, 240, 241, 243, 261, 287, 289, 290-92, 314-15
Dvořák, Anton 298
Dvořák, Tomáš 4, 5, 27

Faulkner, William 88
Fiala, Jiří 281
Fojtík, Jan 13, 23, 49, 59, 125

Gandhi, Mahatma 29, 325
Galuška, Miroslav 80-81, 148, 150
Gorbachev, Mikhail 9, 12-14, 45, 59, 70, 94, 108, 111, 120, 124, 132, 137, 140, 168, 240, 248, 253-54, 263
Gottwald, Klement 172
Guimond, Pierre 2, 3, 5-8, 10-13, 15-16, 22-23, 27, 37-38, 60, 76, 80, 82, 93-94, 115, 173-74, 193, 198, 216, 219, 236

Hájek, Jiří 17, 149, 315
Hanlon, Michael 99, 100, 118
Hasek, John 207-08, 213
Havel, Daša 28-29, 37, 117
Havel, Ivan 14-15, 28-31, 35, 37-38, 59, 60-61, 72, 79, 117, 126, 139, 141, 170, 301, 303-04, 311-12, 315-17, 320, 324
Havel, Olga 17, 28-31, 55, 80, 296, 323
Hegel, G.W.F. 35-36, 74
Hegenbart, Rudolf 263
Heidegger, Martin 17
Hemingway, Ernest 88
Honecker, Erich 69
Hrabal, Bohumil 82, 87-88
Hradílek, Tomáš 33
Hus, Jan 4, 18, 46, 122, 137, 324
Husák, Gustav 5, 10, 110, 121, 124, 132, 144, 150, 153, 162-63, 192, 232, 291
Hussel, Luba 210
Husserl, Edmund 17

Indra, Alois 157

Jackson, Andrew 193
Jakeš, Milan 10, 59, 71, 121, 124-25, 132, 136-38, 140, 144, 263
Jirouš, Ivan 43
Johanes, Jaromir 167, 194

Jones, Allan 53-55, 79, 83
Joyce, James 88

Kafka, Franz 85-86
Kadar, Janos 44
Kant, Immanuel 284
Klaus, Václav 141, 164-67, 172, 176-77, 212, 244-45, 262, 271-72, 274, 282, 295, 312, 314
Klima, Ivan 61, 82-83, 85-86, 87, 200
Klímová, Rita 117, 312
Komárek, Valtr 153, 161, 165-66, 172, 176-77, 231, 270
Koring, Paul 99-100, 118, 189
Kubisova, Marta 127
Kučera, Bohumil 159, 160
Kundera, Milan 56, 61, 82

Labarrière, Pierre-Jean 74
Lis, Ladislav 157
Luther, Martin 16

Maly, Václav 13, 17-18, 47, 76, 126-27, 132, 137, 139, 150, 153-54, 156-58, 168, 184-86, 189, 219, 247, 281, 316-18, 320
Martinu, Bohuslav 298
Marvanová, Hana 27
Masaryk, Jan 178
Masaryk, Tomas Garrigue xi, 10, 18, 20, 44, 130, 137, 169, 172, 177-78, 193, 195, 213, 216-17, 229, 268, 276, 279, 283-86, 307-08, 315, 317, 320-21, 324
Mašek, Bohumil 154
Massicotte, Lynn xii, 7, 12, 54, 67, 103, 193, 204, 205, 301
Matejka, Zdeněk 167-68, 253
Mawhinney, Barry 7-8, 13, 32, 36, 42, 45, 62- 63, 82-83, 93, 103, 129, 145, 154, 159, 164, 172, 198-99, 211, 215, 234-36, 243, 251, 253, 262-63, 266, 274-75
Mawhinney, Islay 13, 211
McLuhan, Marshall 158
McRae, Kevan xii, 204
McRae, Laura xii, 204
McRae, Sean xii

Mečiar, Vladimir 141, 243-45, 272, 275-76, 295, 312
Mikkelsen, Anne-Marie 193
Mikkelsen, Ole 23, 193-94, 298
Mill, John Stuart 284
Miller, Peter 262
Mitterrand, Francois 13, 248
Mlynář, Zdeněk 84, 85
Mohorita, Vasil 187, 264
Mucha, Alfons 80-81
Mucha, Jiří 80-82

Němcová, Dana 60, 72-73, 280
Norman, Robert (Bob) 4, 15-16, 60
Novotny, Antonin 292

Opletal, Jan 99, 101, 103

Palach, Jan 21-24, 27, 32, 117
Palacky, Frantisek 285
Palouš, Martin 14-16, 17, 37, 59, 60, 72, 76, 126, 139, 153-54, 170, 280, 303, 311, 312-13, 315-17, 319, 320
Palouš, Radim 37, 38, 280
Parent, Louise 2, 12, 76
Patočka, Jan 16, 17, 149
Pithart, Peter 262, 266
Prečan, Vilém 280

Rupnik, Jacques 76

Sacher, Rudolf 264,
Salivorová, Zdena 56, 62, 200, 202, 210-11
Sadlaček, Jiří 170-72
Shevardnadze, Eduard 70, 167
Šiklová, Jiřina 280-81
Skilling, Gordon 202, 279-81, 319, 323-25
Škoda, Jan 112-13, 129-30, 137-38
Škvorecký, Josef 56, 61-62, 82, 200, 202, 210-11, 213
Slansky, Rudolph 76, 77
Smetana, Bedrich 298
Šmid, Martin 108
Socrates 17
Sparling, Don 318
Srp, Karel 4, 56-57

Stalin 23, 77, 202, 222
Starek, František 51
Štefanik, Milan 44
Štěpán, Miroslav 10, 124, 130, 135, 140, 144
Strougal, Lubomir 6, 9, 164

Tiso, Monseigneur 165
Thatcher, Margaret 141, 248
Thoreau, Henry 29
Tomasek, Cardinal 32, 46-47, 127, 131-32, 178, 189, 192
Trudeau, Pierre 234-39

Uhl, Peter 108
Urban, Jan 76, 139, 170
Urbánek, Karel 140-41, 154, 159
Urbánek, Zdeněk 15, 72, 76-77, 82-83, 88-89, 118, 126, 200, 280, 316, 319, 320

Vaculík, Ludvík 49, 82-84
Vondra, Alexander (Saša) 139, 198-99, 211-12, 217-18, 255, 281, 313

Wałesa, Lech 154
Wallenberg, Raoul 65

Wilson, Paul 149, 316-19, 323-25

Yakovlev, Alexander 12, 14, 124

Žantovský, Michael 117, 139, 198-99, 311-12
Zielenec, Josef 313